*Traveling
South*

JOHN D. COX

Traveling South

Travel Narratives and the
Construction of American Identity

THE UNIVERSITY OF GEORGIA PRESS

Athens and London

© 2005 by The University of Georgia Press
Athens, Georgia 30602
All rights reserved
Designed by Sandra Strother Hudson
Set in Minion by Bookcomp, Inc.
Printed and bound by Thomson-Shore
The paper in this book meets the guidelines for permanence
and durability of the Committee on Production Guidelines for
Book Longevity of the Council on Library Resources.
Printed in the United States of America

09 08 07 06 05 c 5 4 3 2 1

Library of Congress Cataloging-in-Publication Data
Cox, John D.
Traveling south : travel narratives and the construction
of American identity / John D. Cox.
p. cm.
Includes bibliographical references and index.
ISBN 0-8203-2765-4 (hardcover : alk. paper)
1. United States—Description and travel—Sources.
2. Southern States—Description and travel—Sources.
3. National characteristics, American—History—Sources.
4. United States—Civilization—1783–1865—Sources.
5. Travelers' writings, American.   6. Travel in literature.
7. Southern States—In literature.   8. National characteristics,
American, in literature.   9. American literature—1783–1850—
History and criticism.   10. American literature—19th century—
History and criticism.   I. Title.
E161.5.C69 2005
917.3'04—dc22
2005008515
ISBN-13 978-0-8203-2765-5 (hardcover : alk. paper)

British Library Cataloging-in-Publication Data available

For Amy, the best traveling companion I can imagine

Contents

Acknowledgments, ix

Introduction, 1

CHAPTER ONE
Representing America: The American as Traveler in the Work
of J. Hector St. John de Crèvecoeur and William Bartram, 19

CHAPTER TWO
Moving Slaves: Frederick Douglass, Solomon Northup,
and the Politics of Travel in Antebellum America, 63

CHAPTER THREE
Domestic Travel: The Narratives of Fanny Kemble
and Harriet Jacobs, 103

CHAPTER FOUR
Yeomen All: Frederick Law Olmsted and the Consolidation
of the American Economy and Culture, 141

CHAPTER FIVE
Tourists with Guns (and Pens): Union Soldiers
and the Civil War South, 165

Conclusion, 193

Notes, 199

Works Cited, 231

Index, 243

Acknowledgments

Because this project began as my dissertation at the University of Mississippi, I want first to thank my committee members: Nancy Bercaw; Dan Williams; Bob Brinkmeyer; and especially Jay Watson, my dissertation director, whose comments and suggestions played such an integral role in my writing process. Over the past few years, my friends and colleagues at Georgia College & State University have been tremendously supportive, so I'd like to thank Bruce Gentry and Alice Friman, Sarah Gordon, David Evans, and all of the other members of the English department. I am grateful, also, to those who have helped transform my manuscript into its current, much improved form: the University of Georgia Press's two reviewers, whose careful reading and useful feedback helped me address problems both large and small; Courtney Denney, whose copyediting has made the manuscript both more precise and more readable; and Jon Davies, Andrew Berzanskis, and especially Nancy Grayson, without whose encouragement and assistance this book could not have been published.

In addition, I want to thank both the American Philosophical Society and the Natural History Museum, London, for permission to reprint the two images by William Bartram.

I'd like to thank my family, especially my parents, who have provided unceasing support and love and who have always been, I think, the first audience to whom I am writing. Finally, I would like to thank my wife, Amy, to whom this book is dedicated. Her love and assistance have made this whole process possible, and she has continuously pushed me toward the excellence she herself exemplifies and has helped me place my work, and everything else, into its proper perspective.

Traveling South

Introduction

If God were suddenly to call the world to judgment, He would surprise
two-thirds of the population of the United States on the road like ants.
DOMINGO SARMIENTO

Travel made the United States. As both a country and a concept, America was
founded on movement—of people, of ideas, of goods. Of course, international
immigration has been central to American identity since the earliest European
exploration, but travel within the continent likewise played a significant role in
the creation and maintenance of the American nation.

Struggle, too, has been a defining characteristic of the United States since its
founding. In addition to battling against a colonial power for independence, the
thirteen colonies struggled with themselves to forge a national identity. In fact,
after the Revolutionary War, many Americans wondered whether the bonds
among the original colonies were strong enough to establish a single nation.
They were, but only after the states struggled to define that nation and fought
to keep it intact.

Numerous studies have pointed to these concepts to understand the United
States, but often these works have defined "travel literature" narrowly or made
struggle a precursor to, rather than a central fact of, American national identity.
In both cases, scholars have too readily looked abroad, focusing on international
travel or on struggles between the United States and other nations. Ironically,
even though critics of travel literature often thrive on crossing academic and
intellectual boundaries, many have neglected accounts of travel within national
borders; likewise, many studies of early America have looked primarily at accounts by Europeans in America or by Americans in Europe to understand the
culture of early America. But this international focus fails to appreciate the central role of "travel" itself in American national identity; in fact, far from simply constituting a leisure activity enjoyed only by the wealthy, travel has been
one of the defining characteristics of the American people and their nation
since its very creation. Furthermore, as conflict within the national borders was
obviously central to the creation of the American republic, so, too, was travel
within and among the various regions of the new nation.

Unlike international travelers to the United States, intranational travel writers rarely saw unity among the various regions of the country, especially when visiting the southern states. Using much of the New World rhetoric employed by earlier generations of Old World explorers, many travelers from the northern states to the American South represented the region as backward, wild, uncivilized, or dangerous. Could this area possibly be part of the same country as the home environment of these authors? With the "representative citizen," the "typical home," the economy, or the culture so radically different from that found in New England, for instance, could a single nation be forged from such diverse regions, or must this new political unit called a "nation" necessarily be unified in its economic, social, and cultural qualities? If, as Benedict Anderson suggests, a nation is an "imagined community," could an imagination conceive of a single "American" community with such distinct parts? These questions played a fundamental role in the construction of the new American republic during the period many historians have called the "Age of Nationalism"—the years between the Revolutionary War, when the nation was created, and the Civil War, when the nation confronted the most serious crisis to its national identity. It is the role these intranational travel accounts played in the formation of an American national identity during this period that forms the basis of the current study.

According to article 4 of the Articles of Confederation, "The better to secure and perpetuate mutual friendship and intercourse among the people of the different States in this Union, the free inhabitants of each of these States, paupers, vagabonds, and fugitives from justice excepted, shall be entitled to all the privileges and immunities of free citizens in the several States, and the people of each State shall have free ingress and regress to and from any other State, and shall enjoy therein all the privileges of trade and commerce." Unlike this article, the first three articles in the document address broader issues of governance: respectively, they name the confederacy being formed; give each state the right to retain its "sovereignty, freedom, and independence"; and establish "a firm league of friendship" among the thirteen states. Article 4 is the first one concerned with the rights of the individual inhabitants of the confederacy. Not incidentally, the right to travel among the various states is one of the first individual freedoms established. In fact, the different uses of the term "free" suggest that in a very real sense, freedom *is* the freedom to travel. According to the document, "free inhabitants" and "free citizens" are those who "have free ingress and regress" within the boundaries of the new confederation. The right to travel, it seems, was one of the central freedoms demanded by those who sought independence from Britain, so the first documents drafted to govern the emerging nation sought to guarantee freedom of travel to America's citizens.

Significantly, the Articles of Confederation do not grant the freedom to travel to "paupers, vagabonds, and fugitives from justice," two of which are defined or characterized by their movement. The authors of the Articles of Confederation clearly valued travel as a freedom, but such a right could be misused or abused, they believed, as these excepted categories of travelers demonstrate. Unlike protected colonial citizens, these two classes of Americans traveled in ways that were seen to be counter to the norms of society; that is, they had construed too broadly the freedom to travel and had consequently moved outside of the bounds of state or federal protection. By traveling too freely (and thus subversively), these people had lost the right to travel without restraint and were thus not covered by these articles.

By the time the Constitution was drafted in 1787, in fact, travel apparently seemed to the governing representatives to be as threatening to society as it was liberating. Therefore, the drafters of the Constitution did not include the specific language from the Articles of Confederation that guaranteed the right of "free ingress and regress to and from any other States." Once this "confederation" of states had been transformed into a "nation," even one whose identity was unstable, perhaps the right to travel within the national boundaries was assumed. If the specific right to travel was not incorporated, the new document did include (and make even more specific) the rules pertaining to the movement of those not afforded protection. According to the Constitution, a state must deliver up to another state two types of people: "A person charged in any State with treason, felony, or other crime, who shall flee from justice" and a "person held to service or labor in one State . . . escaping into another." While the right to travel freely is implied in much of the language of the Constitution—"The citizens of each State shall be entitled to all privileges and immunities of citizens in the several States"—travel seems to have become not simply a right to be guaranteed but also a threat to be controlled. Thus, the document explicitly does not grant the freedom of travel to slaves, bondsmen, or criminals. Having gained their own freedom to travel, the men drafting the Constitution were disinclined to grant the same rights to those members of society not already protected. Still, travel remained a central paradigm for imagining the freedoms granted to the citizens of the new nation, despite the potential for subversion that such a freedom entailed, so these documents attempt not only to describe protected actions but also to proscribe acceptable behavior. On the one hand, the Constitution elucidates those laws to which a state had to subscribe in order to join the national union; on the other, it sought to describe a set of values the writers hoped would characterize the American citizenry.

As travel was central to the emerging American national identity (despite the unease it may have raised in the minds of those drafting the Constitution), many Americans during the years after the Revolution believed that freedom to travel—geographically, physically, socially, economically—constituted one of the most obvious differences between American and European society. The vast majority of Europeans, it was argued, were confined to the positions into which they had been born, so they were unable to move from the course determined by their origins; Americans, however, were able to forge new paths for themselves by throwing off their pasts and creating their own futures.

After all, European immigrants to the New World were already travelers in a way that few had been while living in Europe, so the benefits that can accrue to those who travel, such as expanded knowledge of the world, a shift in perspective, or economic opportunities, were felt by an increasing proportion of the American populace. In addition, the widespread availability of travel increased throughout the late eighteenth and nineteenth centuries, as mass tourism became more common and growing numbers of Americans took advantage of cheap transportation both internally and abroad. As Barbara Carson explains, "Almost no Americans traveled for pleasure in the seventeenth and early eighteenth centuries" (373), but this custom changed fairly dramatically in the years following the American Revolution, when "men, women, and children began to travel in unprecedented numbers" (397).

This rise in numbers of touring Americans, both at home and abroad, not only depended on but also contributed to a changing infrastructure and cultural landscape, as Carson points out. Mass tourism depended on convenient travel, often by train or steamship, and required predictable costs for tourists. Thomas Cook's tours to France and Switzerland beginning in the 1850s did much to standardize schedules and fares for railways and hotels in Europe, for instance, and the growth of a transportation infrastructure in the new United States encouraged the development of holiday resorts near springs and other sites of natural beauty. But the increase in travel throughout this period (in both Europe and the United States) also relates to a shifting set of beliefs about who traveled and for what reasons. According to Carson, tourism in the United States depended on changes in attitudes by the middle class, who began to see travel as an activity not limited to the rich.[1] According to many Americans, travel, a cultural practice enjoyed only by the wealthy in Europe, had become democratized in the United States.

From the founding of the nation through the nineteenth century, then, travel came to symbolize the ability of Americans to raise themselves in status, to leave the restraints of European society by transforming themselves into new people, and to move where and when they desired. Furthermore, Americans used this increased (and increasing) ability to travel freely as a means to come to a fuller understanding of their nation. According to Justin Edwards, "The increase in the nineteenth-century tourist industry inspired many travelers and American citizens in general to reflect upon their national identity" (6). International travel and travel writing were especially valued in the United States, argues Mary Schriber, because "foreign peoples, their histories, governments, and cultures provided the 'other' against which Americans sought to define themselves, their mission, and their place in the world" (4). Accordingly, many of America's most prominent antebellum literary figures—most notably, James Fenimore Cooper, Washington Irving, Ralph Waldo Emerson, Nathaniel Hawthorne, and Margaret Fuller—traveled to Europe and wrote accounts of their journeys in attempts to understand more fully the connections between Europe and the United States. By viewing the European cultures from which American society had emerged, these travel writers suggested, they could comprehend more clearly America's distinctions and unique position in the world. In addition, they argued, European travel might allow them to learn how those from outside of their nation viewed the United States. For this same reason, texts by Europeans traveling in the United States were viewed as significant for an understanding of American culture and society; the works of Alexis de Tocqueville, Charles Dickens, Frances Trollope, François August René Chateaubriand, Basil Hall, Charles Murray, and many other European travelers were widely read and discussed in the United States when they were published.

Likewise, critics and historians of early American literature and culture have frequently turned to international travel texts for an understanding of American culture and society. In recent years, especially, as travel literature has begun to be studied more regularly, travel texts by and about Americans have come under increased scrutiny. The vast majority of these studies, however, have continued to investigate either solely or primarily those texts that describe travel across national boundaries and borders.

While international travel is indeed integrally tied to issues surrounding the concept of "nation," the narratives of travel *within* national boundaries, unstable as these boundaries might be, constitute a valuable but neglected source for studies of national identity. In particular, late-eighteenth- and early-nineteenth-century texts of travel to the American South by writers from the North illustrate a continuing struggle to come to terms with those questions of most importance to the new nation: What is American culture? Who are America's citizens? Should or must there be a "national" culture, economy, or identity? Or, in the words of J. Hector St. John de Crèvecoeur, "What, then, is the American, this new man?" (69).

Within theories of nationalism, argues Ernest Gellner, two common models for describing the ties that unite members of a nation are the "cultural" and "voluntaristic." While neither definition is sufficient to explain the phenomenon of nationalism, as Gellner points out, both are useful in attempts to understand the draw of nationalistic feeling for the modern citizen and to comprehend the unspoken beliefs underlying the founding of a modern nation. In the case of the United States, which was supposedly created out of a common desire for freedom from Great Britain but depended on a shared set of beliefs and concerns, what seemed to begin as a voluntary alignment against a common enemy quickly became a confederation of territories and peoples searching for a common culture. The founding documents of this new entity point to this confusion of paradigms, for while each outlines the rules to which member states and citizens agree to comply, these documents clearly grow out of the belief that these members do (or at least should) share a common culture. In the case of travel, the composers and signers of the Articles of Confederation, for instance, agreed to allow "free ingress and regress" to each state's citizens but also established the centrality of *the idea of* travel and freedom of movement within this new national culture.

According to Benedict Anderson, in contrast to dynasties, which are defined by their centers of power and thus generally have "porous and indistinct" boundaries, modern nations are defined by their borders rather than by their seats of government (19). Unlike in a kingship, which "organizes everything around a high centre" and whose "legitimacy derives from divinity, not from populations," in a modern nation, "state sovereignty is fully, flatly, and evenly operative over each square centimetre of a legally demarcated territory" (19). If national identity is at least partly cultural, then, the process of modern nation-building must incorporate the exploration of the areas within the borders and the creation of a hegemonic national culture. Travel provided Americans, as it had Europeans, with information about the natural environment of the New World, but it also taught Americans about the cultures of other regions. As Patricia Medeiros explains, "At the time of the Revolution these travel accounts provided the bulk of the little information most Americans had about the extent and nature of the largely unknown American continent" (195). The publication in either newspaper or book form of accounts that describe these areas is a vital aspect of this process, particularly if newspapers fulfill the crucial function in the creation of a national sensibility, as Anderson argues.

This process of nation-building was especially important in the development of the United States, made up of regions that were in many ways so different from each other. After all, at the end of the American Revolution, the thirteen colonies were only very loosely held together. According to Robert Lawson-Peebles, in fact, "Rent by faction and sedition, divided by topography and animosity, the United States seemed to many to be a fragile, even artificial, construction" (143). The development of this shift, from loose confederation to incipient nation, is illustrated in the country's founding documents, as Anderson points out. While the Declaration of Independence speaks only of the "people," the Constitution, not ratified until 1789, incorporates the term "nation." But this shift, and the process of constructing an American nation, was fraught with difficulty: "Whilst sometimes appearing natural they [national communities] have always been constructed through elaborate ideological and political work which produces a sense of nation and national identity, but a sense which can always be challenged. For there is no one national identity—rather competing national identities jostle with each other in a struggle for dominance" (C. Hall 240). In the United States from the time of the American Revolution to the Civil War, the primary ideologies competing for dominance were increasingly identified with the North and the South. Carolyn Porter concurs, explaining that her primary goal in examining antebellum nonfiction prose is "to understand how many voices were reduced to two, the North's and the South's, and how the former prevailed as 'American' " (349). For a single national identity to emerge, these ideologies had to interact, and the peoples of these regions had to imagine themselves as American. According to Len Travers, this process required the inculcation of a sense of national allegiance: "For the Revolution to be anything more than a war for independence by thirteen temporarily confederated colonies, the minds of the people would have to recognize a preeminent national identity of which they had not previously been aware. This did not mean (and practically could not mean) forsaking an older, more established 'community of allegiance.' Rather, American nationalism required *expanding* the community of allegiance to include not several thousand but several million people, across a vast geographic expanse" (9). For Travers, as for Porter, struggle was central to the emergence of this national identity.

As Porter recognizes, one of the most important literary genres involved in this struggle was the travel literature written by Americans, especially that which concerned journeys within the borders of their national community. These intranational travel narratives fulfilled a number of essential ideological functions. One of these, as Medeiros suggests, was to make those environments that were distant but within the national borders known to a northern, urban population. In addition, argues Medeiros, "Writers who described their travels in settled areas also helped to forge a sense of national identity by making distant places familiar, so that readers could see that they shared some important traits, and had common interests, with their countrymen hundreds of miles away" (196). But these travel accounts did not simply serve to unify diverse groups of people, as Medeiros seems to suggest. Travel narratives frequently sought to differentiate and distance one group or region from another and, in this way, increase a group or region's power and influence over what the narrative had marked as "other." As the variety of discourses circulating at this time began to polarize around the two primary geographical and cultural regions—North and South—intranational travel accounts often confronted issues that served to separate or distinguish these regions from each other as much as to compare and consolidate them.

Partly because America's publishing and printing centers were located primarily in northern cities during the eighteenth and nineteenth centuries, the vast majority of these published accounts of intranational travel describe journeys by northern travelers to the American South.[2] In addition, as Porter recognizes, the voices of these accounts were what came to be regarded as "American." According to Porter, as printing and publishing technologies advanced, and a larger percentage of the American population became literate, Americans came more and more to be tied together "by the threads of a discursive fabric they had come to weave themselves" (349). By the end of the Civil War, the question of which voice would dominate that discursive fabric had been answered: "It was the voice of the white, Protestant male, and whatever its origins, it spoke with a Northern accent" (C. Porter 349).[3]

Because the North finally became the dominant cultural, political, and economic region, its relationship with the South has occasionally been described in colonialist terms. One could contend, for instance, that many of the travel accounts of this period illustrate the different aspects of the colonial process described by V. Y. Mudimbe, who argues that the colonizing structure entails "the domination of physical space," the "reformation" of the minds of the "natives," and "the integration of local economic histories" into a colonialist perspective (2). However, since the North and the South came into being as part of the same nation as they united to rebel against Britain's colonial domination, and because the power relations between North and South did not mirror exactly the typical colonial relationship (if there is indeed a "typical" colonial relationship), one should be careful when applying this paradigm to these regions.[4] After all, although the South was frequently represented as "other," it was unquestionably part of the same nation when most of these travelers were writing. So the South became for many Americans a kind of internal "other," a region seen as the primary barrier to the development of a unified national culture. Therefore, in their attempts to help forge that national identity by exploring their country and traveling within its borders, many American travelers naturally went to the South to confront directly the most obvious national "problem."

The numerous difficulties involved in constructing a unified national identity were increasingly seen to be southern in nature. According to Richard Johnson, this process is common in relation to groups marginalized by or within a dominant culture: "[T]he experiences of subordinated social groups are presented as pathological, problems for intervention not in the organisation of society as a whole, but in the attitudes or behaviours of the suffering group itself" (89). Of course, the South was not simply a marginalized group; while there were many within southern society, especially slaves and women, who were almost completely removed from the centers of power, a significant portion of the white population of the region was hardly "suffering." However, many of the issues of most importance to the new nation—citizenship, race, gender, class—were often transformed into issues represented as having a regional, rather than a national, basis. Thus, throughout the period between the Revolutionary and Civil Wars, northern travel writers increasingly came to believe the primary hindrance to the development of a national community was the South's unwillingness to accommodate itself more fully to northern, represented as "American," cultural, social, and economic practices. I would argue, however, that while the North did indeed exert an extremely powerful influence over the southern states, American national culture truly developed out of the struggle to reconcile these differences. As Homi Bhabha argues, "It is in the emergence of the interstices—the overlap and displacement of domains of difference—that the intersubjective and collective experiences of *nationness*, community interest, or cultural value are negotiated" (2). American national identity, then, has grown out of the struggle as much as it has emerged from any single region, group, or class.[5]

While travel literature has been produced and read or heard since at least the first telling of *The Odyssey*, the scholarly study of this genre is fairly recent.[6] Of course, analysis of individual travel accounts is not a modern phenomenon; the reception of *The Travels of Sir John Mandeville*, originally circulated in Europe around 1360, suggests the lengthy history of interest in that text, for instance. Furthermore, scholars of specific periods or locales have long turned to travel

accounts for particular historical information. The systematic rhetorical analysis of travel literature as genre, however, is a modern phenomenon.[7]

Contemporary scholars of travel writing frequently point to two writers said
to have initiated (or at least signaled) current interest in the genre: Percy Adams
and Paul Fussell.[8] Adams's initial foray into the genre, *Travelers and Travel Liars,
1660–1800*, first published in 1962, investigates the role within the eighteenth
century of what Adams calls "travel lies" and seeks to "ascertain the effects of the
many travel deceptions of the period" (16). According to Adams, his book "deals
. . . with authentic travel accounts that in an Age of Reason told untruths, with
pseudo voyages that were designed to make the public believe them real" (vii).
Adams's next work on travel, *Travel Literature and the Evolution of the Novel*,
traces the impact of travel motifs and structures on the development of the
novel as a genre.[9] While both texts increased interest in travel and travel literature, the former study too easily places accounts of travel into categories difficult
to distinguish upon more careful examination, while the latter focuses primarily
on individual novels rather than travel accounts. Paul Fussell's *Abroad: British
Literary Traveling between the Wars*, on the other hand, focuses exclusively on
travel literature itself and analyzes more thoroughly a specific set of travel texts.
Fussell's study takes as its primary subject a group of British travel writers,
including Graham Greene, Norman Douglas, D. H. Lawrence, Christopher Ish-
erwood, W. H. Auden, Evelyn Waugh, and Robert Byron, whose works exemplified what, for Fussell, travel writing could and should be. *Abroad* still has much
to recommend it, for the analysis of this group of works is both insightful and
highly readable. However, as many recent scholars of the genre have pointed
out, *Abroad* is also deeply flawed, for it sets up and depends on what the author
claims is a fundamental shift, from "true travel" to "tourism," a change that
had apparently taken place only very recently in Fussell's opinion. These British
travel writers are great, Fussell argues, partly because they mark the end of an
era; with the advent of mass transportation (particularly jet airliners), tourism,
not travel, is the only type of movement now available, so these writers' works
purportedly offer us both literary excellence and insight into a world now un-
available.[10]

Because of the somewhat naive distinction it draws between travel and tourism, Fussell's work has become overshadowed by newer, more theoretically sophisticated analyses of the genre. Perhaps the most influential recent critical
study of travel writing has been Mary Louise Pratt's *Imperial Eyes: Travel Writing
and Transculturation*, an analysis of the work travel texts have performed within
European imperialism and a careful reading of works by several authors, including Alexander von Humboldt, Mungo Park, John Stedman, Maria Callcott

Graham, and Flora Tristan. Although Pratt's study focuses primarily on travel writers to South America and Africa, her use of terms such as "contact zone" and "transculturation" has been widely adopted. Furthermore, even though *Imperial Eyes* was hardly the first to recognize such connections, Pratt's analysis of the intimate relationship between travel writing and European imperialism has influenced numerous subsequent studies, including this one.[11] Thus, this specific text (along with the rest of Pratt's work) may be seen to have both marked and encouraged the relative explosion in the past decade of scholarly work on travel writing.[12]

While a large number of critical texts like Pratt's analyze works describing travel in non-Western regions, a significant proportion of recent criticism has focused on travel writing and travelers moving between Europe and the New World. Several studies have analyzed the language of the earliest European discovery and exploration narratives. For example, in *Discoverers, Explorers, Settlers*, Wayne Franklin groups this body of literature into narratives by "discoverers, explorers, and settlers," all of which share at least one common trait: according to Franklin, "More than anything else, the West became an epistemological problem for Europe" (7). In confronting this problem, Europeans used their language to try to understand and, consequently, to control the land before them. Likewise, Stephen Greenblatt argues in *Marvelous Possessions* that early European texts do not offer dependable descriptions of the New World; rather, he states, "We can be certain only that European representations of the New World tell us something about the European practice of representation" (7).[13] Like much other critical work on travel writing, then, these two works seek less to determine the accuracy of specific representations than to analyze more thoroughly the rhetorics and politics of travel writing, as well as the impact the genre may have had on societies on both sides of the Atlantic.

Because texts describing international travel continued to play an integral role in the construction of a national identity, an increasing number of studies have sought to describe the American character or explain the construction of the American nation by contrasting it with territories or nations outside the national borders.[14] Larzer Ziff, for instance, suggests in *Return Passages: Great American Travel Writing, 1780–1910*, that American travel writing not only described peoples encountered elsewhere but also encouraged a "deepened self-knowledge" on the part of the American writer and reader (7). Similarly, Terry Caesar argues, "Americans write of travel abroad, for better or worse, in order to be responsible to their national identities" (5). For Caesar, American travel writing is marked by an "intense skepticism about abroad," so American travelers throughout the nineteenth and twentieth centuries express particularly

ambivalent feelings about their overseas trips (2–3). William W. Stowe, too, focuses on international travel, wondering "what nineteenth-century American
classes, groups, and individuals got out of the expensive, time-consuming, even
dangerous, but extraordinarily popular practice of European travel" (x–xi).
Many Americans traveled to Europe, argues Stowe, in order to construct or
solidify their personal and social identities within American culture.[15] Likewise, James Buzard claims that European travel, available to increasing numbers
throughout the nineteenth and early twentieth centuries, served especially the
social interests of those English and American "travelers" who sought to differentiate themselves from the mass of "tourists" supposedly swarming across the
continent. According to Buzard, "[A]fter the Napoleonic Wars, the exaggerated
perception that the Continental tour was becoming more broadly accessible
than ever before gave rise to new formulations about what constituted 'authentic' cultural experience (such as travel is supposed to provide) and new representations aimed as distinguishing authentic from spurious or merely repetitive
experience" (6). For Buzard, what he names "tourism/anti-tourism" becomes
an especially effective way of understanding modernity, for tourism (or the an-
titouristic impulse) has become, he argues, the "exemplary cultural practice" of
modern society (7).[16]

While all of these studies discuss texts by both men and women, travel traditionally has been a male pursuit and thus not equally available to both sexes.[17]
Despite the differences in access to travel, however, several recent critics note
that more eighteenth- and nineteenth-century travelers were women than has
been recognized. The texts produced by these female travelers deserve careful
analysis, for they provide unique insight into the cultures from which these
women wrote and through which they traveled. In *Imperial Eyes*, for example, Pratt analyzes the gendered discourse of several women travelers, including
Flora Tristan and Maria Graham, who explored "contact zones" but described
these locales and their experiences in much different terms than did their male
counterparts. Mary Suzanne Schriber points out in *Writing Home: American
Women Abroad, 1830–1920*, "[A]lthough the act of writing may require inspiration, the muse is decidedly this-worldly, emanating from economics, technology, politics, ideology, and the various institutions of literature that shape the
writing practice of particular people in particular places at particular times"
(3). For Schriber, "home" is a particularly powerful concept for women travel
writers, who write both *to* and *about* their home. Sara Mills, in *Discourses of
Difference: An Analysis of Women's Travel Writing and Colonialism*, likewise focuses on women's travel narratives and the role of "home" in these texts; Mills is
particularly interested in the rhetorical and cultural influences that determined

the ways in which women's texts were both produced and received.[18] Cheryl J. Fish is similarly interested in women's writing and colonialism, studying the intersections of mobility, domesticity, race, gender, and colonialism. In her recent *Black and White Women's Travel Narratives: Antebellum Explorations*, Fish investigates these issues by looking at the way each of three women—Nancy Prince, Mary Seacole, and Margaret Fuller—published her travel text "as a form of social critique in the 1840s and 1850s . . . and positioned herself as what we would now call a social critic or self-made public intellectual" (2). For all of these critics, travel writing by women illustrates both the pressures women were under in these cultures and the ways in which traveling women in particular have managed to work around those pressures and to subvert the ideologies that have sought to limit their lives.

Despite the large number of travel texts addressed by these various scholars, however, all of these critical studies focus almost exclusively on travel writing describing journeys across national borders. Only rarely, in fact, does travel within national boundaries seem to count as travel at all.[19] This focus may relate to the emphasis within the larger field of postcolonialism on relations between rather than within nations, where critics frequently study the creation of a national identity in relation to colonial or imperial relations. However, while international travel is undoubtedly important for understanding a nation's culture and society, accounts of intranational travel are equally valuable in attempting to understand the creation of an American national identity during the eighteenth and nineteenth centuries, despite Terry Caesar's belief that "[t]ravel within national borders simply lacks the political force of travel across them" (163). In fact, intranational travel accounts highlight the extent to which the creation of a national identity is a complex, tangled struggle, for these texts frequently emphasize the divisions, arguments, and complications within a national culture.

Another problem of many of these studies is the narrow definition of what constitutes "travel literature." In addition to referring solely to accounts of international travel, critics frequently include only those texts that describe leisure travel. This restrictive focus defines the genre too narrowly, however, for people have long traveled and written about their experiences for myriad reasons. Only very rarely, for instance, have slave narratives been studied as travel texts, and the diaries of soldiers are seldom described in these terms. These, too, are travel texts, even though the writers were not in complete control of their movements. One must also be careful of drawing simple distinctions between different types of travel, as Paul Gilroy argues, for travel is too complex an experience to be described in neat categorical terms. Speaking of W. E. B. Du Bois and James

Weldon Johnson, Gilroy writes, "Their work can be used to identify the folly of assigning uncoerced or recreational travel experiences only to whites while viewing black people's experiences of displacement and relocation exclusively through the very different types of travelling undergone by refugees, migrants, and slaves" (133). In contrast to many of these earlier works, this book defines "travel literature" in the broadest terms.

"Travel literature" is less about particular types of travel than it is about almost any kind of published writing that describes the movement of individuals into "contact zones" of one type or another.[20] In addition, however, travel writing also claims a certain amount of veracity. For instance, while novels might describe travel, they are not usefully categorized as "travel literature," for they are not read (at least ostensibly) as factually true. "Travel literature" frequently seeks to establish, and also relies on, a certain trust between the author and his or her readers. The audience generally expects at least an attempt at truthfulness and often assumes the author's sincerity. (Thus, travel texts are frequently attacked vociferously when either of these is found to be lacking.) Furthermore, while travel literature does not necessarily describe journeys across national borders, the crossing of some kind of boundary—geographical, political, ideological, social, racial, or personal, for instance—is a standard feature. In fact, each narrator in the texts described in this study crosses at least one significant boundary, even though all stay within the United States.[21]

Difficulties arise in attempts to define the genre further because people travel into such a wide variety of places and record and transmit their experiences in such a wide variety of written forms. Thus, Mary Louise Pratt thinks of "travel literature" less as a collection of specific conventions than as a site of certain types of discourses:

> While travel literature is certainly a place where imperialist ideologies get created, it is equally certainly a place where such ideologies get questioned, especially from the realm of particularized and concrete sensual experience. In fact, travel literature is a particularly prominent instance of what discourse analysts like to call polyphony, because it is a genre that has never been consigned to professionals or specialists. Even today, it remains a place to which nonspecialist lay voices—an incredible variety of them—have access. You don't have to be a professional writer to write a travel book. Similar to call-in radio, travel literature is ultimately best seen as a genre not in the set of conventions, but in the sense of a discursive space which, like a street corner, is continually crisscrossed by all manner of people. ("Travel Narrative" 215–16)

And, I argue, crisscrossed, too, by all manner of texts.

The study of travel literature, then, should question less what exactly travel literature *is* or what it *describes* but, rather, what travel literature *does*—what cultural, social, political, or ideological work is performed by those texts that describe a narrator's experiences as he or she crosses into and moves within some type of "contact zone." Thus, despite what they might or might not tell us about the South or the traveler narrating the text, more than anything else, travel texts by northern writers about their journeys through the American South worked to establish and maintain an American national identity.

In the following chapters, I describe in more detail the role individual intranational travel narratives played in the complex struggle to define and stabilize an American identity. Accordingly, because struggle and conflict are such fundamental aspects of this process, the structure of most of these chapters attempts to incorporate a sense of this negotiation. While each chapter focuses on a single topic, four of the five chapters describe the work of at least two different writers who were wrestling with similar issues. Unlike the first three chapters, however, chapter 4 describes the work of only one writer; because Frederick Law Olmsted had no peer in terms of his impact—both during his lifetime and for decades afterward—on northern views of the southern states, his work warrants a separate chapter. And due to the sheer volume of texts written and published by soldiers and veterans of the Civil War, the final chapter describes texts by numerous travelers rather than just two, for the real significance of these works is best understood in a broad study. Regardless of the number of texts analyzed in these chapters, I hope that the full significance of each issue will emerge from the distinctions as well as the connections among the various writers both within and between the chapters.

In the first chapter, I investigate the work of two early travelers, J. Hector St. John de Crèvecoeur and William Bartram. Each of these two men in his own way attempts to recreate himself as a representative American man. In *Letters from an American Farmer*, Crèvecoeur uses the paradigm of the American as farmer to suggest the close relationship with the land this "new man" enjoys. This paradigm is complicated, however, by the competing image of the American as traveler, seen clearly in the almost constant meanderings of the narrator, James. Unlike Europeans, Crèvecoeur suggests, Americans are free to travel widely, both geographically and socially, so travel, which is a product of the economic fluidity and social mobility being used to define the idea of America during this period, serves as a sign of American freedom. William Bartram, on the other hand, argues throughout his *Travels* that the American should incorporate within himself a combination of two distinct ways of knowing and understanding the world. By traveling through the South, Bartram seeks to recreate himself as both Enlightenment scientist and proto-Romantic poet, both European and Native American. He, too, represents himself as a traveler and a representative American, but Bartram becomes an American through what travel allows him to know rather than what travel allows him to be.

In chapter two, I investigate the centrality of travel in the slave narratives of Frederick Douglass and Solomon Northup. Although Douglass was frequently forced to move according to his masters' wishes, he learned to alter his required movements in order to accomplish his own goals, at least partially. In this way, he gradually took control of his movements and became an American traveler, so *Narrative of the Life of Frederick Douglass* recounts the author-narrator's transformation from bound slave to free traveler. While Douglass suggests in his 1845 autobiography that his metamorphosis from slave to traveler is essentially complete by the end of the narrative, Solomon Northup is less optimistic. Born a free citizen of New York, Northup argues in *Twelve Years a Slave* that the black American can never truly be free to direct his own travels as long as slavery exists within the nation's borders. Kidnapped during a trip to Washington, D.C., Northup suggests that slavery has infected the very heart of American democracy, for he had been leading an exemplary American life and determining his own movements before he was robbed of his liberty and sold into slavery. Although he is once again with his family in New York at the close of his account, Northup's autobiography does not end on the optimistic note that Douglass's text does, for Northup well knows how tenuous is the freedom to travel (or stay in one place) for the black inhabitant of the United States.

While Crèvecoeur, Bartram, Douglass, and Northup all seek to present themselves as representatives of the American individual, Fanny Kemble and Harriet Jacobs address the issue of national identity through their investigations of the American home. Ironically, provided the opportunity to step outside of their normal domestic routines, these two women use their travels to address the image and ideology of the American household. For Fanny Kemble, author of *Journal of a Residence on a Georgian Plantation in 1838–1839* and wife of a wealthy slave owner, her husband's Georgia plantation constricts her ability to determine her own movements as she seeks to fulfill the duties she sees as essential to a smoothly functioning home. Because the plantation is both household and business, Kemble's husband, Pierce Butler, controls the domestic space, rather than allowing Kemble to control it. The southern household, Kemble concludes, must become more like a northern "home" if the nation is to construct a unified "domestic" ideology. Likewise, Harriet Jacobs argues in *Incidents in the Life of a Slave Girl* that southern domestic space has been corrupted by slavery and has prohibited southern women, free and slave, from fulfilling their duties as wives and mothers. Like Douglass and Northup, Jacobs must learn to direct her own travels in order to escape the bonds of southern slavery. Unlike these two men, however, Jacobs centers her critique of slavery on the home, as she tries to determine her own political and ideological movements by hiding herself within the confines of her grandmother's house. Of course, for Jacobs, too, true freedom means determining her own physical and geographical movement, but she concludes her account by struggling to construct a domestic space for herself and her children in which she will be freed from the necessity of continued or coerced travel.

If travel allowed these earlier writers to investigate the role of the citizen or domestic space in the construction of a national identity, Frederick Law Olmsted's journeys through the South gave him the opportunity to argue for the development of a unified national economy. For Olmsted, slavery's primary fault is its inefficiency, so he seeks to reform the southern economy in order to align it with the emerging industrial capitalism of the North. Olmsted was thus not seeking to *construct* a national economy as much as he was trying to *consolidate* the two regions' economies and societies. Basing his arguments on the ideal of the New England yeoman farmer, Olmsted served as a member of what Mary Louise Pratt calls the "capitalist vanguard," hoping to transform the South into a region more thoroughly dependent on northern capital, expertise, and culture (*Imperial Eyes* 147–51). Travel is an integral aspect of this project, according to Olmsted, for not only must workers be free to travel to those areas where their labor is most needed, but the goods, services, and ideas that form the basis of the economy must be able to circulate freely throughout the entire nation.

While all of these writers differentiated the South and the North in one way or another, Union soldiers during the Civil War—the subject of the final chapter—frequently argued in their journals and travel narratives that the two regions shared much and should be maintained as a single nation. Confronted with the break-up of their country, Union soldiers used their narratives—which are in many ways as much "travel" texts as those previously described—to strive to reincorporate the South and to identify and celebrate those aspects of the region that they found most "American." In addition to giving these Union soldiers a broader understanding of "America" and making them in a sense more representative of the nation because they were travelers, the movement of the Union Army as a whole created a newly unified nation, as the land over which it passed was being reconstituted as American soil. Frequently forced to move in ways that they did not desire, soldiers ironically appear almost slavelike in their inability to travel freely, even as they were fighting to gain political freedom, including the freedom to travel, for the South's millions of slaves. Once again, the travel in which these writers participated became part of a larger struggle to define their nation's identity and thereby determine their country's future.

For all of these writers, from Crèvecoeur to the numerous Union soldiers, travel is constitutive of American freedom and identity, serving as proof of their status (or lack thereof) as American citizens. Like the authors of the nation's founding documents, these writers illustrated the promise (and the dangers) travel, in whatever form, offered both the individual and their society as a whole. Each, then, both re-presents and represents their country and their fellow inhabitants, from whatever region, class, race, gender, or ideology.

CHAPTER ONE

Representing America

The American as Traveler in the Work of J. Hector St. John de Crèvecoeur and William Bartram

In every perception of nature there is actually present the whole of society.
The latter not only provides the patterns of perception in general,
but also defines nature *a priori* in relation to itself.

THEODOR ADORNO

J. Hector St. John de Crèvecoeur's *Letters from an American Farmer* (1782) has long been read as an American national epic, a founding document of the newly emerging United States. D. H. Lawrence famously stated, "Franklin is the real *practical* prototype of the American. Crèvecoeur is the emotional" (29). Albert E. Stone, in his 1963 introduction to the Penguin edition of *Letters*, goes so far as to suggest, "American literature, as the voice of our national consciousness, begins in 1782 with the first publication in England of *Letters from an American Farmer*" (7). These critics, and many who follow their lead, have thus viewed Crèvecoeur's *Letters* as a reflection of the beliefs of a representative individual writing during a particularly volatile, ambiguous period. The ambiguity of the period, most critics argue, is reflected in the lack of coherence so often seen in a book that John Seelye, for instance, calls "deeply disjunctive" (*Beautiful Machine* 131). However, these critics fail to appreciate the role the text itself played in the construction of a national identity. Rather than simply forming the foundation on which Crèvecoeur based his work, American national identity was forged in part through the writing and publication of the text itself.

William Bartram's *Travels* (1791), too, participated in the production of an American national identity during the critical years immediately surrounding the Revolutionary War. While Bartram's book purports to be a rather innocent account of a romantic botanist rambling through the fields and forests of the southern colonies, *Travels* actually addresses questions that were of vital interest

to the emerging republic, particularly those concerning the fundamental identity of the new nation and its inhabitants. As in *Letters*, Bartram's book does not
merely reflect the surroundings in which it was written but actively constructs
the natural, political, social, and cultural environments generally viewed as its
foundation.

Both Crèvecoeur and Bartram participate in this nation-building process
primarily through the construction of a narrator who becomes representative of
American national identity. Through the representation of a narrative persona,
each of these two authors seeks to embody the numerous competing discourses
available to him as an author. In many ways, Larzer Ziff describes both Bartram
and Crèvecoeur when he argues that if we consider that *Letters* constitutes a
reality rather than simply reflects a pre-existing one, "then we see that the eruption of physical conflict at the close is an externalization of irreconcilable differences within the writer's position rather than the intrusion of public events into
an otherwise felicitous private life. These differences exist as a conflict between
what is valorized in the writing and the act of writing itself. To read the *Letters*
as an embodiment of a cultural reality rather than a picture of external reality is to deny the gap between private circumstance and public event" (*Writing*
22). Therefore, the intrusion of revolution, for instance, or the eruption of the
chaos of a hurricane represents the tensions and contradictions of the author's
position as much as the realities of the historical situation. By attempting to
embody the American national identity through the construction of a narrative
persona, each of these two authors recreates the entire nation in his own image
as he reflects the contradictory ideologies that have produced him.

Travel is more than incidental to this process, for movement of many types
determines these representative figures and contributes to the attempted resolution of these contradictory ideological impulses. For both Crèvecoeur and
Bartram, travel is constitutive of national character. Unlike Europeans, they
suggest, Americans are free to travel widely, both geographically and socially,
so travel serves as an indication of Americanness. However, the travel in which
Americans participate further broadens their views and provides them with a
variety of perspectives that together form the American character, so travel not
only serves as an indication of American freedom but also creates the freedom
that Americans enjoy. Thus, Crèvecoeur and Bartram argue, travel is both a sign
and a symptom of American freedom and national identity.

As much as James, the narrator of *Letters*, emphasizes the stability and
"grounded" nature of the farming life, his definition of the American also
depends on movement. Describing the travels of James through the various

regions of the emerging nation, *Letters* constructs a competing image of the American as traveler and thereby complicates from its very beginning the agrarian ideal that so many critics identify as the work's essence. Far from positing at the beginning an ideal that is slowly undermined during the course of the book by the realities of slavery and the American Revolution, as most critics suggest, Crèvecoeur sets up two competing ideals, which are reconciled only in James's closing description of his future life among the Indians. While Crèvecoeur's initial vision of America as the combination of European culture and the New World environment is indeed undermined by the historical contingencies that intrude on the text, as critics have pointed out, this ideal is replaced finally by a new vision in which the representative American figure is constructed as both a farmer and a traveler. Rather than asserting as he does throughout much of the text that this new man, the American, is created solely by the land, James argues finally that the representative American should be a frontier farmer, who is able both to live according to the civilized rules that farming engenders and to participate in a community and a culture—Native American—that is free to move, to travel, and to migrate. Thus, travel finally produces for Crèvecoeur's narrator a new way of *being*, a specifically American ontology resulting from the unique combination of farming and travel constitutive of this "new man."

For Bartram, on the other hand, travel provides the American access to unique combinations of knowledge. If Bartram, too, finally constructs his narrator as both European and Native American, the critical aspect of this union is more epistemological than ontological. That is, Bartram becomes an American because he is able to conjoin not only Enlightenment science with proto-Romantic poetry but also European and Native American ways of understanding the world. Creating a narrative persona allows Bartram to reconcile these competing ideologies, for as a traveler, Bartram's narrator is never bound completely to a single way of knowing his environment—natural, social, or cultural. While travel gives Bartram access to these competing ideologies and epistemologies, his status as a traveler, he suggests, allows him to consolidate these into a single figure.

Although most critics have argued that both Bartram and Crèvecoeur are finally products of the American environment, these two writers in fact produce the environments in which they act. By creating a representative American, each of the authors redefines and recreates the American landscape itself, as a new nation and as wilderness, farmland, and frontier. Through the description of an ideal American citizen, Crèvecoeur and Bartram create also the cultural, social, political, and natural environments this new American will inhabit. Therefore, rather than simply reflecting American society and its environment, these two authors use their texts to produce America itself as a nation and a land.

J. Hector St. John de Crèvecoeur's *Letters from an American Farmer* claims to be comprised of a series of letters written by James, the narrator, to an Englishman, Mr. F. B., describing the New World, its inhabitants, and American society and culture. In the third letter to his correspondent, James attempts to address directly his famous question, "What is an American?" As the title of the book itself strongly suggests, James believes the American to be primarily a farmer. "Some few towns excepted," he explains, "we are all tillers of the earth, from Nova Scotia to West Florida. We are a people of cultivators scattered over an immense territory, communicating with each other by means of good roads and navigable rivers, united by the silken bands of mild government, all respecting the laws without dreading their power, because they are equitable. We are all animated with the spirit of an industry which is unfettered and unrestrained, because each person works for himself" (67). Although James claims throughout most of *Letters* that Americans are loyal subjects of the English Crown and thus do not alone constitute a country, in describing here the inhabitants of America, James uses a number of descriptions that recent theorists have viewed as the standard definitions of a nation. For instance, like Benedict Anderson, who argues that a shared print culture is integral to the formation of a nation, James argues that these people are united by bonds of communication, which are sustained by "good roads and navigable rivers." In addition, the people he describes share common desires, habits, and values, and they are all industrious, independent, and energetic. They also voluntarily obey the same laws and respect their shared government, James suggests. All of these connections—of language, values, habits, and commitments—are possible because all Americans are tied to the land, are "tillers of the earth," according to the passage. For James, it seems, farming and the natural environment bind, even create, Americans as a people.

Certainly James identifies himself from the very beginning of the book as a farmer. For example, in his correspondence with Mr. F. B., James frequently refers to himself as "a cultivator of the earth" (50), and he explains to his friend that he is schooled primarily in agriculture: "I am neither a philosopher, politician, divine, or naturalist, but a simple farmer," he writes (49). But farming is not simply a source of James's physical sustenance, for in the first letter after the introduction, entitled "On the Situation, Feelings, and Pleasures of an American Farmer," James describes the complete contentment he feels on the farm his father has given to him. Nature, argues James, provides him (as it does his countrymen) with everything he could possibly desire. As James explains,

> It feeds, it clothes us; from it we draw even a great exuberancy, our best meat, our richest drink; the very honey of our bees comes from this privileged spot. No wonder we should thus cherish its possession; no wonder that so many Europeans who have never been able to say that such portion of land was theirs cross the Atlantic to realize that happiness. This formerly rude soil has been converted by my father into a pleasant farm, and in return, it has established all our rights; on it is founded our rank, our freedom, our power as citizens, our importance as inhabitants of such a district. (54)

His farm seems to provide everything he and his family need—physically, socially, intellectually, and spiritually. Because the land provides so fully for James's welfare, he rarely has reason to travel elsewhere at all. After the birth of his son, James claims, "I ceased to ramble in imagination through the wide world; my excursions since have not exceeded the bounds of my farm, and all my principal pleasures are now centered within its scanty limits" (53). Thus, James's agricultural life is a stationary one, imaginatively and physically, and his entire existence seems firmly rooted in the local environment of his particular farm. James's intellectual life, too, is tied to his farm, for even though his mind has not been improved "by education, example, books, and by every acquired advantage" as has that of his English correspondent, James explains that "there is not an operation belonging to it [the farm] in which I do not find some food for useful reflections" (53). His primary goal in life, he explains, is to earn enough to provide his children the kind of agricultural lifestyle his father provided for him. According to James, "I envy no man's prosperity, and wi[s]h no other portion of happiness than that I may live to teach the same philosophy to my children and give each of them a farm, show them how to cultivate it, and be like their father, good, substantial, independent American farmers—an appellation which will be the most fortunate one a man of my class can possess so long as our civil government continues to shed blessings on our husbandry" (65). As he received his farmland and farming knowledge from his father, so James hopes to pass on to his children the benefits of an agricultural existence, for James's family members—past, present, and future—are dedicated to an agrarian lifestyle.

If James is thus typical of the members of his own family, so, too, is he representative of the American people in general, according to this account. In fact, he suggests, while most Americans engage in agriculture as their primary pursuit, even those Americans who have other jobs are farmers. For instance, the minister with whom James converses in the introductory chapter both farms and serves as a pastor; he tells James that he cannot help correspond with Mr. F. B. because he must till his farm as well as prepare his sermons. These are not entirely separate tasks, he points out, for like James (and all Americans, the book suggests), the minister has incorporated farming completely into his life: "I have composed many a good sermon as I followed my plough," he tells James (46–47). As the two men both illustrate and contend, Americans are not incidentally farmers but are fundamentally "tillers of the earth," for it is farming that makes the people who they are.

Thus, the primary production of American farming seems to be America's people themselves. The land in America not only provides an environment fertile enough to support large numbers of people, James suggests, but actually recreates the people who live on and work it. Before coming to America, he states, European immigrants "were as so many useless plants, wanting vegetative mould and refreshing showers; they withered and were mowed down by want, hunger and war" (69). However, he continues, "[N]ow, by the power of transplantation, like all other plants they have taken root and flourished!" (69). The soil and the land thus create the American, James suggests, for in this environment the immigrant "takes root" and from it draws his nourishment, becoming in the process an entirely new person. Because the population consists largely of these newly transplanted Europeans or their descendants, Crèvecoeur suggests, American society as a whole has apparently grown out of the land.[1] Furthermore, since the New World possesses such superior soil, James argues, the produce of that soil is likewise of the highest quality. Therefore, he boasts, "we are the most perfect society now existing in the world" (67).

In James's (or Crèvecoeur's) schema, agrarian life in America seems to be situated halfway between the tightly structured civilization of Europe and the chaos of the American wilderness. Significantly, James is a member of the "middle colonies," so his home is located neither in the urban culture of the east, which may be too European, nor on the very edge of the frontier, which exists too close to the savagery of the wilderness. As Patricia Barbeito argues, the book "defines farming as the clearest expression of an ideal social order that is located midway between the corruption of a decaying civilization and the unbridled forces of nature" (35). While European society does not allow most people the freedom to own their own land or to move according to their own desires, according to James, the wilderness encourages too much freedom and does not demand the labor necessary to the health of an individual and a community. Farming, James concludes, offers the American the perfect combination of freedom from the tight bonds of society and responsibility arising from raising crops on a patch of land.

For many critics of Crèvecoeur's *Letters*, the construction of this agrarian ideal as the basis of American society constitutes the book's most significant contribution to American culture. Accordingly, the first three chapters of *Letters*, in which Crèvecoeur carefully constructs this ideal, have long been viewed as the book's most significant sections. These letters are generally seen as optimistic in tone and outlook, and the narrator James is viewed at least initially as an enthusiastic defender of New World Society. For example, A. W. Plumstead suggests that these letters are filled with "joy, pride, wonder" (216). Critics have tended to gloss over the five middle chapters on New England in order to argue that the initial ideal is subverted only in the book's closing chapters, especially by the chapter describing slavery in the American South and by the final letter in which James flees his farm as the dangers of the Revolution are closing in on him and his family. Thus, these final chapters are viewed by most critics as much more pessimistic in tone and focus, due, it is generally believed, either to an alteration on the part of the narrator or to the intrusion of an authorial voice.[2]

Of course, the late chapters on slavery and the Revolution do serve to undermine Crèvecoeur's agrarian ideal, but critics have failed to appreciate the extent to which Crèvecoeur's early construction of this ideal has been qualified from the first pages of the text.[3] James's descriptions of his farm life suggest that nature has been extremely generous to the American farmer, but there are numerous hints that the environment is not always so kind, especially to those marginalized by American society. The status of both slaves and Native Americans is a constant undercurrent to James's descriptions of the beauty of American nature and society, but James is only forced to confront these cultural "others" when he begins to travel throughout his nation. As a result of his journeys, James's belief in the agrarian ideal is further qualified by his growing awareness of the importance of travel, both for his own identity and for the identity of the entire nation as it is being constructed. Travel not only broadens James's perspective but also encourages in him a new, national consciousness in contrast to the local perspective arising from his more stationary, agrarian experiences. While James initially argues that Americans are almost entirely farmers, his own journeys throughout the country convince him that travel is as important to American identity as is agriculture. The whaling culture he encounters in New England, for instance, proves to him that the farming paradigm is insufficient to America's diversity. In addition, his travels south to Charles Town force him to confront the one issue, slavery, that has haunted the book from its very beginning and convince him to revise his beliefs about nature and the natural environment. Although Crèvecoeur does explicitly construct an agrarian ideal in *Letters*, he qualifies that ideal by setting up a competing, contradictory paradigm of the American as traveler. Thus, James becomes most fully American at the end of the book, when he attempts to reconcile the two paradigms into a single identity and becomes a traveling farmer by joining his family with a tribe of Native Americans.[4]

Interestingly, while critics clearly recognize that James undergoes a transformation during the course of the narrative, the full significance of travel on James's perspective and understanding of the American nation has not been adequately investigated.[5] Although few critics have recognized it as such, Crèvecoeur's work is, in a number of ways, a traditional travel narrative, for it follows the journeys of James from his home in Pennsylvania to the coastal islands of New England and the slave plantations of the South. Perhaps this critical reticence to recognize *Letters* as a travel narrative stems from several of the book's unusual characteristics. For one, Crèvecoeur's use of a clearly fictional narrator distances his work from more traditional travel narratives, in which the narrator of the text is more explicitly aligned with the author. Furthermore, Crèvecoeur's *Letters* charts little actual travel on James's part; James describes the regions in which he travels but rarely elucidates how he got there. This lack of detail describing the journeys themselves means that few of the standard generic features of the eighteenth-century travel book—complaints about roads, accounts of lodging, or descriptions of fellow travelers—are included in the work, so only rarely does the reader encounter passages describing the mode of travel or the difficulties overcome. There are few passages, in fact, in which James describes his own movement at all. In one of the rare instances, James explains, "At my landing I was cordially received by those to whom I was recommended and treated with unaffected hospitality by such others with whom I became acquainted; and I can tell you that it is impossible for any traveller to dwell here one month without knowing the heads of the principal families" (141). More exemplary of James's style is the second half of this sentence, in which James describes the experiences a traveler would have rather than relating his own personal experiences, as when he writes, "Let us suppose you and I to be travelling" (74).

Thus, James frequently hints at travel or recounts the travels of other figures in order to describe a certain location or aspect of American life. For instance, much of James's third letter, "What is an American," consists of a history of "Andrew, the Hebridean," an immigrant from Scotland whom James helps to become established in this country. Coming to America with little more than energy and a desire for honest labor, according to James, Andrew soon finds

himself "become a freeholder, possessed of a vote, of a place of residence, a citizen of the province of Pennsylvania" (102). After only four years, James explains,
Andrew is "independent" and "unencumbered with debts, services, rents, or
any other dues" (104). He clearly represents for James the promise that America
offers to the European immigrant. Having immigrated from Scotland, Andrew
is obviously a traveler; however, James represents his success as growing primarily from the beneficence of the American environment and society, as well
as from Andrew's energy and honesty, both of which have been given room to
grow and mature in America.

Immediately following James's account of Andrew is a chapter entitled "Description of the Island of Nantucket, with the Manners, Customs, Policy, and
Trade of the Inhabitants." As is common in *Letters*, James does not include a
description of his journey to Nantucket, nor does he describe many of his experiences on the island; instead, he describes the island and its people with a
kind of detachment only occasionally interrupted by details (or hints) of his
own wanderings. Perhaps Crèvecoeur includes this chapter after describing Andrew's success in order to contrast the culture found on Nantucket with that of
the Hebridean island from which Andrew had emigrated. Although James does
not explicitly relate the two islands, he does suggest that the people of Nantucket benefit greatly from their participation in American society. "Had this
island been contiguous to the shores of some ancient monarchy," James argues,
"it would only have been occupied by a few wretched fishermen, who, oppressed
by poverty, would hardly have been able to purchase or build little fishing barks,
always dreading the weight of taxes or the servitude of men-of-war" (109). The
similarity of this description to his suggestions about Scotland's coastal islands
is difficult to ignore.

James is fascinated by New England's islands, he claims, because the inhabitants have managed to accomplish so much in an unforgiving natural environment. While he loves to describe the natural fecundity of the American
continent, he finds in his travels that he is drawn to those spots "where extraordinary exertions have produced extraordinary effects, and where every natural
obstacle has been removed by a vigorous industry" (108). The society that has
grown out of the continent's generous environment thus benefits even those
areas that are not as naturally blessed. On Nantucket, James suggests, he has
met with "barren spots fertilized, grass growing where none grew before, grain
gathered from fields which had hitherto produced nothing better than bram-
bles, dwellings raised where no building materials were to be found, wealth acquired by the most uncommon means" (108). In fact, the land is so barren and
unable to support an agricultural society that it initially seems hardly a section

of the same continent. However, the inhabitants of this island do possess the industry typical of the American character, argues James, so they have transformed themselves into a different kind of farming culture. As James explains, "If these people are not famous for tracing the fragrant furrow on the plain, they plough the rougher ocean, they gather from its surface, at an immense distance and with Herculean labours, the riches it affords; they go to hunt and catch that huge fish which by its strength and velocity one would imagine ought to be beyond the reach of man" (110). By redescribing these islanders as "farmers of the sea," James can more easily incorporate them into his agricultural paradigm and continue to describe them as essentially American figures. Significantly, James shifts his use of pronouns as he works to incorporate these inhabitants of Nantucket fully into his definition of the American. Although he initially describes the people as "they" or "them," he uses the first-person "we," "us," and "our" with more frequency as the chapters on Nantucket progress. In letter 7, for instance, entitled "Manners and Customs of Nantucket," James explains, "[N]o marriage articles are drawn up among us by skilful lawyers," and, "We give nothing with our daughters" (144).

Because he continues to define the American primarily as a farmer, James explains that the native peoples of Nantucket, another group he encounters during his travels in New England, are not members of American society. Unlike those "American" inhabitants of Nantucket originally from Europe, who are now flourishing on the island, the native population has decreased dramatically in recent years. "What is become of those numerous tribes which formerly inhabited the extensive shores of the great bay of Massachusetts?" James wonders (122). While the islands, like the American continent, were formerly inhabited by numerous tribes of Native Americans, James explains, the native population has almost completely vanished. James seems to view the extinction of the native people as inevitable, and he blames the diminishing numbers on fate or chance rather than on the other inhabitants of the continent. "Wherever they [Native Americans] happen to be mixed, or even to live in the neighbourhood of the Europeans," James argues, "they become exposed to a variety of accidents and misfortunes to which they always fall victims: such are particular fevers, to which they were strangers before, and sinking into a singular sort of indolence and sloth" (121). Perhaps James believes these natives are not worthy of full participation in American society because they are not farmers. Instead, he claims, they have traditionally lived on what the sea provided them, and now they are too indolent and slothful. Unlike the ever-expanding society of European Americans, James concludes, the native people "appear to be a race doomed to recede and disappear before the superior genius of the Europeans" (122). Despite the tone of inevitability that James uses here, however, his description of these peoples seems to qualify slightly his earlier exuberance concerning the limitless opportunities offered by the American continent.

However, it is not only James's encounter during his travels with the native peoples of Nantucket that encourages him to revise his earlier definition of the American. As he slowly comes to realize, if the European people of Nantucket are American farmers, they are also travelers, and James begins to incorporate some amount of travel into his description of the American character. After all, James himself learns about his fellow countrymen during a journey through New England. Because the livelihood and success of these New Englanders depend on their almost continual travels, James is forced to admit that at least a portion of the American population are regular travelers as well as farmers (as he defines them). He realizes also that farming itself is dependent on travel, not only the local movement of farmers but the extensive transfer of American produce; in fact, the more successful American farmers are, the more travel is required to support and satisfy them. According to James, "[A]s our internal riches increase, so does our external trade, which consequently requires more ships and more men" (145). Farming is thus integrally tied to travel, both local and international.

Although his earlier description of Americans as immigrants presupposed a certain amount of travel, James has suggested in the early chapters that further travel is unnecessary for Americans, who, like himself, generally choose to remain on their farms. While he initially argues that the soil transforms these immigrants into Americans, James comes to realize that travel is another essential aspect of this alteration, as travel becomes so important to his own evolving self-identity and to his understanding of the American nation. Like a European immigrant, James expands his vision when he no longer stays so close to home. Thus, while he had originally told his English correspondent that he would limit himself to topics related to agriculture, James begins to use his travels to broaden his own perspective and the scope of subjects addressed in his letters. Like the recent immigrant to America he has described who "suddenly alters his scale," James is being forced out of his initial agrarian perspective by his movements as he is confronted by difference within his own country's borders (82).

As James comes to broaden his national perspective and to gain knowledge from the travels in which he participates, so, too, do the people of Nantucket expand their horizons and gain information essential to their futures as they travel throughout the nation and the world. The result of this wide travel is the acquisition of important information concerning those regions most conducive to immigration, James explains. "They everywhere carry admonition and useful advice," he states, "and thus by travelling, they unavoidably gather the most necessary observations concerning the various situations of particular districts, their soils, their produce, their distance from navigable rivers, the price of land, etc." (145). According to James, because they are such a vigorous, healthy group, the island is not large enough to contain their expanding population. As a result, many people leave Nantucket and immigrate to the mainland. "Emigration is both natural and easy to a maritime people," James suggests, so "[t]hey yearly go to different parts of this continent" (145). Travel clearly serves this island population well, for it both provides them with their present livelihood and ensures their continued success as they outgrow the small, barren island on which they live.

Interestingly, James indicates that one group of Nantucket emigrants has suffered from the incredible fertility of the region in North Carolina where they have founded "New Garden." "No spot of earth can be more beautiful," James claims; "it is composed of gentle hills, of easy declivities, excellent lowlands, accompanied by different brooks which traverse this settlement. I never saw a soil that rewards men so early for their labours and disbursements" (146).[6] The soil of New Garden is incomparably fertile, and even the highest grounds bear "the most luxuriant grass and never-failing crops of grain" (147). Given James's initial enthusiasm for the promise offered by America's fertile farmland, this settlement might seem to illustrate the pinnacle of American possibility. However, here the soil is too rich, so these immigrants are not forced to toil as hard as their Nantucket brethren. Thus, the New Garden settlement "does not breed men equally hardy, nor capable to encounter dangers and fatigues," and the extensive fertility of the region "leads too much to idleness and effeminacy" (147). Because they don't work, according to James, these settlers seem, like the native inhabitants of New England's islands, somehow unqualified to be counted as fully American. Even if James were to begin life again, he argues, he would not choose to live in the rich lands of North Carolina, "where mankind reap too much, do not toil enough, and are liable to enjoy too fast the benefits of life" (147). Instead, James explains, he would settle "on the rougher shores of Kennebec" in Massachusetts, for it "will always be a country of health, labour, and strong activity, and those are the characteristics of society which I value more than greater opulence and voluptuous ease" (148). Thus, James qualifies his early ideal by arguing that extreme fertility can be detrimental to American identity; in fact, the whalers of Nantucket seem more American than these immigrants who so effortlessly extract their livelihoods from the rich southern soil.

James reaches similar conclusions about the inhabitants of Charles Town in letter 9, entitled "Description of Charles Town; Thoughts on Slavery; On

Physical Evil; A Melancholy Scene." On Nantucket, James has argued, nature has not been overly generous, so the inhabitants are forced to toil in order to carve out their existence. However, this labor is the source of their pleasure and the secret of their happiness, so the absence of fertility seems to have produced the community that flourishes there.[7] In contrast, few people in Charles Town—besides the slaves—must labor, so their time is available for entertainment and vice: "The rays of their sun seem to urge them irresistibly to dissipation and pleasure," James states (167). The southern environment is seen as particularly dangerous to men, many of whom die young. Most women, James observes, outlive several husbands (167). Here the land has become deadly, more an alluring but dangerous seductress than a nurturing mother. In the words of Annette Kolodny, the danger here is that the land's "embrace may turn to engulfment" (58).[8]

James's journey to Charles Town is even more significant because it forces him to confront directly one issue—slavery—that has troubled him throughout his narrative. Prior to his travels to New England and the South, James argues briefly that slavery in the North is not harmful to slaves, and he generally ignores the full significance of African enslavement. However, the issue of slavery frequently interrupts his narrative, suggesting some conflict within or between the narrative and authorial voices. Clearly Crèvecoeur seems to place slavery at the center of the book, for the issue arises even in the early, "optimistic" chapters, qualifying James's reverie about the promise of American society. While he initially suggests that slavery is a regional, rather than a national, issue, James comes to argue after he has traveled to the South that slavery actually underlies American society as a whole and undermines its promise of rebirth and renewal.

In fact, before the book proper even begins, the initial ideal of America as a land of freedom and opportunity is undermined by Crèvecoeur's dedication to Abbé Raynal, author of *A Philosophical and Political History of the Settlements and Trade of the Europeans in the East and West Indies*, which suggests that slavery will constitute one of the book's central concerns. The dedication of the book to Raynal essentially calls into question James's representations of America before they are even constructed. In this way, then, the initial ideal James describes is always already undermined by the extratextual apparatus of the book. In *The Transformation of Authorship in America*, Grantland Rice concurs, stating, "Much of the confusion about *Letters from an American Farmer* has stemmed from a failure to take into account Crèvecoeur's dedication to Abbé Raynal" (102). In his dedication, Crèvecoeur juxtaposes slavery and freedom and thus highlights the institution's central role in New World society and the connections between American freedom and chattel slavery. Addressing Raynal,

Crèvecoeur writes, "As an eloquent and powerful advocate, you have pleaded the cause of humanity in espousing that of the poor Africans. You viewed these provinces of North America in their true light: as the asylum of freedom, as the cradle of future nations and the refuge of distressed Europeans" (37). As its placement in this excerpt suggests, the "true light" in which Raynal viewed America here illuminates two seemingly opposite phenomena, freedom and slavery, so Crèvecoeur's description of America as the "asylum of freedom" is undercut by the previous reference to the plight of African slaves. For both Crèvecoeur and Raynal, it seems, the existence of the former depends on the continuation of the latter. As Christine Holbo suggests, "Just as Raynal discerned slavery at the dark heart of commercial humanist societies, James sees community as founded upon the extremities of slavery" (47). Through this dedication, Crèvecoeur both acknowledges that slaves are indeed human and argues that slavery is an issue that affects all of the "provinces of North America." Thus, the attentive reader will begin the book with the enslavement of Africans firmly attached to the concept of freedom that America apparently promises to "distressed Europeans."

But it is not only the dedication to which most critics have failed to attend adequately. From almost the very first page, the issue of slavery intrudes on the text through the comments, anecdotes, and descriptions of James and other characters. In the introduction, for instance, James, his wife, and their minister discuss the proposal by the Englishman Mr. F. B. to James, requesting that James write the series of letters that will eventually form the book. Contrasting the life of the mind enjoyed by his correspondent with the active, demanding life led by her husband, James's wife explains that in England, according to Mr. F. B., "they have no trees to cut down, no fences to make, no Negroes to buy and to clothe" (48–49).[9] Along with clearing land and marking property as one's own, buying and providing for slaves is said to be an essential task for an American farmer, one of the first three that comes to mind. James's wife further hopes that travelers passing their farm will not say, "Here liveth the scribbling farmer," but, "Look how fat and well clad their Negroes are" (49). Writing, at least in America, she sees as purely recreational (or dangerously political) compared to the more important tasks required by the demands of farm life, such as protecting one's property, in land or slaves.

At the beginning of the second letter, James himself begins to call into question the ideal he will describe more fully within a few pages. Generally read as one of the two most important chapters for James's establishment of an American agrarian ideal, this letter has long been pointed to by critics as exemplifying James's belief that the American farm is an ideal world in which all creatures, human or not, cooperate for the good of the entire community. "[W]here is that station," James wonders, "which can confer a more substantial system of felicity than that of an American farmer possessing freedom of action, freedom of thoughts, ruled by a mode of government which requires but little from us?" (52). James thanks Mr. F. B. for describing the lot of the "Russian boor" or the "Hungarian peasant" while on his trip to America, for, James exclaims, by contrasting his situation with that of others, "I am happier now than I thought myself before" (51). He then notes, "Hard is their fate to be thus condemned to a slavery worse than that of our Negroes" (52). For the reader, of course, the irony is immediately apparent, since James is himself a slave owner. He will later conclude that slavery in any form is insupportable, but here his thoughts remain particularly ambivalent and confused.[10] Even though he may not at this point be able to apply his commentary to his own situation, his ability to do so will change by the end of the book, once his own perspective has been enlarged and altered by his travels south.

James's ambivalence also arises in an anecdote he relates of his bees and a kingbird. Long recognized as one of the central scenes of the book, James's story of his bees has generally been read, as by D. H. Lawrence, as an allegory concerning the importance of colonial solidarity in the struggle for independence from the English monarchy. This tale's significance changes, however, if the subsequent sections are included in the analysis, an interpretative move few critics make, oddly enough, perhaps because the topic seems to change in midparagraph to a discussion of quail. If we take Crèvecoeur's paragraphing seriously and read the two descriptions as integrally connected, then these descriptions can be seen as James's oblique method of describing the treatment of oppressed peoples in America and the role the law should play in their defense, rather than simply as an allegorical view of the Revolution. This hermeneutically rich tale can most productively be read as encouraging numerous interpretations, so through what purports to be a purely personal anecdote concerning his experiences in nature, James expresses his thoughts on a number of social and political issues and his responsibilities concerning them.

As James is preparing to shoot a kingbird that has been feeding on bees from his hives,

> a bunch of bees as big as my fist issued from one of the hives, rushed on one
> of these birds, and probably stung him, for he instantly screamed and flew, not
> as before, in an irregular manner, but in a direct line. He was followed by the
> same bold phalanx, at a considerable distance, which unfortunately, becoming
> too sure of victory, quitted their military array and disbanded themselves. By this

inconsiderate step, they lost all that aggregate of force which had made the bird
fly off. Perceiving their disorder, he immediately returned and snapped as many
as he wanted; nay, he had even the impudence to alight on the very twig from
which the bees had driven him. I killed him and immediately opened his craw,
from which I took 171 bees; I laid them all on a blanket in the sun, and to my great
surprise, 54 returned to life, licked themselves clean, and joyfully went back to the
hive, where they probably informed their companions of such an adventure and
escape as I believe had never happened before to American bees! (56)

Immediately following this anecdote, within the same paragraph, James describes the pleasure he draws from the quail that inhabit his farm. As is often the
case, James's thoughts then seem to move suddenly in a new direction, and he
discusses the importance of maintaining and protecting these animals during
the long winter. James explains that unlike most of his neighbors,

> I permit them to feed unmolested; and it is not the least agreeable spectacle which
> that dreary season presents, when I see those beautiful birds, tamed by hunger,
> intermingling with all my cattle and sheep, seeking in security for the poor, scanty
> grain which but for them would be useless and lost. Often in the angles of the
> fences where the motion of the wind prevents the snow from settling, I carry them
> both chaff and grain, the one to feed them, the other to prevent their tender feet
> from freezing fast to the earth as I have frequently observed them to do. (56–57)

Why are these two anecdotes together? What is it, beyond the obvious natural settings, that binds them in James's mind? Both, I would argue, concern
the weak and the powerless, seen through James's participation in the "natural
order."

The meaning of these stories becomes clearer in the following paragraph
when James explicitly compares himself to the colonial legal system, which,
he points out, should protect those who are unable to take care of themselves.
"[T]he law is to us," James proclaims, "precisely what I am in my barnyard, a
bridle and check to prevent the strong and greedy from oppressing the timid
and weak" (57). Certainly no group in eighteenth-century America was more
oppressed by "the strong and greedy" than the African American slave (except
perhaps Native Americans, about whom James also shows some concern). If
James represents the legal system in his anecdote concerning the bees and the
kingbird, the bees, unable to unify themselves for any length of time against
their enemy, can easily be viewed as American slaves who rarely had opportunities to organize into groups for effective mass resistance against their oppressors. African Americans, the story foretells, would "return to life" were they

freed from the bonds of slavery by the legal codes of the colonies. These legal codes should sustain the oppressed, as James does the quail, rather than support the powerful, so the law is failing to fulfill its purpose by not serving as a "bridle and check" as intended.[11]

James's use of nature as a vehicle for relating his ambivalent political thoughts is particularly significant. As Christopher Looby points out, "In the thought of cultural leaders of the early national period, there is a kind of automatic metaphorical exchange between images of natural order and ideas of social and political order" (253). The passages quoted above are perfect examples of how this language operates in Crèvecoeur's text, for James simultaneously relates a personal anecdote, a natural description, and a political treatise. James is ambivalent enough about the political issues that he is obliquely discussing as to be unable to address them directly; only through allegory, disguised as natural description by the inclusion of irrelevant detail, can James confront the treatment of slaves and his participation in the institution of slavery and the political situation in the colonies.

For Crèvecoeur, influenced as he was by the European Enlightenment, the natural, individual, and political spheres should relate and correspond to each other. His narrator retreats into the natural in order to discuss the political, both because he is trying not to confront these issues directly and because, more important, he believes that the political ought to be derived from the natural. Individuals and governments should act in accordance with nature; human society, rather than existing in opposition to nature, should strive to exist in harmony with it.[12] Through these anecdotes, James is thus addressing his own personal actions, the politics of his community and his society, and the laws of the natural order. So, if the American government and its individual constituents can draw power and authority directly from the natural environment, then there is the possibility of perfect agreement between an individual, the government, and natural law.

But, of course, "natural law" is not a stable concept, and as he travels more widely, James is confronted by signs that nature is inherently both nurturing and violent, both just and unjust.[13] In the early pages of letter 9, in which he describes his travels in Charles Town, James represents nature as he has throughout much of the text, as a nurturing mother who provides the inhabitants of the city with incredible abundance. Of Charles Town he writes, "Its situation is admirable, being built at the confluence of two large rivers, which receive in their course a great number of inferior streams, all navigable in the spring for flat boats. Here the produce of this extensive territory concentres; here therefore is the seat of the most valuable exportation" (166). The result of the region's natural abundance is predictable. The fertility of the land is reflected in the beauty of the city, so "[a]n European at his first arrival must be greatly surprised when he sees the elegance of their houses, their sumptuous furniture, as well as the magnificence of their tables" (167).[14] The people of Charles Town, James claims, "are the gayest in America; it is called the centre of our beau monde and is always filled with the richest planters in the province, who resort hither in quest of health and pleasure" (166–67).

But then James's tone changes, as he wonders if perhaps nature doesn't spoil her children through overabundance, as in New Garden. As a result of this fertility and the slavery that is the foundation of Charles Town society, James realizes, the most prosperous are those who do the least amount of work: "The three principal classes of inhabitants are lawyers, planters, and merchants," none of whom James views as contributing to the welfare of American society (167). Lawyers, in particular, hold the reins of power here; they have, in fact, "reached the *ne plus ultra* of worldly felicity," and are now "far above priests and bishops" (167). In addition to suggesting a certain lack of piety among southerners, James's comment on lawyers' superiority to the clergy draws a parallel between the society of the South and that of Europe. (His use of Latin here—the first in the book—is telling.) For James, American society's superiority is dependent on the absence of a ruling class, so the power that lawyers yield is particularly disturbing; as James has stated in letter 3, "We have no princes for whom we toil, starve, and bleed" (67). His trip South forces James to reconsider his earlier statements, for the distinctions he has drawn between the Old and the New Worlds are failing him.[15] James pushes this idea of southern degeneracy further by explicitly comparing the South to Rome. As was Rome, the South is corrupted by slavery, the effects of which are felt not only by the slaves but by the society as a whole. Thomas Philbrick argues, "Still more dismaying are the effects of slavery on the masters, for—whether in the North or the South, whether ancient or modern—slavery encourages those who profit by it to indulge their most brutal impulses" (46). Because of the influence slavery has on the leaders of society, James finally realizes, slavery undermines the attempt to create an agrarian utopia in America.[16]

Slavery has undermined this attempt because it has inverted the natural order. "Strange Order of Things! Oh, Nature, where art thou?" James exclaims (169). Nonlaborers hold power, and labor yields the workers no harvest: "Day after day they drudge on without any prospect of ever reaping for themselves" (169). Parenthood is deadly rather than life affirming: "If Negroes are permitted to become fathers, this fatal indulgence only tends to increase their misery"

(169). Slave parents, he continues, "are not permitted to partake of those ineffable sensations with which nature inspires the hearts of fathers and mothers; they must repel them all and become callous and passive" (169). The reason for "this unnatural state," as James calls it, is that according to the institution of slavery, the master is in complete control of the slaves, who are not even able to act according to their most basic needs. James states, "the very instinct of the brute, so laudable, so irresistible, runs counter here to their master's interest; and to that god, all the laws of Nature must give way" (170). In these passages, James views nature as nurturing and positive; thus, slavery exists in direct opposition to nature.

By the end of the chapter, however, James's view changes as he comes to understand fully that nature can also be violent and deadly. Significantly, this shift in James's view is attributable directly to the effects of his personal travels and his participation in new experiences. Introducing his famous tale in which he encounters a horribly mutilated slave hanging in a cage, James attempts to explain the change that has overcome him: "The following scene will, I hope, account for these melancholy reflections and apologize for the gloomy thoughts with which I have filled this letter: my mind is, and always has been, oppressed since I became a witness to it" (177). James stumbles across this scene when he is going to dinner at a planter's home, literally walking along a path on which he has never before traveled. "I was leisurely travelling along, attentively examining some peculiar plants which I had collected," he explains, "when all at once I felt the air strongly agitated, though the day was perfectly calm and sultry" (177). Perceiving some birds of prey on a cage, James involuntarily fires his gun and scares them off, "when, horrid to think and painful to repeat, I perceived a Negro, suspended in the cage and left there to expire" (178). Unable to travel to safety, the slave is literally being eaten alive by birds and swarming insects. Appalled by the torture the natural world is helping to inflict on this slave, James wants to put the man out of his misery, but, of course, he has no more ammunition. After providing the wretch a small drink, James "muster[s] strength enough to walk away" to his host's, and the slave master's, house (167). There he hears that the slave had killed his overseer and learns that the "laws of self-preservation" necessitate such punishments.

Thus, James finally concludes that acting according to nature can bring about violence and death as easily as it can peace and life. "The history of the earth!" James exclaims, "Doth it present anything but crimes of the most heinous nature, committed from one end of the world to the other? We observe avarice, rapine, and murder, equally prevailing in all parts" (173). Since the "most heinous nature" of these crimes is "equally prevailing in all parts," then this state of affairs must to some degree be inherent in humanity. Of course, his realization of this prevalence is dependent on his having traveled widely.

Furthermore, James states, "If Nature has given us a fruitful soil to inhabit, she has refused us such inclinations and propensities as would afford us the full enjoyment of it" (174), suggesting in the end that the fertility of the American continent is more a danger than a blessing. As fertile a continent as North America is, according to *Letters*, this idea has broad implications for James's schema. Norman Grabo points out this irony, arguing, "[I]f fertility is inevitably the source of misery instead of happiness . . . then the ideal American farmer is trapped in a terrible bind" (170). The farmer confronts greater danger the more fertile his land is and the more success he enjoys. As James himself states, "[T]he extreme fertility of the ground always indicates the extreme misery of the inhabitants" (176). James does not attempt simply to dismiss slavery as perverse and unnatural; on the contrary, he sees slavery by the end of this epistle as indicative of the natural order.

Slavery is a national, rather than a regional, issue, James believes, because the South is intimately connected to the rest of American society. In fact, James begins the chapter by suggesting that Charles Town represents all of the North American colonies by calling it the center of the richest region in the hemisphere. He begins, "Charles Town is, in the north, what Lima is in the south; both are capitals of the richest provinces of their respective hemispheres" (166). By explicitly placing Charles Town in the context of all of North America, James both asks the reader to see it as a city representative of the entire continent and subtly brings up the connections between the northern colonies and the slavery that supports the economy of this city and the entire nation. By so doing, James questions the clear distinctions between northern and southern colonies that were so often used as a justification for the supposedly "benevolent" version of slavery practiced in the North, even by James himself.

Clearly the farming paradigm is no longer sufficient to represent either James himself or American society in its entirety. During the course of *Letters*, James's agrarian ideal has been qualified by his experiences, as he has traveled throughout his country and transformed himself from James the farmer to James the traveler. Although he cannot naively reestablish himself on his farm and reassume his status as a representative American, James does remain somewhat committed to his agrarian dream. But once he has gone on his journeys, he is larger than that dream, so he becomes, in the final chapter, a combination of his two ideals, ending his account attempting to establish himself as both a farmer and a traveler.

Letter 12, "Distresses of a Frontier Man," recounts James's experiences after the outbreak of the American Revolution as he makes plans to move his family to the frontier in order to join a Native American tribe.[17] James's response to the Revolution and to the new knowledge he has garnered by traveling is not simply to reassert his belief in an earlier ideal, as many critics have suggested. James instead revises his beliefs and creates a different version of the American individual and, thus, of an ideal America. James will become this new man by taking his family to the frontier in order to join a nomadic culture and, at the same time, to establish a new farm. Thus, James hopes paradoxically both to farm and to travel.

However, his family will not become the frontier folk James has described in an earlier chapter. Those inhabitants of the frontier had forsaken their European heritage entirely and had become more savage than human, their actions "regulated by the wildness of the neighbourhood" (76). "[T]his is the progress," James explains; "[O]nce hunters, farewell to the plough. The chase renders them ferocious, gloomy, and unsocial" (76). This mode of life provides these frontier people with new habits and manners: "These new manners being grafted on the old stock produce a strange sort of lawless profligacy, the impressions of which are indelible. The manners of the Indian natives are respectable compared with this European medley. . . . [T]hey grow up a mongrel breed, half civilized, half savage" (77). In contrast, James will be careful to maintain a civilized life when he is with the Indians. Unlike hunters, who are completely mobile and unattached to any piece of earth, James will stay rooted to the land by tilling the soil and growing crops he, his family, and the community will enjoy. As he says, "As long as we keep ourselves busy in tilling the earth, there is no fear of any of us becoming wild; it is the chase and the food it procures that have this strange effect" (220). Thus, he will remain a member of a community, unlike the frontiersmen who forsake the society of others.[18]

Nor will James be like those Europeans who only visit the Indians briefly in order to study them; he will live with and among them. While Europeans do not generally "carry to the wilderness numerous families," but go as "speculators" and "as visitors, as travellers" or visit "to study the manner of the aborigines," according to James, he will go "to conform to them, whatever they are," and will be not simply a visitor but "a sojourner" and "a fellow-hunter and labourer" (226). James will travel to the Native Americans, but he will also travel with them.

Accordingly, James will adapt himself and his family to native society and culture. He will do whatever is necessary to fit his family into this village; for instance, he claims, "As soon as possible after my arrival, I design to build myself a wigwam, after the same manner and size with the rest in order to avoid being thought singular or giving occasion for any railleries" (219). And, he will depend more fully on hunting to supplement his family's needs. His children, too, will adopt Indian habits, although, he earnestly hopes, they will not become too charmed by native life. James seems especially concerned that his children will gain "such a propensity to that mode of life as may preclude their returning to the manners and customs of their parents" (219). They might, he worries, neglect farming for the pleasures of the hunt. James seems to fear, that is, that his children will become pure travelers, unfettered but also uncontrolled. Instead, he hopes to combine the movement and freedom promised by a nomadic society with the stability and discipline of a more "civilized" one.

In order to ensure this balance between movement and stasis, James will resume his farming and will demand that his children continue to plow. In addition, he will pay his children for their labor by providing them with the future promise of land. James explains his system as follows: "I will keep an exact account of all that shall be gathered and give each of them a regular credit for the amount of it, to be paid in real property at the return of peace. Thus, though seemingly toiling for bare subsistence on a foreign land, they shall entertain the pleasing prospect of seeing the sum of their labours one day realized either in legacies or gifts" (223). Since the ownership of land is central to James's philosophy, this keeping of accounts is essential to his new society. But neither he nor his children will actually own the land that they farm, so James will farm but will also remain free to travel to new areas and experiences. Now that he has become a traveler, dependent on the insight and expanded perspective that his journeys have provided, this freedom to move is an essential component of James's new life.[19] In fact, he realizes, in order for him to be fully American and to continue to be representative of American national identity, James will have to embody both the opportunity and stability of the agrarian life and the understanding and freedom of travel.

Once he has joined the tribe and begun his new life, James argues, he will become a completely new person. To begin with, he and his family will become members of an entirely new community, even family. As he explains, "[M]y wife, my children, and myself may be adopted soon after our arrival" (219). In fact, he continues, "[W]e shall likewise receive names from them" (219). In return, James hopes to found a new society. He will not adapt himself completely to native culture but will continue the agricultural practices he learned from his father and even try to inculcate a sense of the importance of farming in the members of the tribe: "Half a dozen acres on the shores of ———, the soil of which I know well, will yield us a great abundance of all we want; I will make it a point to give the overplus to such Indians as shall be most unfortunate in their huntings; I will persuade them, if I can, to till a little more land than they do and not to trust so much to the produce of the chase" (221). He will also incorporate American and European technology into his farming, and he will try to serve as an example to those around him. "[M]y example alone," he hopes, "may rouse the industry of some and serve to direct others in their labours" (221). He hopes to discourage his native neighbors from depending entirely on the hunt and turn them into more dedicated farmers. While becoming more native himself, he will help "civilize" Indian society.

Thus, James seeks finally not simply to be a representative American but to establish an entirely new American society. Ironically, in order for James to become fully American, to transform himself into an amalgam of both the farming and the traveling personae, he must move with his family to the margins of American society and seek to reestablish a new cultural and social center. He has come to understand the necessity for this shift by traveling himself through what he thought were the margins of the country and confronting directly the oppression of those people marginalized by his society. He discovered, of course, that the problems he believed to be marginal were actually central to the American nation's identity. James's search for a middle ground thus takes him beyond the scene of the battles into his own utopia. He realizes that in relation to slavery and to the American Revolution, there is no middle ground, so he rhetorically produces his own.[20] James's middle colonies simply could not escape what were initially represented as regional abnormalities. Philip Beidler argues that James "depicts a society in which the bustle and activity of urban life and the barbarous disorder of the frontier are reconciled in the middle landscape of an agrarian America. . . . [T]he pattern is repeated in subsequent attempts to detail the regional peculiarities of north and south" (60). But the reconciliation Beidler describes has been undermined by James's realization that these "regional peculiarities" are neither simply regional nor peculiar but are central to the nation as a whole in its present form. Because James and his family are part of American society, they must either suffer the consequences of the problems that plague that society or quit that society. So, James elects to leave the colonies and found a new American society by establishing a new farming-traveling life and culture.

Letter 11 of Crèvecoeur's *Letters to an American Farmer* concerns a visit by the Russian correspondent, Iw——n Al——z, to the home and gardens of Mr. John Bertram, "the celebrated Pennsylvanian Botanist" (187). The model for this figure was unquestionably John Bartram, Royal Botanist to the British colonies and a man whom Linnaeus called the greatest natural botanist in the world, although the portrait in *Letters* is clearly idealized. Bartram was not, for instance, the strong opponent of slavery that Crèvecoeur's Bertram is, though he was, as the letter suggests, a dedicated disciple of Linnaeus and an important colonial figure. As an "enlightened botanist" (197), in the words of Crèvecoeur's narrator, John Bartram sought to increase knowledge of the New World and to expand Linnaeus's classification system to incorporate all of those plant species indigenous to the North American continent. As the Royal Botanist to the colonies, his role was to be of use to the English Crown.[21]

John Bartram fulfilled both of these responsibilities admirably, introducing to Europe between 25 and 50 percent of all New World species and, through the first botanical garden in North America, carrying on an extensive trade in plant species with numerous members of English society. He traveled extensively in North America, notably in Pennsylvania and Canada, as well as along the eastern coast and in Florida. During these travels, John Bartram had the development of the regions always in view, exemplifying the belief that, in the words of the publisher of his *Travels in Pensilvania and Canada,* "Knowledge must precede a settlement" (iii). In the journals of his travels, Bartram frequently mentions that the rivers he traverses are suitable for the large, flat-bottomed vessels often used for trade, and he regularly measures nature in terms of productive potential, stating in the journal of his northern travels, for instance, "We travelled to a fine creek big enough to drive two mills" (67). Josephine Herbst explains that John Bartram's journal of his Florida journey "was a precise account written with an eye to what might interest a mercantile King. Bartram knew he was sent to Florida with an eye to development of natural resources, not to enthuse over Nature and its blessings" (197). In one way, then, Crèvecoeur's description of Bertram is faithful to the original, for Bartram was an exemplary Enlightenment scientist who explored the American environment for products that could be put to practical use.

Although he was much less successful professionally than his father, John's son William continued his father's botanical work. An accomplished artist of flora and fauna from an early age, William was as drawn to nature as was his father and accompanied John on many collecting and exploring trips, most significantly to Florida in the 1760s. From 1773 until 1778, William himself traveled through the southern colonies and Florida under the patronage of Dr. Fothergill, an English medical doctor interested in botany. Instructed to collect new plant species and to forward seeds and botanical samples to Fothergill in London, William was also told he might keep a journal of his travels throughout the southeastern colonies. While William was not particularly conscientious in his duty to his European patron, he did eventually send Fothergill a collection of forty-seven drawings, numerous dried plant specimens, and a two-part written report. In all three of the "texts" that he provided to Fothergill, William seems closely aligned with his father, attempting to categorize the flora and fauna of a region in order to assist the future development of the area and the exploitation of its natural resources. Thus, William's primary work, like his father's, was part of a larger Enlightenment project that attempted to map, and thus to know and to dominate, an area of the country that was then largely unknown. For the William who narrates the report to Fothergill, as for John, travel does not signify a broadening of being, as it did for Crèvecoeur, but rather the broadening of civilization, empire, and trade.

However, William "was not the same explorer for empire that his father became," for in his public work, entitled *Travels through North and South Carolina, Georgia, East and West Florida, the Cherokee Country, the Extensive Territories of the Muscogulges or Creek Confederacy, and the Country of the Chactaws. Containing an Account of the Soil and Natural Productions of Those Regions; Together with Observations on the Manners of the Indians,* he is much less obviously an Enlightenment figure (Slaughter, *Natures* 188). While parts of *Travels* do illustrate this same imperial project in which he participated with his father, in this text William's proto-Romantic impulses temper his Enlightenment ideals. If in his report to Fothergill he is still the son of John Bartram and the disciple of Linnaeus, in *Travels* he works to create a much more complex narrator-figure. Unlike the more concise report to Fothergill, *Travels* lists and classifies but also waxes poetic; it attempts to know nature as it celebrates the unknown. It reflects, in other words, the many competing and contradictory aspects of William Bartram himself. It reflects Billy Bartram, son of the famous Royal Botanist, who learned at his father's knee but struggled to free himself from his father's influence and control, but it also reflects William Bartram, the renowned artist of nature, who was appreciated by his father's patron, Peter Collinson, and whose drawings were admired by the Royal Society in London. And it reflects Puc-Puggy, "flower hunter," the gentle admirer of flora who was understood by Native Americans and accepted into a tribe through his new name. According to Thomas Slaughter, "As narrator of the *Travels,* he has myriad identities available to him—Billy, William, Puc-Puggy, the representative of a superior culture, the brave man among cowards, the scientist, the artist, the Romantic, the Quaker, a man scared and alone who is unsure of his nature and of nature itself" (*Natures* 145). It is exactly all of these contradictions that make *Travels* such an interesting and enduring book, for by reading *Travels* one can watch an author attempt to come to terms with his past in the very act of creating a new identity, an identity that frees William from his earlier failures as a businessman and as a slave-owning master of a plantation, that reflects Enlightenment ideals and

Romantic impulses, and that pays homage to his European past and celebrates his American present.

Travels was published in Philadelphia in 1791, almost fifteen years after William's Florida journey had ended. During these years, Bartram revised his journals and tried to produce both a unified text and a coherent narrator. The William Bartram of *Travels* is thus "a persona, a character in a book whom the author imagined back in his plantation swamp and whom he became over the course of his travels, in writing his *Travels*, in the garden after his traveling was done" (Slaughter, *Natures* 177). Bartram's attempt to create this narrative persona constitutes the most significant production of the text, for through this figure William seeks to refashion himself as a traveler and as an ideal American individual. Through the writing and revising of the text, Bartram works to produce what Crèvecoeur had attempted to create years earlier, an ideal figure, the representative American. Crèvecoeur's "new man" is largely a combination of contradictory cultural and political allegiances, not only a European but also a Native American, both a farmer and a traveler. Bartram's ideal is more complex, however, for Bartram's narrator-figure combines the Enlightenment scientist with the proto-Romantic poet, as well as the European with the native. Ironically, while travel tends to proliferate the discourses included in his texts and the subjectivities available to him, Bartram's representation of himself as a traveler allows him to consolidate these competing ideologies and discourses and to re-create himself as the perfect representative American. Through the figure of the American traveler, then, Bartram attempts to embody the great variety of cultures, ideologies, and peoples of the American nation itself.

Critics of Bartram's *Travels* seem to be as divided as are those of Crèvecoeur's *Letters*. On the one hand, many critics see Bartram as an early proponent of nature and an important forerunner to such later figures as Thoreau and Emerson, the latter of whom greatly admired Bartram's work.[22] Critics in this school also chart Bartram's influence across the Atlantic on European Romanticism, finding traces of Bartram in such writers as Coleridge, Wordsworth, and Chateaubriand.[23] Another group of critics, however, downplays Bartram's proto-Romanticism, insisting that he is more like his father than unlike and arguing that his exploitive tendencies outweigh his "environmentalist" sensibilities.[24]

Despite their final judgment on Bartram, however, almost all of these critics agree in their use of *Travels* as a conduit to a clearer understanding of the author himself.[25] Ernest Earnest perhaps speaks for many readers of *Travels* when he suggests, "There is a strong lyric quality that makes the *Travels* throughout a revelation of the personality of William Bartram. Few books are so completely synonymous with their creators" (131). Even Thomas Slaughter, author of the excellent *The Natures of John and William Bartram*, who clearly recognizes the author's conscious construction of a narrative persona, uses his insightful readings of numerous Bartram texts to uncover the two historical figures themselves. Thus, the vast majority of critics maintain their focus steadfastly on William Bartram himself.

However, many readers have failed until quite recently to differentiate between William Bartram and his alter ego in *Travels* or to recognize the degree to which both his travels and his *Travels* created Bartram as an author, a traveler, and an American. Furthermore, the William Bartram who narrates *Travels* is not the same William Bartram who narrates the report to Fothergill. These distinctions, both between Bartram's two narrators and between his two texts, highlight the construction of these narrative figures and illustrate the ideological structures with which William grappled. However, *Travels* is the more significant of the two texts, for, despite William's attempt to produce a unified text and narrator, it illustrates most clearly the competing beliefs that Bartram tried to combine in order to produce the ideal American figure. The William Bartram of the report does not so clearly exhibit the contradictions inherent in this project.

The report remains important, however, for the light it sheds on the Enlightenment beliefs that are often minimized in *Travels*. In the report, William attempts to account for the time he has spent in the Florida wilderness and to justify his patron's financial outlay, so he seems very much like his father before him, an explorer for empire. As disciples of Linnaeus, the Bartrams sought to categorize the plants of those regions of the New World that remained largely unexplored for botanical specimens. In *Imperial Eyes: Travel Writing and Transculturation*, Mary Louise Pratt points out that the natural history project that followed the publication of Linnaeus's *Systema Naturae* in 1735 attempted to categorize and define every plant (and later animal and mineral) according to genus and species and thus to map out the entire globe; Linnaeus's system, Pratt argues, "launched a European knowledge-building enterprise of unprecedented scale and appeal" (25). John Bartram had helped classify the plants of the New World in midcentury but had focused his early travels on the northern parts of the continent. Once the South began to appear as a distinct region, the Bartrams sought to include it within the domain of natural history, so they traveled south and sent collections of plants and animals, as well as written reports, north and to Europe.[26]

During this period, Pratt argues, "Specimen gathering, the building up of collections, the naming of new species, the recognition of known ones, became standard themes in travel and travel books" (27). What these travel texts exemplify is the narrative Pratt terms the "anti-conquest," in which "the naturalist naturalizes the bourgeois European's own global presence and authority" (28).[27] Traveling in the guise of harmless scientists simply attempting to understand the world, these botanical travelers constituted the advance guard of a much larger Enlightenment project.

But these Enlightenment figures were far from harmless, as Pratt clearly shows in her study of travel writing, for the goals of Enlightenment science correspond closely to the aims of an ever-expanding European (and later American) capitalism. Natural historians' attempts to map the world in terms of flora and fauna were particularly useful in this economic process. "Like the rise of interior exploration," Pratt argues, "the systematic surface mapping of the globe correlates with an expanding search for commercially exploitable resources, markets, and lands to colonize, just as navigational mapping is linked with the search for trade routes. Unlike navigational mapping, however, natural history conceived of the world as a chaos out of which the scientist *produced* an order. It is not, then, simply a question of depicting the planet as it was" (30). Natural historians such as the Bartrams led the charge in the search for exploitable natural products as they helped to transform the abundant chaos of American nature into shapes more easily comprehended and used.[28]

William Bartram's role in this project is most obvious when in the report he describes his traveling companions. While he often travels alone or with just one companion, Bartram is frequently in the company of European traders and others seeking to extract value from the land and the indigenous peoples. After a meeting in which the Indians have seceded large tracts of land, Bartram accompanies the surveyors appointed by the colonial governor. He writes, "The Surveyors, Indian, Deputies, with their attendants, together with Packhorsemen, and hunters; The guides, and a Number of People who went to view the lands, being all ready, June 7th we set off from Augusta to the number of 70 or 80 People" (440). As this expeditionary force makes its way through the lands recently come under European control, Bartram literally leads the group into the wilderness: "I chose to keep a small distance ahead of the Main body; by which I avoided the heat & dust rais'd by such a Number of People; & at the same time had leisure & oppertunaty to pick up any curiosities within view" (440). The image is almost ludicrously symbolic—quiet Billy Bartram stooping over a flower as a rumbling mass of surveyors, guides, and land prospectors tears through the southern wilderness behind him. While his position in front might suggest a certain isolation from the rest of the imperialist group, Bartram does fulfill an important role, if not in this specific group then in the larger Enlightenment culture of which this small army is a part. In this passage, then, Bartram is a southern traveler whose primary ideological function is to bring a certain region of the South under European (or northern) epistemological control. Rarely is the role of natural history in the project of imperialism and colonialism so neatly drawn.

Although Bartram does not often place himself at the front of a literal surveying party of European colonialists as he does in this passage, he does represent himself as keenly aware of his duty to his patron, thus maintaining his advance position. He frequently tells Dr. Fothergill in the report that in a certain region, for example, he has "discover'd nothing new, or much worth your notice" (431), or, more hopefully, that the "Soil is a black Rich mud or Clay & looks fit for Rice, Corn, Sugar Cane &c" (475). Uncultivated land seems somehow unnatural according to the Bartram of the report. Describing land near St. Simon's Island in Georgia that belongs to absentee landowners, for instance, Bartram writes, "thus one of the most valuable Parts of the Province lays as useless as any part of the Indian Country" (433). Neither absentee owners nor Native Americans, according to Bartram, make proper use of the land and help it fulfill its productive potential.

Bartram is most explicit concerning the future development of a region when describing the area near the Little Saint Johns River in Florida. Bartram describes this land as the perfect site for a future settlement and through his language thus converts the wilderness into standing reserve, seeing in the present only signs of future development:

> Before I leave off in treating of this part of Florida, beg leave to observe that about this Part of the River of Little St. Juane appears to be a very proper & important place for a Settle ment and very necessary to strengthen a communication with the Province of West Florida; This River is large & Navigable, a great ways up, & the clearest & finest water I have seen in this Province, prodigiously replenish't with a variety of excellent River Fish. The Land on its banks fertile, & remarkebly well Timbered with Cypress & vast Pine Forest of as large a growth as any I have ever seen, & no country can well exceed it for extensive Savanahs & range for Cattle. The Indigo Plant grows so plenty & Luxurient, that the planters have only the trouble of cutting away the Trees & stir up the soil. I have seen the greatest quantity of rich Iron Ore in these Hills near this River that I have ever seen, of the species call bog Ore. & the greatest Plenty of Stone, for building with, & there is a great likelyhood of other Valuable Minerals, in this unknown Country. (498)

According to Bartram, the beauty of this land rests entirely in its potential. The soil is fertile and will thus support large crops; the land is well "timbered," meaning it is capable of producing much processed lumber; and the range he fills with future cattle and farmers who will need to perform little work in transforming the region to their purposes. Furthermore, the fertility is not simply a surface feature, for vast reserves of valuable minerals lie underground waiting to fulfill their purpose by being mined. The land in Bartram's descriptions seems incomplete without the human intervention that will allow the region to fulfill its proper destiny.

In contrast, *Travels* contains no passages that so explicitly favor the development of the wilderness, for the William Bartram who narrates that text expresses particularly ambivalent feelings toward the development of nature. Rather than simply fulfilling his function as a member of an imperialist project, the William Bartram of *Travels* seems more aware of the numerous contradictory ideologies in play as he moves through the South. The most obvious illustration of the differences between the report to Fothergill and *Travels* can be seen in the drawings of the Alachua Savanna Bartram completed for each. The sketch he drew for Fothergill (figure 1) is more map than anything, while that which he included in *Travels* (figure 2) is a much more idealized representation of the savanna. The Fothergill map exemplifies Bartram's dedication to his patron's Enlightenment project, practically providing instructions for the future development of the savanna.[29] The *Travels* sketch, however, illustrates Bartram's ambivalent feelings about his travels in the South and about uncultivated nature, particularly the Alachua Savanna, which seems to have been especially important to him.

The sketch sent to Fothergill includes the features standard to any map: In the lower right corner is a scale to indicate distance, in the top left is the compass rose, and in the lower left corner is a key that relates particular descriptions to letters on the drawing. In addition, the sketch is largely realistic; beyond the one animal drawn out of proportion in the middle of the savanna, most of the features included are drawn to scale. The one building Bartram includes is indicated in the key to be the Seminole village, Cuscoela. Finally, and perhaps most important, roads leading to and through the savanna are clearly drawn and labeled.

The picture included in *Travels*, on the other hand, is not as realistic a representation of the savanna. The frame on the left indicates immediately that this work is not as directly representational as the map. This column suggests classical times, but it could also be seen to represent "the present, civilization, and the structures of man," as Slaughter argues (*Natures* 181). The viewer is, then, essentially looking backward in time, into a past prior even to European antiquity. Accordingly, there are no roads in this version of the savanna, as if the drawing shows a prelapsarian state of nature. The inclusion of numerous animals not drawn to scale to their environment furthers the lack of representational authenticity and might imply by contrast that realism and accuracy are further colonizing techniques. The Native American structure is again included but is not labeled, making it seem as natural as the other aspects of the picture. Thus, this romanticized Alachua Savanna seems as much a state of mind as an existing natural phenomenon.

In the text of *Travels*, Bartram describes the savanna in the following terms:

> This little lake and surrounding meadows would have been alone sufficient to surprise and delight the traveller; but being placed so near the great savanna, the attention is quickly drawn off, and wholly engaged in the contemplation of the unlimited, varied, and truly astonishing native wild scenes of landscape and perspective, there exhibited: how is the mind agitated and bewildered, at being thus, as it were, placed on the borders of a new world! On the first view of such an amazing display of the wisdom and power of the supreme author of nature, the mind for a moment seems suspended, and impressed with awe. (168–69)

This description illustrates, as does the sketch, William's desire to maintain Alachua Savanna in its pristine condition, a condition no longer available except, of course, as an ideal. A necessary aspect of the scene, it should be noted, is the viewer's emotional response, suggesting that the land itself is incomplete or inadequate without the participation of Bartram himself.

The more Romantic, idyllic aspects of his sketch and descriptions do not necessarily exclude features that point to a tradition of imperialist drawing and writing. Particularly important is the perspective from which the scene is viewed, the "lord-of-all-I-survey" height from which the image was apparently drawn, or at least imagined. But even the romanticization of nature, as well as the "naturalization" of the native inhabitants, plays a role in the imperialist project of knowledge-building and domination, for these rhetorical devices serve to erase the relationship established between the imperial subject and his surroundings.[30] Bartram might in this image be urging us to view the Alachua Savanna in ways other than the one that encourages development, but he continues to be trapped within an Enlightenment paradigm even as he struggles against it.

Much of the larger text of *Travels* in which this image appears illustrates the same tension between an Enlightenment project to categorize and to know and a proto-Romantic reverie on nature and an individual's place within it. Many critics have noted that Bartram's language alternates rapidly between the scientific and the poetic.[31] For instance, describing the banks of the Altamaha River, Bartram writes, "Drawing near the high shores, I ascended the steep banks, where stood a venerable oak. An ancient Indian field, verdured over with succulent grass, and chequered with coppices of fragrant shrubs, offered to my view

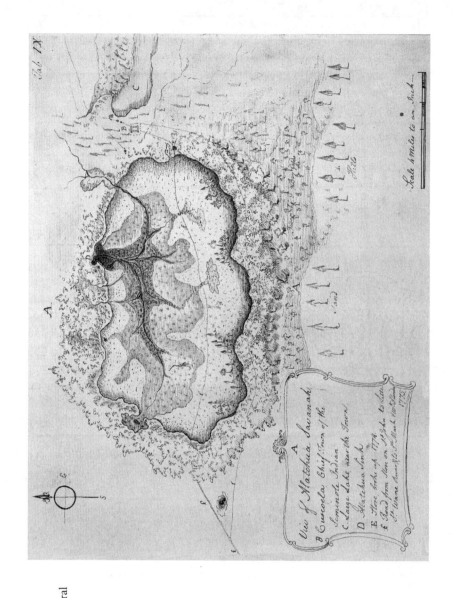

Map of the Alachua
Savannah, by William
Bartram. (© The Natural
History Museum,
London.)

Drawing of the Alachua Savannah, by William Bartram. (Courtesy of the American Philosophical Society.)

the Myrica cerifera, Magnolia glauca, Laurus benzoin, Laur. Borbonia, Rham-
nus frangula, Prunus Chicasaw, Prun. laurocerasus, and others" (64). As several
critics state, and as this passage exemplifies, the sudden changes in Bartram's
rhetoric in *Travels*, and the contradictory impulses that produce them, can at
times be almost comic.[32] Bartram moves among several rhetorics of travel available to him, most notably between the objective method of Enlightenment classification and the subjective mode of proto-Romantic evocation. His inclusion
of perspectives alternatively suggesting either distance from or immersion in his
immediate surroundings accentuates this rhetorical complexity.

While Bartram's preference in *Travels* may lean toward the more sublime
aspects of nature, he expresses even in this text an awareness of his duty to
his patron and thus an acknowledgment of his Enlightenment background and
project. Bartram begins the first chapter, in fact, by acknowledging his dependence on Fothergill's patronage. He writes, "At the request of Dr. Fothergill, of
London, to search the Floridas, and the western parts of Carolina and Georgia, for the discovery of rare and useful productions of nature, chiefly in the
vegetable kingdom; in April, 1773, I embarked for Charleston, South Carolina"
(27).[33] As he searches for both "rare" and "useful" plant species, Bartram the
botanical explorer takes his orders from Europe, represented here as the seat
of power and knowledge. In fact, at times Bartram looks to London for further directions, as if he is unqualified to determine his own route. Unable to
travel in the western regions of Carolina because of the danger of Indian attack,
Bartram explains, "I now formed the resolution of travelling into East Florida;
accordingly, I immediately wrote to Doctor Fothergill, in order that he might
know where to direct me" (68). There, as in Carolina, Bartram will continue
what he calls his "proper employment," "discovering and collecting data for the
exercise of more able physiologists" (45), again suggesting that the most important knowledge and understanding reside elsewhere. In fact, here Bartram
represents himself as unable to act or travel at all without the guidance of his
patron, whom he suggests is firmly in place within, and oriented to, European
civilization and the American environment.

The role of these "more able physiologists" is, one assumes, to verify the
correct Linnaean classification of Bartram's discoveries, re-placing the natural
products of the New World into a European knowledge formation and recreating Bartram as a hybrid figure halfway between the wilderness and civilization.
Accordingly, Bartram is intent on naming everything he comes across with a
Latin designation; any native name it might have is not, it seems, a plant or
animal's "real" name. Mary Louise Pratt writes, "Natural history extracted specimens not only from their organic or ecological relations with each other, but

also from their places in other peoples' economies, histories, social and symbolic systems" (31). This naming by natural history "extracts all the things of the world and redeploys them into a new knowledge formation whose value lies precisely in its difference from the chaotic original. Here the naming, the representing, and the claiming are all one; the naming brings the reality of order into being" (33). For these Linnaean botanists, a plant or animal essentially exists only after it has been placed within this European system of classification. Even though this system of classification is as culturally determined as is any other, the "native" view of the plant is disregarded in favor of the supposedly "objective" Linnaean designation.[34] Bartram himself is able to travel between the two systems, for he retains both his European name, William Bartram, and his native appellation, Puc-Puggy.

However, while Bartram focuses on those plants that have some value for the natives—particularly medicinal—and might thus prove especially useful for his patron, Bartram does include native names in this work, often those of animals. "There is inhabiting the low shores and swamps of this river and the lakes of Florida, as well as Georgia," Bartram explains, "a very curious bird, called by an Indian name (Ephouskyca) which signifies in our language the crying bird. I cannot determine what genus of European birds to join it with" (135). This comment might suggest that the European system of knowledge is inadequate to the study of nature in the New World were it not for the footnote appended by Bartram to the bottom of the page that provides the reader with the "correct" classification, *Tantalus pictus*.[35] As Linnaean lists cannot convey the myriad relationships of a single species with its environmental surroundings, Bartram here resorts to a footnote because of his inability to incorporate the Linnaean designation within his description of the Native American view, as if the two languages and epistemes are irreconcilable.[36] In ways that his report rarely does, *Travels* thus illustrates Bartram's ambivalence toward two competing systems of knowledge, both of which he respects and appreciates but neither of which is adequate to the task of providing him with a complete understanding of his world.

A similar ambivalence marks Bartram's descriptions of Native Americans and their cultures. As in his sketch of the Alachua Savanna, Bartram often places Native American individuals and structures into a scene and thus suggests that they are simply a part of nature. Furthermore, his attempts to classify native cultures and societies parallels his struggle to place plants indigenous to the region into the Linnaean system. The six chapters of part 4 of *Travels*, dedicated to various native tribes and their customs, contains sections entitled, for instance, "Persons, characters, and qualifications of the Aborigines," "Government and civil society," "Marriages and funeral rites," and "Language and monuments."

In this attempt to lay out a clear chart of native society and culture, Bartram is heeding his Enlightenment training and dedication to the Linnaean project. He is simultaneously acknowledging, however, that Native Americans do have a government and a civil society, for instance, and are thus not entirely different from Europeans. Still, in the projects of naturalization and classification, the Indian is decidedly "other" to Bartram.[37]

However, Bartram actually argues directly for an identification between Europeans and natives when he encounters a lone male Indian on the trail, frequently represented as a liminal space in which cultures meet. Having "passed the utmost frontier of the white settlements on that border," Bartram describes himself as enjoying the tranquility of early evening when, "on a sudden, an Indian appeared crossing the path, at a considerable distance before me" (43). "On perceiving that he was armed with a rifle," Bartram continues, "the first sight of him startled me, and I endeavoured to elude his sight, by stopping my pace, and keeping large trees between us; but he espied me, and turning short about, sat spurs to his horse" (43).[38] According to the text, Bartram realizes that he is in the Indian's power, so he decides "to meet the dreaded foe with resolution and chearful confidence" (43). Bartram offers his hand, simultaneously "hailing him, brother," but "the intrepid Siminole" initially jerks his arm away (43). After a moment, however, "he instantly spurred up to me, and with dignity in his look and action, gave me his hand" (44).[39] "In fine," Bartram concludes, "we shook hands, and parted in a friendly manner, in the midst of a dreary wilderness" (44). Even though he had described the natural surroundings before this encounter as "varied and beautiful" and drawn himself as enjoying "the happy moments of evening contemplation," by the end of the passage the forest has become "dreary." As in other passages, the beauty of nature is dependent on human participation. After this encounter, the human relationship established between these two men offers the only light in the dark wilderness.

Arriving at the trading house, William learns that the man he encountered had been "ill-treated" the day before but had escaped, promising to "kill the first white man he met" (44). Both men, it seems, conquered their initial responses and approached the other as individuals. By doing so, Bartram suggests, each overcame his individual identity and became a representative of his respective society. Slaughter concurs, arguing, "The story is about two representative men, about two cultures, two civilizations, two ways of life come together in nature to reveal their true selves. The story ultimately tells us that their natures were one" (*Natures* 208). Bartram's anecdote suggests that this type of unity can occur only when each culture is ready to accept the other with respect and openness. This respect and openness occurs significantly on the road, so both men are in fact travelers when they meet, rather than simply "representative men," as Slaughter suggests. Because they are travelers, both men are neither fully within nor outside of their "home" cultures and environments, so they seem to establish a middle space here in which they can meet on an equal footing.

Interestingly, *Travels* has not traditionally been read as espousing any politics whatsoever, despite the politically charged nature of passages such as this one.[40] Critics have traditionally ignored the passages in which Bartram expresses strong political feelings, even though he frequently interjects such political points into his general discussions of the natural environment. Immediately following the story of his encounter with the "Siminole," for instance, Bartram asks, "Can it be denied, but that the moral principle, which directs the savages to virtuous and praiseworthy actions, is natural or innate?" (44). Even without "the assistance of letters, or those means of education in the schools of philosophy," Bartram argues, Indians understand "the dignity, propriety, and beauty of virtue" (44–45). Written in a period when Native Americans were regularly treated as animals and widely regarded as dangerous and violent "others," Bartram's discussion here is particularly noteworthy.

But it is not only these explicitly political passages that illustrate Bartram's beliefs concerning the development of the American nation and the promises of the American political system. As critics are increasingly coming to understand, *Travels*, written during and immediately after the American Revolutionary War, is very much a political book, despite its pretenses to the contrary. As Charles Adams points out, earlier critics who represent Bartram as either an "earnest naturalist" or an "American mythologist" share the assumption "that Bartram was a man strangely unconcerned with the great events of his day, and that the *Travels* reveals an astounding lack of historical consciousness" (112–13).[41] In contrast, Adams argues that Bartram's South is "a deliberately constructed place, a metaphorical region that expresses a distinct conception of history directly related to contemporary events" (113). Christopher Looby, like Adams, argues that Bartram and others used the structure of the Linnaean classification system as "a figure for social stability and . . . for an intensely desired end to the flux of revolutionary social-historical change" (257).[42] These critics see Bartram expressing his political beliefs and his desires for an end to the chaos brought about by the American Revolution through his dependence on the stability of Linnaeus's system.

However, Bartram also expresses his political beliefs through his representations of nature and with his descriptive language, not only by his use of an Enlightenment classification system, as these critics suggest. Particularly through his descriptions and anecdotes concerning his trip up the Saint Johns River and back again, Bartram expresses his thoughts on the contemporary political scene and the promise of the new nation's future through his representations of the natural environment.[43] By separating his descriptions of two different fountains with a story of the chaos brought about by a hurricane, Bartram sets up a clear parallel between his trip and the course being followed by the nation as a whole. Bartram simultaneously argues that American identity is also determined by travel, as he recreates his narrative persona into a representative national figure. Bartram's use of his trip on the Saint Johns River as an allegory for the course of the emerging nation is particularly significant, for the river played a clear geopolitical role at this time. As John Seelye points out, the Saint Johns River "separated the lands claimed by the British from Indian country. . . . [T]he western side of Bartram's St. John's is literally *the* West, for the river served as a frontier line separating savagery from civilization" (*Beautiful Machine* 144). The distinctions between the two are clearly illustrated by the contrast Bartram draws between his trip upriver, during which he camps on the western side of the river and faces the numerous dangers of the wilderness, and his return trip down the river, during which he stays with farmers on the eastern side and enjoys the beauty of the cultivated fields and pastoral ideal. Thus, his journey represents a middle course between a native, precolonial system of rule and the civilization of the eastern shore. The American, Bartram suggests, should exist between these two cultures and partake of the understanding and experience offered by the two sides, refusing to settle on either shore but continuing instead to travel on the passageway between both.

Before leaving the lower trading post on his journey, Bartram engages an Indian to assist him, but he drops off this young man earlier than expected, "knowing the impossibility of compelling an Indian against his own inclinations, or even prevailing upon him by reasonable arguments, when labour is in the question" (112). As Bartram's canoe reached the shore, the Indian "sprang out of her and landed, when uttering a shrill and terrible whoop, he bounded off like a roebuck, and I lost sight of him" (112). The Indian is obviously more at home in the wilderness, so after this companion has run off, Bartram is alone, paddling up the river in his canoe, a craft that links Bartram with Native American culture but also provides him his only means of returning to the "civilization" that he has left behind. For this trip, then, Bartram is on his own.

He quickly realizes that the surface beauty of the natural environment hides extreme danger lurking underneath. Even though "the evening was temperately cool and calm," Bartram writes, "[t]he crocodiles began to roar and appear in uncommon numbers along the shores and in the river" (113). The connection between the roar of the alligators and the whoop of the Indian is unmistakable.

Much of Bartram's ensuing discussion of the dangers of alligator attack can easily be read as relating to his fears of Indians. Although Bartram was a friend to
many tribes of Native Americans, particularly the Seminole, he was often dis-
suaded from pursuing a planned course for fear of attack. In fact, in several
passages Bartram makes explicit the metaphorical connection between Indians
and alligators in his writing. Spending nights so near the haunts of so many
alligators, he suggests, "appeared to me as perilous as running the gauntlet betwixt two rows of Indians armed with knives and firebrands" (119). And an "old
champion" alligator, Bartram explains, "acts his part like an Indian chief when
rehearsing his feats of war; and then retiring, the exhibition is continued by others who dare to step forth, and strive to excel each other, to gain the attention of
the favourite female" (122). Bartram argues in the parallels he draws here that,
like the alligators, Native Americans are part of nature and are thus ruled more
by force and violence than by reason and virtue.[44]

In perhaps the most frequently quoted passage in the book (as well as the
one most often questioned for its veracity), Bartram describes a battle between
two almost mythic alligators.

> Behold him rushing forth from the flags and reeds. His enormous body swells.
> His plaited tail brandished high, floats upon the lake. The waters like a cataract
> descend from his opening jaws. Clouds of smoke issue from his dilated nostrils.
> The earth trembles with his thunder. When immediately from the opposite coast
> of the lagoon, emerges from the deep his rival champion. They suddenly dart
> upon each other. The boiling surface of the lake marks their rapid course, and
> a terrific conflict commences. They now sink to the bottom folded together in
> horrid wreaths. The water becomes thick and discoloured. Again they rise, their
> jaws clap together, re-echoing through the deep surrounding forests. Again they
> sink, when the contest ends at the muddy bottom of the lake, and the vanquished
> makes a hazardous escape, hiding himself in the muddy turbulent waters and
> sedge on a distant shore. The proud victor exulting returns to the place of action.
> The shores and forests resound his dreadful roar, together with the triumphing
> shouts of the plaited tribes around, witnesses of the horrid combat. (114)

Like the rest of the natural world, these creatures are ruled by the one who ex-
hibits the most force, and all of nature seems to participate in this epic struggle,
as "the earth trembles," and the "shores and forests resound his dreadful roar"
(114). Many critics argue that Bartram has discovered hell on earth here, and
John Seelye suggests in "Beauty Bare" that this Great Sink "provides a counter-
part to the paradise of fish on the other side of the Saint John's" (49). After the
fight ends in "the muddy bottom," the vanquished retreats into the safety of the

"muddy turbulent waters and sedge" to hide from the victor. The murky water thus provides both a battleground and a refuge for the alligators.

After fighting among themselves, however, the alligators join forces as they attack Bartram, "several endeavouring to overset the canoe" (115). After he discovers that the alligators will not pose such a threat if he paddles close to the shore and keeps his enemies on one side of him, Bartram decides to procure some provisions and "then return to my harbour" (115). He realizes he must stay with his boat, for without it, there would be no hope of "returning in safety to any settlements of men" (115). Bartram does manage to return to his camp and, despite the occasional incursion by a bold alligator, to regain relative safety. He realizes, however, that even though the alligators are feasting on incredible numbers of fish in the river, his campsite is open to attack, both from alligators in the water and bears and wolves on land. In fact, Bartram does have to scare off two bears by firing his gun.[45] After a night fraught with danger, in which the "noise of the crocodiles" kept him awake, however, Bartram finds that, "when I arose in the morning, contrary to my expectations, there was perfect peace" (119).

After several more nights in which he is in constant danger of attack, Bartram finally finds "a very convenient, open, airy encamping place, under the protection of some spreading Oaks" (129). Even though he "found the surface of the ground very uneven, by means of little mounts and ridges," Bartram here for the first time on this trip "enjoyed a night of peaceful repose" (129). The battles, it seems, are finally over, and Bartram is in no further danger of attack. "In the morning," he explains, "I found I had taken up my lodging on the border of an ancient burying ground, containing sepulchres or tumuli of the Yamasees, who were here slain by the Creeks in the last decisive battle, the Creeks having driven them into this point, between the doubling of the river, where few of them escaped the fury of the conquerors" (129). The Indians, too, are no longer fighting, so the peace that Bartram finds is the result of the absence of warfare of several kinds.[46] After this, Bartram will proceed to the eastern, "civilized" side of the Saint Johns, having survived the danger of the wilderness and convinced himself of the possibility of peace.

After surviving one kind of battle, however, Bartram is unprepared for the next disaster awaiting him. Describing the approach of a hurricane he has failed to predict, Bartram writes,

> Being heretofore so closely invested by high forests and deep swamps of the great river, I was prevented from seeing the progress and increase of the approaching tempest, the terrific appearance of which now at once confounded me. How pur-

ple and fiery appeared the tumultuous clouds, swiftly ascending or darting from the horizon upwards! they seemed to oppose and dash against each other; the skies appeared streaked with blood or purple flame overhead, the flaming lightning streaming and darting about in every direction around, seemed to fill the world with fire; whilst the heavy thunder kept the earth in a constant tremor. (131)

Traveling during the height of the American Revolution, Bartram describes in this passage, as he does in much of his writing, both a natural phenomenon and an historical event, as well as a personal anecdote. Since he revised this text in the years following independence, perhaps Bartram is explaining why he failed to participate in the Revolution.[47] While he may not have fought, this passage suggests, he did feel the full force of the storm's fury. Bartram finds a spot where he "intended to seek shelter and abide till the fury of the hurricane was overpast," but he is caught in the middle of the storm, "and to my utter confusion and astonishment," he exclaims, "I could not find from what particular quarter its strongest current or direction came, whereby I might have a proper chance of taking measures for securing a harbour or running from it" (131). Despite his relative safety next to the shore, "All seemed a frightful chaos" (132).

"When the wind and rain abated," Bartram concludes, "I was overjoyed to see the face of nature again appear" (132).[48] The storm seems to have created a new world, and, immediately afterward, Bartram arrives at his destination, a farm owned by a friend and situated on the eastern bank of a now beautiful lake. The farm, despite the devastation caused by the storm, sits in an ideal setting. Bartram writes,

Here is a vast body of land belonging to this estate; of high ridges fit for the culture of corn, indigo, cotton, batatas, &c. and of low swamps and marshes, which when properly drained and tilled, would be suitable for rice. . . . The farm is situated on the East shore of the beautiful Long Lake, which is above two miles long, and near a mile broad. This lake communicates with the St. Juan, by the little river that I ascended, which is about one mile and an half in length, and thirty or forty yards wide. The river, as well as the lake, abounds with fish and wild fowl of various kinds, and incredible numbers, especially during the winter season, when the geese and ducks arrive here from the north. (133)

This plantation seems to have everything Bartram might desire in a farm. The environment around it possesses incredible natural beauty, there is an overabundance of fish and game, the land is particularly fertile, and the river provides an adequate means of transporting the products of the farm to market. The dangers of the wilderness have been domesticated by the colonial farmer, and nature has been made even more beautiful through the wise use of its productive potential.

Bartram's descriptions of an idyllic landscape continue after he leaves this farm and makes his way downriver along the eastern shore. The dangers of the wilderness have been overcome, and now even the normal unpleasantries of travel seem bearable. For instance, Bartram writes, "Having agreeably diverted away the intolerable heats of sultry noon in fruitful fragrant groves, with renewed vigour I again resume my sylvan pilgrimage" (139).[49] The first leg of the trip was certainly never described as a "sylvan pilgrimage." Elsewhere he exclaims, "What a beautiful display of vegetation is here before me! seemingly unlimited in extent and variety" (141). Nature on this side of the Saint Johns River is utterly benign and comforting.

Bartram's views of the political possibilities for this new republic are expressed in his description of a fountain he discovers, one whose inhabitants all live in apparent peace. Looking at the fountain, Bartram invites the reader to join him in imagining the scene he sees before him. "Behold," he urges, "a vast circular expanse before you, the waters of which are so extremely clear as to be absolutely diaphanous or transparent as the ether" (150). The fountain is surrounded by "a great variety of fruitful and floriferous trees, shrubs, and plants" (150). And, the creatures inhabiting the pond live in perfect harmony:

> At the same instant innumerable bands of fish are seen, some clothed in the most brilliant colours; the voracious crocodile stretched along at full length, as the great trunk of a tree in size; the devouring garfish, inimical trout, and all the varieties of gilded painted bream; the barbed catfish, dreaded sting-ray, skate, and flounder, spotted bass, sheeps head and ominous drum; all in their separate bands and communities, with free and unsuspicious intercourse performing their evolutions: there are no signs of enmity, no attempt to devour each other; the different bands seem peaceably and complaisantly to move a little aside, as it were to make room for others to pass by. (150–51)

The violence of the western shore seems completely absent, and here in this fountain exists an earthly paradise. But, Bartram warns, these animals maintain their natural antipathy toward each other; only their environment has changed: "And although this paradise of fish may seem to exhibit a just representation of the peaceable and happy state of nature which existed before the fall, yet in reality it is a mere representation; for the nature of the fish is the same as if they were in Lake George or the river; but here the water or element in which they live and move, is so perfectly clear and transparent, it places them all on an equality with regard to their ability to injure or escape from one another" (151). The east, civilized side of the river has provided these fish an environment in which they can freely act without fear of violence. Unlike the murky, muddy fountains Bartram witnessed in the wilderness, this fountain is perfectly transparent, so the creatures can keep their enemies always in sight. No leader rules by force here, for all make room for the others, not because their "natures" have changed, but because their environment has in a sense made them equals.

As before, however, when he was camping in the wilderness, Bartram must leave this apparent paradise and return to the river and his canoe, resuming his journey down the middle passage between the hazards of the wilderness and the ideals of civilization. For it is this position with which Bartram seems most comfortable, neither on one bank nor the other, an inhabitant of neither the wilderness nor a farm. Bartram is a traveler, so he explains, "I left these Elysian springs and the aromatic groves, and briskly descended the pellucid little river, re-entering the great lake," from which he eventually makes his way back to his point of origin, the lower trading house (152).

Bartram's passage on the geopolitical frontier of the Saint Johns River parallels his journey in the South as well as his movement through *Travels* itself as a figure equally comfortable in both the city and the country. While he represents himself as the product of a European society transplanted to a new land, he at least partly rejects that culture in favor of a more "natural" existence. Likewise, he both accepts and rejects Native American culture, for although there are many aspects that he greatly admires, he believes the native societies he experiences to be too violent and undependable. By combining the positive qualities of both systems, Bartram suggests he can refashion himself as the perfect combination of European and Native American characteristics and re-create himself as the ideal inhabitant of the newly formed American nation.

Bartram has traditionally been viewed as a character who managed to miss the American Revolutionary War. John Seelye remarks, for instance, "Like his father before him, William Bartram set out in 1773 as an agent of British empire, but when he returned to Philadelphia, in 1777, it was like Rip Van Winkle to a new nation" ("Beauty Bare" 53). Unlike Rip Van Winkle, however, William Bartram did play an active role in the emerging nation, spending ten years revising his journals into a coherent narrative of travel through the American South. In so doing, he was attempting to unify not only the various discourses within himself but also the diverse regions and ideologies that would together come to constitute the United States.

Like J. Hector St. John de Crèvecoeur, William Bartram used his text to create a vision of the American as fundamentally a traveler, for both authors created narrators who not only expand their understanding of the world by traveling

but also seek to incorporate within themselves the diverse perspectives encountered in their journeys throughout the American nation. For both, also, the
South becomes critical as the region where they can confront both their own
and the American "self" and "other." Travel through the region provides the
ideal journey toward personal and national self-definition, because the South
is within the national boundaries, even as these boundaries are just beginning
to be delineated, but is also decidedly different from the more urban society of
the North. Despite these similarities, however, the projects of Crèvecoeur and
Bartram are not identical. Crèvecoeur suggests finally that American being can
be enlarged through the combination of farming and travel, so his traveling
narrator hopes to fashion a new American ontology. Bartram regards travel
as providing an opportunity to incorporate within himself a diversity of cultural methods of understanding the world, so his traveler is uniquely American
because of his unique combination of epistemologies, Native American and European. Still, his narrator, like Crèvecoeur's, is an American because he is a traveler, for travel through the South provides each with the opportunity to forge a
unique personal, and national, vision.

CHAPTER TWO

Moving Slaves

Frederick Douglass, Solomon Northup, and the Politics of Travel in Antebellum America

Freedom, the ability to choose one's own direction, makes life beautiful and pure.
HOUSTON BAKER

On April 6, 1846, Dred and Harriet Scott filed petitions in St. Louis, Missouri, suing the widow of John Emerson for their freedom on the grounds that they were no longer slaves, having previously resided for two years in a free state, Illinois, and having been transported by their owner, John Emerson, into a free territory, the Wisconsin Territory. Because they had traveled outside of Missouri, they argued, they were no longer the slaves of the Emerson family, even though they had since returned to that slave state. The Missouri circuit court agreed and ordered the Scott family emancipated, concluding that their residence in a free state had made them free. The Missouri Supreme Court disagreed, however, and overturned the circuit court's earlier decision, ruling that their freedom had been lost upon return to a slave state. When Dred Scott was subsequently sold to another owner, he appealed to the federal courts. Since he was a citizen of Missouri and his new owner, John Sandford, was a citizen of New York, Scott believed, the case was now under the jurisdiction of the federal legal system. During the December term of 1856, however, the Supreme Court disagreed, ruling five to two that the United Stated Supreme Court had no jurisdiction in the case. No difference of citizenship existed, Chief Justice Taney wrote in the majority opinion, because Dred Scott was not a citizen.[1] Taney concluded his decision by stating, "Upon the whole, therefore, it is the judgment of this court, that it appears by the record before us that the plaintiff in error is not a citizen of Missouri, in the sense in which that word is used in the Constitution" (*Historic* 190). The Constitution, Taney believed, was written and adopted by and for the white inhabitants of the United States; therefore, black residents were not accorded citizenship by the Constitution.[2] Justice McLean disagreed, however,

arguing that the Constitution's definition of citizenship should not be so narrowly defined. He explained that several states that had ratified the Constitution
had given citizenship to black Americans, so a percentage of the population that
had passed the Constitution had not been white. Justice McLean also recognized that this case, *Dred Scott v. John F. A. Sandford*, had a bearing on many
of the most important issues then facing the American republic, including the
definition of slavery, the definition of citizenship, the relationship between the
state and the national governments, and the constitutionality of the Missouri
Compromise.[3] All of these issues were raised, the courts learned, when a slave
traveled.

Perhaps the central, even defining, freedom promised to citizens of the
United States has been the freedom of movement. Certainly movement is the
first freedom denied those sold into slavery, signaled by the presence of iron
chains and bound hands and feet. American slavery can thus be defined as an
institution that forbade the movement of a person according to his or her own
will and demanded movement according to the wishes of another. According
to the ideology of slavery, in fact, slaves were incapable of acting or moving
in their own interests, for they were not fully human and did not understand
what was best for their own welfare. They could be moved as objects, according to this ideological system, but they could not direct themselves as subjects.
Dred and Harriet Scott undermined this definition of slavery, however, by arguing that their movement—even though supposedly under the guidance of
their master—had set them free. Slavery, they suggested, was not a permanent
state, as Taney's majority opinion argued, but a political condition that could
be altered through travel to a new locale. By traveling to (and residing in) a
free state, they argued, they had proven their personal subjectivity and thus had
become people who were no longer slaves. Not objects to be moved, they were
subjects who traveled. So, even though they had initially been moved in accordance with the wishes of their owner, they proved that their travels had also
been guided by their own purposes by initiating a court case upon their return.
In changing the purposes of their journeys to meet their own ends, Dred and
Harriet Scott suggested that they should no longer be considered slaves, for by
redefining their movement as travel, they had become free.

In addition to using the movement demanded by their masters for their own
purposes, however, slaves traveled in numerous other ways that directly contradicted the laws and ideology of slavery. In fact, for American slaves, participation in movement forbidden by their owners was one of the most common and
significant forms of subverting the ideology and fighting the daily restrictions
of slavery. For instance, Frederick Douglass describes "accidentally" letting his

master's horse escape so that he would have to go recapture it at the neighboring plantation, where he could receive some badly needed nourishment from his relatives. In addition, slaves not only escaped North but also visited friends and family members on other plantations, met spouses or lovers in secret, or gathered in groups away from the watchful eyes of owners. For all of these activities, travel—the ability to move in a self-directed fashion toward a specific goal—defined their subversion.

Despite the centrality of movement and stasis in the life of American slavery, however, the fundamental role of travel has been neglected by many historians of slavery and readers of nineteenth-century narratives by former slaves. While most recognize the importance of movement, few have analyzed its role in these narratives. Travel is, in fact, a fundamental precondition to the publication of a "slave narrative," for slaves were simply not afforded any opportunity to produce such accounts while they remained slaves. Likewise, the construction of a textual identity, which many have argued is the central issue of these narratives, was not accomplished without some sort of intervening journey between slavery and publication. In order to produce a slave narrative and create a textual identity, a slave had to travel. In the process, he or she had to become something (and someone) decidedly other than a slave. Many critics have argued that the literacy that was also an essential component of the production of a slave narrative served as a sign that the writer was no longer simply a slave, for textual skills necessarily wrought changes in those who possessed them. For instance, Houston Baker writes, "The voice of the unwritten self, once it is subjected to the linguistic codes, literary conventions, and audience expectations of a literate population, is perhaps never again the authentic voice of black American slavery. It is, rather, the voice of a self transformed by an autobiographical act into a sharer in the general public discourse about slavery" (*Journey* 43). Although Baker's comment depends on a problematic belief in an "authentic voice of black American slavery," it does help to explain the significance of literacy, for entrance into new discursive communities profoundly altered the slave's identity.[4] Likewise, travel was a necessary prelude to the publication of a narrative by a slave, for slavery could not be simultaneously experienced and written. Slavery could only be narrated and published from a space at least partially removed from the institution itself. Thus, narratives are written not by slaves but by "ex-slaves," by "escaped slaves," or, in the representations of slave ideology, by "fugitive slaves."

The significance and power of these different phrases used to describe slaves who have effected self-directed travel highlight the centrality of movement to the very definition of slavery. For abolitionists a slave who has escaped is no longer a slave but is, rather, a completely different person. The phrase "fugitive slave," on the other hand, represents a linguistic attempt to maintain a slave identity for one who is now someone and something else. The phrase "fugitive slave" is therefore an attempt to deny the significance of self-directed travel, to extend the power of slavery over a group of people who no longer acted according to slave ideology, and to incorporate into the identity of "slave" those who lived in territories where slavery did not legally exist. The adoption of the Fugitive Slave Law in 1850, then, effectively redefined a significant portion of the national population not as people but as slaves, redefining slavery itself in the process, or at least adopting or acquiescing to a southern definition of slavery. The dispute hinged on whether the legal identity of the person in question would ultimately be determined by the master—in which case the person is a "fugitive slave"—or by the person him or herself—in which case the person is an "ex-slave" or a "former slave." By robbing travel of its value as a sign and vehicle of freedom, subjectivity, and citizenship, slavery destroys travel. Slave narratives, however, suggest that travel and slavery are mutually exclusive, so travel transforms the slave's movements into self-directed action and consequently destroys slavery.

These narratives, as well as contemporary legal and legislative battles such as the Dred Scott case or the Fugitive Slave Act, also highlight the struggle occurring at this time over the political meaning of space in American culture. This struggle centered on whether the paradigm of "slavery" or "freedom" would govern American space and determine American identity. The Fugitive Slave Act, for instance, was an attempt to expand the institution of slavery across the entire nation and to make all of the United States, even those areas where slavery was illegal, supportive of southern ideology. Furthermore, intimately tied to this struggle over the meaning of American space was the political significance and meaning of movement. If "fugitive slaves" are no longer safe from recapture even in Massachusetts, for instance, then slave travel does not produce or signify the freedom it promises to American citizens. On the other hand, if slaves who escape to the North are safe from recapture, then they can be seen as having become more fully American by participating in the fundamental right to self-directed travel. After all, if one of the basic qualities of the American individual is his or her freedom to travel, then slaves should be able to join the republic as citizens once they have proven themselves legitimate by participating in the self-directed movement that defines so many as Americans.

For many readers of these texts, slave narratives get their power and their authority from the author-narrator's combined experiences of slavery and escape to freedom. An outsider does not have access to the same insight as does one who has experienced slavery, but slaves who have not escaped are rarely if ever able to report honestly their experiences, much less to publish accounts of their lives. For instance, describing Frederick Douglass's comments about the significance of slave songs, Albert Stone argues, "Neither the slaves themselves nor a sympathetic outsider—like, say, the sympathetic English actress Fanny Kemble who could not fathom the significance of the slave singing on her Georgia plantation—is in a position to tell the truth about this music. Only by *being* black and *becoming* free has Douglass earned the rank and right of interpreter" ("Identity" 70). Stone's remarks suggest that the right to speak for the slave, or the ability to interpret correctly the experiences of those enslaved in the South, depends on an ontology not of slavery but of blackness, combined with an epistemology of travel. However, texts published by former slaves describing their experiences in slavery do not depend on an ontology of blackness (whatever that might be) but actively produce the narrator-authors as travelers and as identities-in-progress. Rather than relating the experiences of a "black" subjectivity that has traveled, these narratives create traveling narrators as central to the experience of American slavery. In fact, because travel was central to the American experience as a whole, as Crèvecoeur and Bartram had shown at the end of the eighteenth century, slaves not only freed themselves by traveling but defined and positioned themselves as Americans.

In Frederick Douglass's *Narrative of the Life of Frederick Douglass, an American Slave*, freedom of movement and the antithetical barriers to self-directed action constitute major, though largely neglected, themes.[5] The importance of these themes can be seen not only in the role of streets in Douglass's achievement of literacy but also in the centrality of such symbols as the sailboats on the Chesapeake Bay or the description of his life as a journey to freedom. In fact, the *Narrative* recounts Douglass's growing ability to direct his own travels as he concurrently moves from under the control of a series of people and institutions that demand of him only specified types of movement. As a slave, Douglass is not allowed to direct his own movement, for his master, the people for whom he works, and the ideology of slavery itself all control how and where he is able to move. By the end of his narrative, however, Douglass has learned fully how to travel for himself. Douglass the traveler has overcome Douglass the slave. Thus, the book traces the narrator's journey from that of bound slave to that of free traveler and, simultaneously, representative American.

Solomon Northup's account traces a very different journey. Described in the opening pages of the text as a happy, stable homeowner, Northup is represented as a traveler and an American who becomes a slave. Unlike Douglass, for whom a sense of membership in a political entity is one of his ultimate goals, Northup begins the book as a citizen of New York but loses his rights as he travels and is then kidnapped and sold into slavery. After he is taken, Northup's movements are severely constrained both by the physical bonds and by the ideology of the slave South. Like Douglass's text, then, *Twelve Years a Slave* is founded on movement and travel; for both narrators, travel is the precondition of their authority and their textual existence. Even though Northup's book, describing a circular journey that begins and ends with freedom in the North, is in many ways a more traditional travel narrative than is Douglass's, travel has a more profound effect on Northup's text. While Douglass's text seems to suggest that with citizenship in the North comes a certain amount of sought-for stability, Northup's text argues that even American citizens are not exempt from forced movement. Northup's account illustrates, then, what could still happen to the African American citizen Frederick Douglass has struggled to become. Ultimately, Douglass's text suggests that the slave can become a traveler and free himself or herself from bondage. Northup's text, on the other hand, questions the extent to which unhindered travel is available to any black American, slave or free. No black citizen of the United States is truly a free traveler, argues Northup, for all are open to transportation South, causing their freedom to travel to be transformed and degraded into mere movement. Thus, as both Douglass's and Northup's experiences clearly show, the travels (and movements) of black Americans, slave and free, raised issues of the significance of space and travel that were fundamental to the definition and identity of America and its citizens.

According to Frederick Douglass's *Narrative of the Life of Frederick Douglass, an American Slave*, movement had been an important factor in his life as a slave almost from the time of his birth. For instance, he saw his mother only at nighttime, for she lived on another plantation and was forced to steal away after her duties were completed in order to visit her son. As Douglass explains, "She made her journeys to see me in the night, travelling the whole distance on foot, after the performance of her day's work" (40). Because his mother had to travel over twenty miles without being caught to see Frederick, he saw her only a few times before she died, and then only very briefly. But Douglass also experienced physical movement firsthand. For much of his youth he was shuttled back and forth between the Lloyd plantation on the Eastern Shores of Maryland, where he was born, and the Hugh and Sophia Auld household in Baltimore, where he worked and lived for a number of years. He was forced to move onto the farm of Edward Covey and, once there, forced to move around the plantation and work as a field hand. While a slave, his movements were controlled by others, particularly by his various masters, but also by the ideology of slavery and the cultural expectations of American society. However, not all of his movements were determined by others, for like many slaves Douglass often traveled in ways counter to those prescribed by slavery. For instance, he met with other slaves in secret, he traveled throughout Baltimore, and, most important, he escaped to freedom in the North.

Thus, it is not simply Douglass's ultimate travel north that makes movement so important to the *Narrative*, for throughout the text, Douglass creates a narrator who becomes more and more of a traveler as the book progresses. That is, Douglass the slave is contrasted throughout the text with Douglass the traveler, and once the narrator fully becomes a traveler who can direct his own movements, he is, according to the text's logic, no longer a slave. His narrative describes his growing awareness of his identity as a traveler and follows his journey from the confinements of southern slavery to the freedom of American travel. For much of the story, Douglass represents himself as both slave and traveler, simultaneously moving according to his owner's wishes and beginning to incorporate his own goals and values into his wanderings. He is only truly free once he can determine fully his actions and his travels, he argues. Accordingly, Douglass explains, he is still at least partially a slave until he stands up to speak at the abolitionist meeting, for by traveling from the audience to the speaker's podium and from silence to speech, Douglass finally breaks free of the ideological restraints that have held him in bondage and completes his journey from slavery to freedom. By freeing himself physically from the bonds of slavery and by emancipating his identity from the ideology of the southern slave system, Douglass becomes fully a traveler, a speaker, and, simultaneously, a representative American figure. If, as Houston Baker argues, "[T]he expressive, married, economically astute self at the close of Douglass's work represents a convergence of the voices that mark the various autobiographical postures of the *Narrative* as a whole" (*Blues* 49), the voices at the end are primarily those of the ex-slave and the traveler. Thus, perhaps this moment at the close of the narrative is the book's true climax, for only here do the two modes of self-definition converge, as Douglass illustrates the vast distance he has come from bondage and silence to freedom and self-expression.

Despite the central importance of travel in all of its manifestations, however, most critics of Douglass's three autobiographies have focused their attention on the role of literacy and language in the texts and in the life of their author. In fact, the significance and meaning of literacy has been the single issue around which almost all Douglass criticism has revolved. Broadly construed, literacy has proven a rich avenue of investigation into the meaning of Douglass's oeuvre and has provided critics a way to analyze not only Douglass's writing but also his construction of a textual subjectivity and historical persona. Some critics have investigated Douglass's use and knowledge of literary forms, genres, and rhetorical devices, simultaneously arguing about his place in the American literary canon. For instance, Henry Louis Gates Jr. argues that the slave narrative "is a 'countergenre,' a mediation between the novel of sentiment and the picaresque, oscillating somewhere between the two in a bipolar moment, set in motion by the mode of the Confession" ("Binary" 214).[6] Furthermore, Gates argues, Douglass's *Narrative* presents an extended meditation on the nature of language and suggests "the completely arbitrary relation between description and meaning, between signifier and signified, between sign and referent" (223). Thus, Douglass serves as a trickster who moves back and forth between the world of the slave and that of the master.

Gates's essay presaged the Douglass criticism that followed, for much has addressed more thoroughly the difficult question of Douglass's relationship to language. For instance, many recent critics have focused on the ideological impact of Douglass's linguistic usages and his ability (or inability) to resist language's hegemonic power. As William Andrews explains in his introduction to the 1991 volume *Critical Essays on Frederick Douglass*, criticism of Douglass's work during the 1980s attempted to answer Houston Baker's implicit question: "Does the *Narrative* signify Douglass's mastery of literary discourse—or its mastery of him?" (10).[7] Valerie Smith, for instance, argues that Douglass fails to free himself completely from the representational system he uses, mirroring in his text not only the cultural definitions of masculinity but also, and more fundamentally, a representation of the myth of the self-made man.[8] Smith, like a number of Douglass critics, concludes that even though Douglass does learn to manipulate the language of his oppressors, he is unable to subvert that language because of his participation in some of the most basic American myths.[9]

Many recent critics disagree, however, and conclude that Douglass does manage, in one way or another, to subvert the ideological systems in which he finds himself. For instance, while Rafia Zafar argues, "The life of Douglass, in history and in print, operates as an extension and amplification of that of the ideal American set forth in Franklin's *Autobiography*" (99), he adds that Douglass is writing himself into a tradition that was then limited to white males (115).[10] Zafar and others argue that Douglass fits into American literary or cultural traditions primarily through the tensions illustrated in his uses of language in his texts. It is exactly these tensions, they suggest, that show Douglass to be a representative American figure.[11] Thus, most recent writing that addresses Douglass's complicity with the ideology of his time and the limitations or opportunities provided by the representational system argues that Douglass both used language for his own purposes and remained somehow bound to it.

Related to these questions is the issue of Douglass's creation of a textual and historical subjectivity, for it was primarily through print, these critics argue, that Douglass was able to forge a unique and lasting personal identity. Expressing the sentiments of many critics, Eric Sundquist argues, "Douglass demonstrates that literacy is linked to the power to enslave and, alternatively, to the power to create one's own subjectivity and redeem one's community" (Introduction 11).[12] Henry Louis Gates Jr. has famously stated, "Surely this must be the literary critic's final judgment of Frederick Douglass: that he was Representative Man because he was Rhetorical Man, black master of the verbal arts. Douglass is our clearest example of the will to power as the will to write" (*Figures* 108). For Gates, it is Douglass's use of literary conventions and linguistic codes in his construction of a textual identity that makes him an American representative man. Douglass is not the self-made man some critics accuse him of pretending to be, Gates argues, for he depended on language in his struggle for freedom and identity.[13] Thus, language is what makes Douglass representative.

But Frederick Douglass is not solely a language-user, and his status as a representative American comes not simply from his rhetorical abilities or the tensions manifested in his texts. It is, in fact, his status as a traveler that makes Douglass most representative as an American. Like Crèvecoeur and Bartram before him, Douglass illustrates that the defining freedom for the American is the freedom to travel, and it is exactly this freedom that he seeks and finally attains in his 1845 *Narrative*. Interestingly, when describing the centrality of language to Douglass's most famous autobiography, his 1845 *Narrative*, many critics describe the narrator's quest for and attainment of literacy as a journey, during which Douglass had to overcome obstacles in order to reach his final destination, literacy and freedom. In fact, Frederick Douglass himself frequently describes literacy as the route to freedom.[14] However, few readers have placed this metaphorical journey into the broader context of literal movement that runs throughout the text.

The centrality of travel and its relationship with literacy are illustrated force-fully in Douglass's description of the methods he employs in learning to read and write. Forbidden by his master Hugh Auld to be taught to read by his new mistress, Sophia Auld, Douglass becomes determined to learn when he realizes how opposed to his literacy Hugh Auld is. According to Auld, "If you give a nigger an inch, he will take an ell. A nigger should know nothing but to obey his master—to do as he is told to do" (57). If Sophia were to teach Douglass to read, Auld reasons, "there would be no keeping him. It would forever unfit him to be a slave. He would at once become unmanageable, and of no value to his master" (57). Auld would be unable to "keep" Douglass, who would become "unmanageable"; that is, his movements and actions would not be determined by Auld. Given the slightest loosening of his bonds, his master claims, Douglass will move as freely as possible, pushing against the limits of his bondage and slowly expanding his freedom. If Douglass were allowed to determine his own movements even minimally, argues Auld, he would soon refuse to move according to his master's commands. Hugh Auld realizes, as his wife initially does not, that reading can become a form of intellectual and social travel, and, in addition, that travel of any kind not controlled by the master is antithetical to slavery.

Denied this opportunity to attain literacy, however, Douglass turns to the streets in order to step outside of his slave status and learn what has been forbidden him. Describing his method of learning to read, Douglass writes,

> The plan which I adopted, and the one by which I was most successful, was that of making friends of all the little white boys whom I met in the street. As many of these as I could, I converted into teachers. With their kindly aid, obtained at different times and in different places, I finally succeeded in learning to read. When I was sent to errands, I always took my book with me, and by going one part of my errand quickly, I found time to get a lesson before my return. I used also to carry bread with me, enough of which was always in the house, and to which I was always welcome; for I was much better off in this regard than many of the poor white children in our neighborhood. This bread I used to bestow upon the hungry little urchins, who, in return, would give me that more valuable bread of knowledge. (60)

Like Dred and Harriet Scott, Douglass performs the movement his master has demanded but alters the purpose to his own advantage. Thus, Douglass is able to perform several types of movement simultaneously, not only geographical but also social, racial, and intellectual. In the streets, where the rigid strictures (and structures) of the slave household are in some flux, Douglass crosses social and racial boundaries, by befriending white children, for instance. Furthermore, in his relationships with these white children, Douglass relocates himself outside of his normal cultural roles in order to assume new ones, particularly those of student and provider instead of slave. These children, too, move outside of their prescribed roles when Douglass "converts" them into teachers. In fact, these children are teachers even before they begin to instruct Douglass in reading, for their ability to wander these urban streets at will exemplifies for Douglass the paradigmatic freedom of travel he seeks eventually to attain. Although the social and educational institutions established for the purpose of teaching children to read and write are closed to him, Douglass learns to read "at different times and in different places" instead, in those spatial and temporal spaces that existed on the margins of slave ideology. Only the city's streets offer Douglass this type of space, for in the streets those social, racial, and cultural roles and identities that seem most solid become fluid and unstable.

Douglass learns to write in a similar fashion, by using lessons he picks up as he travels throughout the city and by taking advantage of those opportunities provided by the mobile nature of life in America's urban thoroughfares. Douglass's first writing lessons come about as a result of his work outside of the home and his presence in a shipyard. He writes, "The idea as to how I might learn to write was suggested to me by being in Durgin and Bailey's ship-yard, and frequently seeing the ship carpenters, after hewing, and getting a piece of timber ready for use, write on the timber the name of that part of the ship for which it was intended" (63).[15] Douglass again introduces self-direction into his movements throughout the shipyard, where he has been sent by his master. Instead of acquiescing to his status as an object within the economic system, Douglass becomes a subjective manipulator of his environment. In a sense, he transforms himself from shipyard cargo to shipboard sailor, redefining himself and determining, at least partially, his movements around the ships.

After learning his first few letters, Douglass again depends on the young boys he meets in the city to teach him the rest of the alphabet. "After that," he explains, "when I met with any boy who I knew could write, I would tell him I could write as well as he. The next word would be, 'I don't believe you. Let me see you try it.' I would then make the letters which I had been so fortunate as to learn, and ask him to beat that. In this way I got a good many lessons in writing, which it is quite possible I should never have gotten in any other way. During this time, my copy-book was the board fence, brick wall, and pavement; my pen and ink was a lump of chalk. With these, I learned mainly how to write" (63). As when he is learning to read, Douglass realizes how he can alter his relationships while in the street to his best advantages. Furthermore, he reconfigures those structures that served to support slave ideology—fences, walls, pavement—in order to put them to his own use and subvert that ideology. In this way, the roles of various parts of the city change as Douglass appropriates the city for his own ends.[16] Douglass thus proves his agency both by marking his world—inscribing his name on the parts of the city—and by leaving evidence of his movement—traveling throughout the urban landscape. His destination is less important to him than his ability to travel and to write.

By moving socially, geographically, and intellectually, Douglass takes a step in his transformation from slave to traveler. When Douglass is a traveler in the streets of Baltimore, he steps out of his roles as a slave, momentarily leaving behind his status as an object by assuming the status of a person desiring an education.[17] Instead of depending on others, they depend on him. Rather than passively accepting his situation, he actively recreates himself as a person who is willing to make deals in order to receive what he wants. Trading bread for lessons with the white children he meets in the streets of the city, he is no longer an object within the economy but a purposeful participant in that economy. Rather than fulfilling the roles that slave ideology assigns him and assuming the identity provided, Douglass attempts to become one who crosses borders and produces his own identity as a traveler.

This type of movement would have been far more difficult had Douglass not already traveled from the Lloyd plantation to Baltimore. As Douglass explains, "A city slave is almost a freeman, compared with a slave on the plantation" (58). The primary freedom allowed slaves in the city was, of course, freedom of movement. In fact, as soon as he is chosen to go to Baltimore, Douglass realizes that his travels will afford him a sense of freedom extremely rare among slaves. His first trip to Baltimore, therefore, begins what will turn out to be a life of travel. Without that first trip from the plantation, Douglass suggests, he might never have freed himself from slavery: "I look upon my departure from Colonel Lloyd's plantation as one of the most interesting events of my life. It is possible, and even quite probable, that but for the mere circumstance of being removed from that plantation to Baltimore, I should have to-day, instead of being here seated by my own table, in the enjoyment of freedom and the happiness of home, writing this Narrative, been confined in the galling chains of slavery. Going to live at Baltimore laid the foundation, and opened the gateway, to all my subsequent prosperity" (56). Had Douglass not traveled, he explains, and not been given the chance to move outside of the normal routes and routines of a plantation slave's life, he would have remained a slave.[18] The physical trip to Baltimore, then, encourages and symbolizes all of his subsequent journeys—psychological, social, geographical, and intellectual.

Douglass had learned early in life that travel and movement, particularly to the city, were to be greatly valued. In contrast to the majority of slaves whom he sees on the plantation, Douglass knows a few who work aboard his master's sloop. It is their responsibility to carry the farm's crops to market, so these sailors were fortunate in being allowed to visit Baltimore. The sloop, Douglass explains, was captained by his master's son-in-law, but "she was otherwise manned by the colonel's own slaves. Their names were Peter, Isaac, Rich, and Jake. These were esteemed very highly by the other slaves, and looked upon as the privileged ones of the plantation; for it was no small affair, in the eyes of the slaves, to be allowed to see Baltimore" (43). For slaves who are rarely given any opportunity to stray outside of the clearly demarcated boundaries of the plantation, the opportunity to travel to a city such as Baltimore seems to represent a degree of freedom to be very highly prized.[19] Furthermore, the travel afforded these four men serves in the text to differentiate them from the majority of Colonel Lloyd's slaves and to provide them, therefore, with personal identities such as few of the "from three to four hundred" slaves owned by Lloyd enjoy in Douglass's *Narrative* (43). In addition to granting them a certain status among Colonel Lloyd's other slaves, travel has to a real degree created these men's textual identities, for had they not participated in regular journeys to Baltimore, they would have instead remained a part of the unnamed mass of slaves on the plantation. Travel has, in a sense, created their being, transformed them from objects into subjects, and given them a degree of freedom enjoyed by very few who were enslaved.

The freedom offered by boats and sails recurs in Douglass's text and, during the period of his most restrictive bondage, lifts his spirits and causes him to hope and to strive once again for freedom. In one of the most famous passages of the *Narrative*, Douglass stands on a hill above the Chesapeake Bay and dreams of possessing the freedom he sees in the boats sailing on the water. The only section mentioned by both authors of the two prefaces preceding Douglass's narrative, this description of the freedom of travel has been viewed by many readers as one of the defining passages of Douglass's story. In what could be described as his personal Declaration of Independence, Douglass prays to God, "with an apostrophe to the moving multitude of ships," as he watches these boats from the hillside overlooking the bay: "You are loosed from your moorings, and are free; I am fast in my chains, and am a slave! You move merrily before the gentle gale, and I sadly before the bloody whip! You are freedom's swift-winged angels, that fly round the world; I am confined in bands of iron! O that I were free! O, that I were on one of your gallant decks, and under your protecting wing! Alas! betwixt me and you, the turbid waters roll. Go on, go on. O that I could also go! Could I but swim! If I could fly!" (74–75). Enclosed in quotation marks in Douglass's text, this passage can be seen as an attempt by the slave who later becomes known as Frederick Douglass to break through the account and free himself rhetorically. Having captured his rhetorical freedom, the slave produces a passage widely recognized as one of the book's most eloquent. But rhetorical freedom is not sufficient, as the enslaved narrator understands, for true freedom is based on the ability to direct one's own physical movement. In this passage, then, the freedom Douglass envies is primarily one of travel. The boats are loosed from their moorings, so they are free; Douglass is fast in his chains, so he is a slave. The movement of the boats is assisted by the wind but not directed by it, for they "move merrily before the gentle gale." In contrast, when Douglass does move, it is without pleasure, for he is forced to move in specified ways "before the bloody whip." He imagines himself a sailor on the deck of the ships, enjoying the winds that bring and symbolize the freedom he so desires. Furthermore, as Rowe notes, Douglass's wish to become a sailor is particularly significant because his probable father, Captain Anthony Auld, acquired his title "by sailing a craft on the Chesapeake Bay" (41). Thus, bondage is especially difficult for Douglass because of his inability to claim what he considers his birthright. Were he not bound by the institution and ideology of slavery, Douglass seems to suggest, he would be a traveler like the father who refuses to recognize his own slave child.

This incident occurs during the year Douglass is working for Mr. Covey, the harshest master Douglass faces. Unlike all of Douglass's previous masters, Covey succeeds in "breaking" Douglass, "in body, soul, and spirit" (74).[20] "Behold a man transformed into a brute!" Douglass exclaims, comparing himself to a creature that never moves autonomously but only at another's command or by instinct. Reassured by the white sails he views from the hillside, Douglass eventually seizes control of his own future. "You have seen how a man was made a slave," Douglass famously states; "you shall see how a slave was made a man" (75). This rebirth is precipitated by Douglass's refusal to work—to move according to Covey's commands—and his subsequent flight, during which he controls his own movements. Described in the masculinist language of Douglass's attainment of manhood, this scene is integrally tied to issues of travel and movement. Douglass does not work according to Covey's directions, so Covey beats him. As a result, Douglass leaves the farm in blatant disregard for Covey's attempts to control his movements.[21] Several times Douglass acts according to his own desires rather than Covey's commands, so Covey finally seeks to restrain Douglass's movements completely by binding him. Douglass's refusal to submit to even this type of control constitutes the almost total subversion of Covey's authority to determine Douglass's movements. Consequently, Douglass explains, "I now resolved that, however long I might remain a slave in form, the day had passed forever when I could be a slave in fact" (79). It is Douglass's resolution to control his own actions that determines his status. Here Douglass has become as much a traveler as a slave.

Of course, Covey is not the only bar to Douglass's unrestricted movement, and Douglass must also overcome the institution of slavery as a whole by escaping to the North. This travel is particularly difficult, however, because of the dangers associated with the rural roads, unlike the relative freedom represented by the urban streets of Baltimore. Although roads can function as conduits to freedom, they can also represent danger for slaves who are attempting to move outside the bounds of slavery, as is forcefully illustrated in Douglass's description of his first attempt to flee north. Douglass describes numerous fears that haunt him and his companions as they plan their escape, explaining, "At every gate through which we were to pass, we saw a watchman—at every ferry a guard—on every bridge a sentinel—and in every wood a patrol. We were hemmed in upon every side" (86). Douglass continues, "[W]hen we permitted ourselves to survey the road, we were frequently appalled" (86). The fears of the group were not unfounded, for the roads of the South did indeed hold countless dangers for runaway slaves, such as the bloodhounds and other dogs slave owners often used in their attempts to catch them. In addition, because of the extreme instability to the institution of slavery that traveling slaves represented, defenders of slavery frequently patrolled the roads of the South in order to minimize slaves' movement from their places on the plantations to which they belonged.[22] In fact, any white person had the right to stop any black person and demand to see his or her papers; because of this widespread practice, every white person a slave met was a potential enemy, legally able to detain any black person until determination could be made concerning the right of the slave (or free black person) to be traveling. Thus, defenders of slavery sought to control, use, and define the roads to uphold the institution and to assist in the submission of the slaves, while slaves attempted to use the roads for their own purposes and to redefine them as channels to freedom.

Throughout the *Narrative*, roads both promise liberty and signal danger, for the mobility that provides positive contact with others can also bring disastrous outcomes for slaves. For instance, Douglass describes a slave of Colonel Lloyd who one day happens to meet his master out on his horse. Not realizing that the white man riding down the road is his owner, the slave responds honestly to questions concerning the unkindness of his master. After the conversation, the slave "went on about his business, not dreaming that he had been conversing with his master" (49). Several weeks later, however, the slave is sold "down the river" to a Georgia trader and not even given time to say good-bye to his family or friends. Instead, "[h]e was immediately chained and handcuffed" (49), thus ensuring that he did no further traveling on his own, geographically, rhetorically, or otherwise. Sometimes the result of a slave's travels could be even more unfortunate, as Douglass explains: "Colonel's Lloyd's slaves were in the habit of spending a part of their nights and Sundays in fishing for oysters, and in this way made up the deficiency of their scanty allowance. An old man belonging to Colonel Lloyd, while thus engaged, happened to get beyond the limits of Colonel Lloyd's, and on the premises of Mr. Beal Bondly. At this trespass, Mr. Bondly took offence, and with his musket came down to the shore, and blew its deadly contents into the poor old man" (53). This old slave's offence was traveling outside of the appropriate borders, and the fact that he did this accidentally apparently has no bearing on the fatal punishment. Douglass also describes a slave, Demby, who is shot by Mr. Gore for refusing to leave the river to which he had run in order to escape a whipping; consequently, Demby is killed both for moving and for remaining stationary against the commands of the overseer. While the text seems to differentiate these two acts—moving on his own and not moving for his master—in reality these are always conjoined actions in instances of slave travel, for the fulfillment of one necessitates the negation of the other. As the stories of Demby and the old man illustrate, any movement whatsoever by a slave that contradicted the orders or expectations of his or her master was severely, often brutally, punished. The severity of the punishments suggests the threatening power of undirected travel in the minds of the slave owners and overseers, for even the slightest failure to move for a master could be a radical subversion of slave ideology.

In addition to representing the manifold dangers of movement outside of the normal roles and routines of slave life, the road further serves as a sign of Douglass's lack of knowledge of the world beyond his own limited realm. As Russell Reising argues, "When he and a band of friends plan an escape, it is their *ignorance* of geography that intimidates them most" (266). They do not know where they can find freedom, safe from recapture, for they have never traveled outside of a very limited area; Douglass writes, "We knew nothing about Canada" (86). At this point, Douglass seems to believe freedom is more a destination or a place than a state of being; only after he begins to direct his own movement more fully does he come to understand that travel in and of itself can bring about, even constitute, the freedom he seeks. If travel brings knowledge and freedom, Douglass realizes, lack of travel can result in an ignorance of the world beyond one's own arena and a bondage both physical and mental.

Not surprisingly, this ignorance is most effectively eradicated by the knowledge gained from travel, as Douglass realizes when he is returned from Baltimore to the household of Thomas Auld. Douglass writes, "I sailed from Baltimore for St. Michael's in the sloop Amanda, Captain Edward Dodson. On my passage, I paid particular attention to the direction which the steamboats took to go to Philadelphia. I found, instead of going down, on reaching North Point they went up the bay, in a north-easterly direction. I deemed this knowledge of the utmost importance. My determination to run away was again revived. I resolved to wait only so long as the offering of a favorable opportunity. When that came, I was determined to be off" (67). Not only does travel here provide Douglass with knowledge, but it also revives his determination to gain freedom and encourages further, more subversive, travel on his part. It is travel that provides Douglass with the necessary information about the direction to freedom. Travel, then, gives Douglass knowledge, determination, and courage. He has used the small amount of freedom afforded him as he is moved by (and between) his various masters to plant and partake of a more significant level of freedom and travel. As Hugh Auld had warned his wife, given an inch, Douglass has taken an ell.

Of course, his initial attempt to escape fails because he and his friends are exposed prior to their attempt, perhaps, Douglass suggests, by Sandy, a slave initially included in their plans. For Houston Baker, "Sandy seems to represent the inescapable limiting conditions of Afro-American slavery in the South; he is the pure, negative product of an economics of slavery. . . . Sandy represents the virtual impossibility of an escape from bondage on the terms implied by the attempted escape from Freeland's" (*Blues* 47). I would argue, however, that Sandy also represents the slave who is unable to travel freely, so determined by slavery that he cannot imagine movement that directly contradicts the ideals of slavery. Even though Sandy had earlier assisted Douglass in his attempts to escape physical torture, he seems unable to imagine or participate in a more liberating type of travel. He seeks to find a space within slavery in which to move more comfortably rather than searching outside the institution for more significant types of travel and freedom, and he seems to have carved out a life for himself within slavery in which he has limited freedom of movement. As a root doctor, Sandy is planted firmly within the ideology of slavery, unlike Douglass, whose less firm connection to the land allows him a much greater flexibility and fluidity.

Douglass's second attempt is successful because by then he has traveled more widely and gained the further knowledge necessary for his escape. According to Jonathan Arac, during this second attempt Douglass used the newly opened railroad between Baltimore and Philadelphia, borrowing a free sailor's papers and taking advantage of the crowds. "The train's speed," writes Arac, "meant that before he was even expected home from his workday in the shipyards, he had already reached freedom" (671). In his *Narrative*, however, Douglass refuses to describe his escape route, ironically failing to narrate the text's most vivid story of travel. He explains that he will not describe these travels because such a disclosure would endanger other slaves. This form of travel, Douglass explains, can be narrated only at a cost, putting in danger not only those who assisted in his escape but also those who will come after him. "I deem it proper to make known my intention," Douglass states, "not to state all the facts connected with the transaction" (94).[23] Because travel can so effectively subvert the institution and ideology of slavery, Douglass suggests, those who are fighting for abolition and for the unfortunate multitude still enslaved should continue to keep hidden the most effective means of encouraging slave emancipation. In addition, however, there is a sense in which this travel cannot be narrated, for with this escape, Douglass realizes, comes his personal transformation from bondage to freedom. Despite his willingness to describe the many times he began to move against the wishes of his various masters, perhaps he is unable to describe adequately this manifestation of his transformation. Instead, Douglass can narrate only his preparations for and the results of this revolutionary travel.

Once he has physically escaped from slavery, he is more able than ever before to direct his own movements. His travels are no longer determined by a master or by those for whom he works, as they were on the plantations or even during his various jobs in Baltimore. He still does not control his actions completely, however, for he continues to be influenced by the ideology of slavery. Only after he has confronted how his own beliefs about his position in the world are determined by the ideology of the system under which he struggled for so long can he become the citizen-traveler he has dreamed of becoming. As a result of his interest in learning more about the abolitionist movement, Douglass begins to attend abolitionist meetings once he has found employment in New Bedford. As he explains, he "never felt happier than when in an anti-slavery meeting" (104). He continues:

> [W]hile attending an anti-slavery convention at Nantucket, on the 11th of August, 1841, I felt strongly moved to speak, and was at the same time much urged to do so by Mr. William C. Coffin, a gentleman who had heard me speak in the colored people's meeting at New Bedford. It was a severe cross, and I took it up reluctantly. The truth was, I felt myself a slave, and the idea of speaking to white people weighed me down. I spoke but a few minutes, when I felt a degree of freedom, and said what I desired with considerable ease. From that time until now, I have been engaged in pleading the cause of my brethren—with what success, and with what devotion, I leave those acquainted with my labors to decide. (104)

Traveling to the podium to address a room of white abolitionists, Douglass finally feels himself fully capable of determining his own movements. Until he feels himself worthy of addressing this abolitionist meeting, he explains, "I felt myself a slave." Only by overcoming the internal doubts that slavery had provided him does Douglass see himself as fully a traveler and not a slave, and only by traveling the crucial distance from audience to podium does he overcome these doubts. The final segment of Douglass's travels is primarily ideological or psychological. As Donald Gibson points out, in Douglass's description of his movement from slavery to freedom, the emphasis is more on his psychological journey than on his physical one ("Reconciling" 553). As a result of this new freedom, Douglass becomes a traveler for the cause of abolition, traversing the country (and later the world) in order to lecture on slavery and to eradicate the institution from the United States, simultaneously demonstrating both his freedom to travel and his entitlement to that freedom. [24]

In his roles as an abolitionist and a traveler, Douglass seeks to become an inspiration to others who are bound by slavery. As Houston Baker explains, "Douglass's narrator not only secures his own liberty, but also becomes something of a mythic figure, taking his place in the same framework that includes the drinking gourd, the underground railroad, and the North Star" (*Long* 79). [25] Furthermore, according to Eric Sundquist in *The Cambridge History of American Literature*, "More so than many other slave narrators, Douglass was aware of his ability and his need to create a paradigmatic story" ("Literature" 324). As Baker and Sundquist recognize, Douglass hopes to become a representative figure for other slaves struggling for their freedom and a place in the American nation. In order to become someone other than a slave, Douglass argues through this text, the slave must become a traveler.

But Douglass does not become a representative figure only for other slaves. As numerous critics have recognized, Douglass recreates himself as an exemplary national character, a representative American. And for Douglass, as for Crèvecoeur and Bartram before him, the American is first and foremost a traveler, for freedom of movement is a fundamental freedom upon which the nation is founded. [26] Douglass's desire to become this type of national character is illustrated throughout the text, particularly in passages in which he compares slaves to members of Congress or links himself with national heroes. For instance, describing his first attempt to escape from freedom, Douglass writes, "In coming to a fixed determination to run away, we did more than Patrick Henry, when he resolved upon liberty or death. With us it was a doubtful liberty at most, and almost certain death if we failed" (86). Thus, Douglass becomes a revolutionary traveler, writing himself into an American historical tradition. By explicitly comparing himself to a figure from the American Revolution, Douglass seeks to re-create himself as a national hero, but one who is seeking to subvert southern ideology and is having to fight to become a citizen of the country that he so desperately wants to join.

This representative American figure, "Frederick Douglass," is very much a creation of travel, for only after he has become free does the narrator take the surname "Douglass." As he explains in the last chapter of his narrative, he was known as "Frederick Bailey" while a slave and traveled under an assumed name during his escape:

> On the morning after our arrival at New Bedford, while at the breakfast-table, the question arose as to what name I should be called by. The name given me by my mother was, "Frederick Augustus Washington Bailey." I, however, had dispensed with the two middle names long before I left Maryland so that I was generally known by the name of "Frederick Bailey." I started from Baltimore bearing the name of "Stanley." When I got to New York, I again changed my name to "Frederick Johnson," and thought that would be the last change. But when I got to New Bedford, I found it necessary again to change my name. The reason of this necessity was, that there were so many Johnsons in New Bedford, it was already quite difficult to distinguish between them. I gave Mr. Johnson the privilege of choosing me a name, but told him he must not take from me the name of "Frederick." I must hold on to that, to preserve a sense of my identity. Mr. Johnson had just been reading the "Lady of the Lake," and at once suggested that my name be "Douglass." From that time until now I have been called "Frederick Douglass;" and as I am more widely known by that name than by either of the others, I shall continue to use it as my own. (101)

Thus, there was not a slave named Frederick Douglass, the narrator explains, for that is the name of a free man. As a free man, Douglass seems unwilling to keep the name his mother gave him when he was a slave; of course, his status as a fugitive slave demands that he conceal his former identity as much as possible to avoid recapture. In addition, once he has freed himself and is no longer "following the condition of the mother," perhaps he finds the name "Bailey" too closely associated with Harriet Bailey, the mother who spent her entire life in slavery. Furthermore, because he does not know his paternity and has not been recognized by this other, unknown parent, his father's name is not available to him. So, he takes a name from a Scott poem, foreshadowing the importance of the written word to his future identity. Because he has traveled so extensively as an abolitionist and is "widely known" by the name "Frederick Douglass," he concludes he will "continue to use it as my own," once again confirming the central importance of travel to his life and to his identity.

Like Frederick Douglass, Solomon Northup, author and narrator of *Twelve Years a Slave*, has different names when he is free and when he is enslaved. Unlike Douglass, however, Northup begins his life, and his account, as a free man. Kidnapped into slavery during a visit to Washington, D.C., Northup's name is changed to "Platt," by which he is known during the entire twelve years of his captivity. He quickly learns not to announce that he is legally a citizen of New York named Solomon Northup, for the slave traders who transport him to Louisiana beat him mercilessly after the one time he tries to plead his case to them. He does not try again until he meets Samuel Bass, a sympathetic carpenter from Canada who is opposed to slavery; in fact, Bass is the man responsible for bringing Northup's plight, and slave identity, to the attention of his northern friends. Northup's struggle for freedom, then, becomes a struggle to be recognized legally as Solomon Northup, rather than as Platt. Northup seeks to recover an identity rather than create one. By the end of the narrative, Northup's legal name has been restored to him, and he is once again in New York with his family and community of friends.

Because Douglass's 1845 autobiography has for many years served as the model of the American slave narrative, critics have traditionally ignored or given scant attention to those narratives that do not chart a similar course from bondage to freedom or illiteracy to authorship.[27] As a result, even those narratives that initially sold more copies than did Douglass's have been ignored in favor of those that trace a comparable route out of servitude. Solomon Northup's *Twelve Years a Slave* is a case in point. While Douglass's *Narrative* sold approximately five thousand copies in the first four months of its publication, the first printing of eight thousand copies of Northup's narrative sold within its first month; by 1856, within three years of its initial printing, Northup's text had sold over thirty thousand copies.[28] Although historians and other students of the slave narrative have consistently mentioned Northup's narrative in their studies, the book is very rarely given anything other than passing notice. Most writers who mention him simply use Northup in order to make a particular point about slavery or to support further their reading of other slave narratives.[29] For instance, while Houston Baker holds, "The narratives of Solomon Northup and Henry Bibb are on a par with Douglass's," Baker fails to follow this point with an extended analysis of the work of either writer (*Long* 80). Similarly, while Robert Stepto does include Northup's narrative in his study of the slave narrative form, he does not grant it nearly the attention he gives to *Narrative of the Life of Frederick Douglass*. Ironically, one historian who showed Northup's text respect was U. B. Phillips. Published in 1918, his controversial history *American Negro Slavery* incorporated little evidence from slave narratives, for Phillips believed them unreliable sources concerning the institution of slavery. He did, however, single out Northup's narrative as more useful than most. "Though the books of this class are generally of dubious value," he writes in a footnote to the text, "this one has a tone which engages confidence. Its pictures of plantation life

and labor are of a particular interest" (445).[30] Certainly Northup's contempo-
raries gave his narrative a good deal of attention. Frederick Douglass called it "a
strange history," (qtd. in Eakin and Logsdon ix), and in her *Key to Uncle Tom's
Cabin* Harriet Beecher Stowe pointed to Northup's experiences as providing
credence to the representations in her abolitionist novel (340–43).

One aspect of Northup's book that has perhaps kept it from being as critically appealing to modern readers as other narratives by ex-slaves is its description of an unusual course of events: Northup was born free but was kidnapped
into slavery. Even though the narrator does describe one man with whom he is
housed in a cell and another whom he meets on a boat as having also been kidnapped from freedom (38, 42), historians have generally agreed that this was a
fairly rare occurrence.[31] In fact, even the narrative itself suggests that once it was
known that Northup had been kidnapped, southern authorities, including the
justice system, expediently secured Northup's freedom. In many ways Northup
was an exceptional rather than a typical slave, so, critics have indicated, the plot
of Northup's narrative is simply not as representative as is Douglass's. As a result,
the narrative has been bypassed in favor of those that supposedly speak about
the experiences of a larger number of slaves.

Furthermore, unlike Douglass's *Narrative*, which was, the book's title page
proudly claims, "written by himself," *Twelve Years a Slave* is actually the product
of a joint effort between Solomon Northup and David Wilson. Many readers
have favored those narratives produced without the assistance of an amanuen-
sis, even denying that Northup's narrative is an autobiography. Robert Stepto,
for instance, is "not prepared to classify Solomon Northup's *Twelve Years a Slave*
(1854) as an autobiography," though he does think it "a more sophisticated text
than Henry Bibb's" (11).[32] This joint authorship is indicative of a larger issue
that may also have troubled a number of critics: the authors' representation of
Northup the narrator not as the strong-willed individual man fighting alone
to free himself from slavery but rather as one who, because he is enmeshed
in a number of communities, depends on the cooperation of others to help
him secure his freedom. The narrator of *Twelve Years a Slave* is simply not an
"American" hero in the way that Frederick Douglass's narrator is. Nor does
Northup condemn slavery in the same uncompromising tone as does Douglass.[33] Of course, this is not to suggest that Northup did not hope to abolish
slavery—he was fervently against the institution—but the book does not express the same degree of moral certainty as does Douglass's *Narrative*. Neither
Northup nor Wilson was ever the active abolitionist that Frederick Douglass
became.

Ironically, the very qualities that may have discouraged readers in the past from focusing on *Twelve Years a Slave* actually point to a rhetorical and thematic complexity long overlooked by critics of Northup's narrative. Because Northup is not as propagandistic as is Douglass, the views of slavery expressed in Northup's narrative are perhaps more subtle than are those in Douglass's *Narrative*. In addition, while Northup does not represent himself as the powerful individual Douglass does, his descriptions of the relationship between the individual and his or her society are both incisive and original. Douglass argues through his narrative that slaves should be regarded as human and are worthy to become fully participating members of American society. Northup, on the other hand, argues that black Americans, both slave and free, already are fully participating in American society, and particularly in the American economy, so they should be granted full legal rights as well. Finally, because Northup's text is in many ways a more traditional travel narrative, his representations of travel are even more intertwined into the narrative as a whole. While Douglass generally represents the freedom to travel as an emancipatory activity and seems to reach his goal of freedom at the end of the narrative, Northup argues that he is unable to travel as freely as are white citizens of the United States, even when he is legally a free man. Thus, while Douglass seeks to earn his citizenship, Northup seeks to prove his. Douglass works to illustrate that slaves are worthy of complete integration into the American republic, but Northup tries to show that even free black Americans do not fully benefit from their citizenship and thus that not all American citizens enjoy the same rights and freedoms. Douglass earns his freedom by himself, according to his autobiography, but Northup's freedom comes about through the cooperation of the communities of which he is a part. Through descriptions of the movement and travel he has undergone, then, Northup's text performs a more incisive critique of American society, suggesting not only that black Americans, both slave and free, are members of American society that are denied their rights but also that those rights are dependent on the active consensus of the society as a whole. Thus, Douglass's critique of slave society may prove the more powerful, but Northup's text performs a more biting critique of American society as a whole.

Northup's very first sentence signals an account dramatically different from the one published by Douglass in 1845: "Having been born a freeman, and for more than thirty years enjoyed the blessings of liberty in a free State—and having at the end of that time been kidnapped and sold into Slavery, where I remained, until happily rescued in the month of January, 1853, after a bondage of twelve years—it has been suggested that an account of my life and fortunes would not be uninteresting to the public" (3). The differences between being born a freeman and being born a slave are immediately obvious. Rather than growing up with little knowledge of his relatives, as Douglass did, Northup was born into a well-established, financially secure family. His father had once been a slave but had been emancipated at the death of his former owner, a member of the Northup family. After his liberation, Solomon Northup's father spent much of his life farming in various counties across New York, never settling permanently in any one position. "His whole life," Northup writes, "was passed in the peaceful pursuits of agriculture" (5). Because of his "diligence and economy," his father eventually acquired "a sufficient property qualification to entitle him to the right of suffrage" (5). Thus, in stark contrast to Douglass, Northup was born into a stable family and was offered a solid education, and his father was a citizen of New York who participated in the political process of his state.

Northup follows in his father's footsteps once he is married, spending at least part of his time as a farmer. Northup also works in a number of other jobs, however, that allow him to move around the state. He works as a repairman on the Champlain Canal and learns to transport lumber on the rivers. In fact, after learning "the art and mysteries of rafting," Northup even hires a number of other hands to help him and goes into business for himself, gaining several contracts to transport "large rafts of timber from Lake Champlain to Troy" (8). During one of these trips down the lake, Northup actually crosses the border into Canada and visits several cities, particularly Montreal and Kingston. If Northup's father was a farmer who occasionally moved, Northup seems to be a traveler who farms.

Northup and his wife, Anne, finally decide to settle into a farming life full-time. They rent part of a farm his father had worked earlier and settle into their new home. Northup, "accustomed from earliest youth to agricultural labors," enjoys the work and "commence[s] farming upon as large a scale as my utmost means would permit" (8–9). Despite his happiness with farming life, however, Northup continues to travel, primarily to play his violin at local dances. "Wherever the young people assembled to dance," he explains, "I was almost invariably there. Throughout the surrounding villages my fiddle was notorious" (9). Anne, too, travels throughout the region, frequently finding employment as a cook. Even when Northup is primarily a farmer, he spends much of his time traveling about New York. In fact, despite his skills and experience with farming, Northup and his wife eventually leave the farm and move to Saratoga Springs, a famous northern tourist destination, even living and working for a time in the United States Hotel, verifying, in a way, their status as American travelers.

While they seem to enjoy their freedom to travel around Saratoga Springs, however, they do not live as well as they had on the farm, according to Northup. As he explains, "The flattering anticipations which, seven years before, had seduced us from the quiet farm-house, on the east side of the Hudson, had not been realized. Though always in comfortable circumstances, we had not prospered. The society and associations at that world-renowned watering place, were not calculated to preserve the simple habits of industry and economy to which I had been accustomed, but, on the contrary, to substitute others in their stead, tending to shiftlessness and extravagance" (10–11). Travel, then, brings Northup and his wife a sense of freedom but also fails to satisfy their desires and even seems somewhat dangerous or corrupting. As he has already stated, "Well, indeed, would it have been for us had we remained on the farm at Kingsbury" (9).

As he provides his early history to his readers, Northup strives to place himself and his family firmly within American society. He is careful to point out that his father was a successful farmer who had acquired enough property to gain the right of suffrage and had also provided his children with a work ethic, a sense of morality, and an excellent education. Northup thus characterizes his early life as one of stability and comfort. As Northup matures, his connections to the national republic are only strengthened. As Sam Worley explains, "He moves into a building which, as he specifically points out, had played a role in the Revolutionary War, thereby further implying his connection to American life and history. Similarly, when he tells us that he worked on the construction of the Champlain Canal, he implies a connection between his personal labor and success and the national prosperity" (247). Thus, despite a period in Saratoga Springs in which he doesn't prosper, Northup's life before he is kidnapped seems an almost idyllic expression of the American dream.

Northup seems to be living the life Douglass seeks throughout his *Narrative*. He is an American citizen, he travels freely about the countryside, he earns (and keeps) his own wages, and his marriage is recognized by law. In addition, Northup is part of a complex network of relationships, based both on his extended family and on the larger communities in which he and Anne are involved. As he describes his personal history, Northup consistently names the people with whom he has connections: Henry B. Northup, a family friend; Timothy Eddy, who married Northup and his wife; Mr. Baird and the Reverend Proudfit, for whom his wife worked before their marriage; David McEachron and William Van Nortwich, his superintendents on the Champlain Canal; Lewis Brown, from whom Northup purchases some livestock; Isaac Taylor, who employs Northup as a hack driver in Saratoga Springs; and a host of other named individuals with whom Northup comes into contact. Unlike Douglass, who represents himself as an almost isolated individual who rarely depends on others, Northup shows himself to be deeply immersed in the community.[34] Northup seems to define himself through the relationships he makes, and the travels he participates in are always communal in one way or another, particularly when he travels with his fiddle. This dependence on his ties to others serves him well when he travels only within the limited area of his immediate region, but he discovers he cannot depend on the larger, national community to the same degree when he travels to Washington, D.C., with two men he meets.

Ironically, it is as Northup is taking a walk that he meets the two men who later sell him into slavery. They give their names as Merrill Brown and Abram Hamilton, although Northup later learns that these were aliases used during their travels to hide their true identities. They tell him they are circus performers who are traveling through the North, primarily for pleasure: "They were connected, as they informed me, with a circus company, then in the city of Washington; that they were on their way thither to rejoin it, having left it for a short time to make an excursion northward, for the purpose of seeing the country, and were paying their expenses by an occasional exhibition" (13). These two men seem almost the polar opposite of slaves, for they are traveling freely and earning their own money, thereby seeking economic opportunity in movement. They explain that their theatrical act needs musical accompaniment and hire Northup to travel with them to New York. Northup immediately accepts their offer, "both for the reward it promised, and from a desire to visit the metropolis" (13). Since these two men are traveling so freely and earning money, Northup naturally assumes that he is as free to travel as they are. After only one performance in New York, the three change their plans and head to Washington, D.C., stopping on the way to procure Northup papers stating that he is free.

As Northup quickly learns, while the freedom of his two companions is written on their bodies and guaranteed by their white skin, his freedom is revocable, since it is entrusted only to the papers he carries. Carrying evidence of his freedom, Northup and the two men continue their journey to the nation's capital. Once Northup loses his papers, he also loses his freedom. At some point during his stay in Washington, Northup is drugged and sold into slavery, he assumes by his two companions. He falls into a deep sleep in his hotel, but, he explains, "when consciousness returned, I found myself alone, in utter darkness, and in chains" (19). For Northup, whose identity seems to be so tied to his relationships with other people, being alone is as difficult as the tight bondage and complete darkness he experiences. "What had I done to deserve imprisonment in such a dungeon?" he wonders (19). "It could not be," he continues, "that a free citizen of New-York, who had wronged no man, nor violated any law, should be dealt with thus inhumanly" (20). Of course, Northup's transgression is not that he has committed a crime but that he is not white. In America, Northup realizes, to be black is necessarily to travel always and only under risk, for all black Americans are potential slaves, whose freedom to travel can always be transformed into forced movement.

The irony of being kidnapped and sold into slavery while visiting the nation's capital is not lost on Northup. He is kept for several days in a small prison that is "so constructed that the outside world could never see the human cattle that were herded there" (22). Northup writes,

> The building to which the yard was attached, was two stories high, fronting on one of the public streets of Washington. Its outside presented only the appearance of a quiet private residence. A stranger looking at it, would never have dreamed of its execrable uses. Strange as it may seem, within plain sight of this same house, looking down from its commanding height upon it, was the Capitol. The voices of patriotic representatives boasting of freedom and equality, and the rattling of the poor slave's chains, almost commingled. A slave pen within the very shadow of the Capitol! (22–23)

Northup's description of his enslavement here is significant, for the inclusion of chains and the slave pen mark his inability to travel as the primary right denied him. Although the two circus performers who have sold him into slavery are still free to wander throughout the country, Northup's freedom of movement has been taken; unlike white people, whose rights are assumed because they are white, black citizens such as Northup must always prove their citizenship and right to travel. The Capitol building, too, is belied by its exterior, for although it serves as the symbol of American freedom and liberty, it fails to protect all of its citizens and thus supports the enslavement of its own people. According to Worley, "The Capitol itself becomes a false front for corruption" (251). At the heart of the American legal system, Northup argues, lies the institution of slavery; as a result, the rights and freedoms of all Americans are jeopardized.

After a few days in this pen, Northup and his fellow slaves are taken under the cover of night to a waiting boat to be shipped to the South. "So we passed, hand-cuffed and in silence, through the streets of Washington," Northup explains, "through the Capital of a nation, whose theory of government, we were told, rests on the foundation of man's inalienable right to life, LIBERTY, and the pursuit of happiness! Hail! Columbia, happy land, indeed!" (34). In the streets he had enjoyed freely only a few days earlier when they "were black with people"

(17), Northup now passes, bound and silenced, into a life of slavery, his travel almost completely transformed into movement directed by others.

Once enslaved, Northup does not again hear the name by which he has been known since birth until he is freed twelve years later. On the boat trip to New Orleans, he is "appointed to superintend the cooking department and the distribution of food and water" (42). As a result of these duties, he explains, "I was called steward—a name given me by the captain" (43). Once he reaches New Orleans, however, he learns the name he had been given upon becoming a slave. When a trader comes on board and begins calling out the names of those slaves he has purchased, no one answers to the name "Platt." After all of his other slaves have been accounted for, this trader, Mr. Theophilus Freeman, asks the captain where Platt is. "The captain was unable to inform him, no one being on board answering to that name," Northup explains:

> "Who shipped *that* nigger?" he again inquired of the captain, pointing to me.
> "Burch," replied the captain.
> "Your name is Platt—you answer my description. Why don't you come forward?" he demanded of me, in an angry tone.
> I informed him that was not my name; that I had never been called by it, but that I had no objection to it as I knew of.
> "Well, I will learn you your name," said he; "and so you won't forget it either by—," he added. (49)

Now that he is a slave, Northup realizes, he is no longer "Solomon Northup" but "Platt," even though "this was the first time I had ever been designated as Platt—the name forwarded by Burch to his consignee" (49–50). Of course, Platt has no rights, although Northup was a citizen. Likewise, while Northup was an American, Platt is a slave; Northup, a subject, but Platt, an object. When he was Northup, the narrator traveled about the country as an autonomous person; now that he is Platt, he is shipped as cargo. Northup traveled; Platt is moved.

Because travel is the defining freedom of the American nation and the primary right denied those enslaved in the South, one of the first skills Platt must be taught is to move in an appropriate manner. Upon reaching New Orleans, Northup is placed in a holding pen with other newly acquired slaves. Mr. Theophilus Freeman and his partner, James H. Burch, proceed to arrange the slaves according to their physical appearance, tallest to shortest, men and women on opposite sides of the room. "Freeman charged us to remember our places," Northup explains, and "exercised us in the art of 'looking smart,' and of moving to our places with exact precision" (51). Northup's owners are here hoping to destroy any previous identity Northup may have by creating or confirming

"Platt's" identity as a slave. Not accustomed to being instructed about exactly where to move, Northup must learn to ignore his own desires concerning his body's movement and to obey whoever currently has control over him.

Northup learns, however, that he can never train his body to move completely in the service of another person. The narrator's most intense experience of slavery occurs after he has fought with Mr. Tibeats, for whom he works as a carpenter and who owns but half of "Platt," the other half being owned by a previous master, Mr. Ford. So enraged is Tibeats by his slave's inability to follow exactly his contradictory demands, he and three others attempt to lynch Northup. After they have bound him tightly and placed a rope around his neck, they are stopped and chased off by Mr. Chapin, the overseer of Mr. Ford. While they are gone, the overseer sends for Mr. Ford at a neighboring farm and inexplicably leaves Northup exactly as he has found him. According to the description in his narrative, Northup has here entered the fiery center of slavery:

> As the sun approached the meridian that day it became insufferably warm. Its hot rays scorched the ground. The earth almost blistered the foot that stood upon it. I was without coat or hat, standing bare-headed, exposed to its burning blaze. Great drops of perspiration rolled down my face, drenching the scanty apparel wherewith I was clothed. Over the fence, a very little way off, the peach trees cast their cool, delicious shadows on the grass. I would gladly have given a long year of service to have been enabled to exchange the heated oven, as it were, wherein I stood, for a seat beneath their branches. But I was yet bound, the rope still dangling from my neck, and standing in the same tracks where Tibeats and his comrades left me. I could not move an inch, so firmly had I been bound. To have been enabled to lean against the weaving house would have been a luxury indeed. But it was far beyond my reach, though distant less than twenty feet. I wanted to lie down, but knew I could not rise again. The ground was so parched and boiling hot I was aware it would but add to the discomfort of my situation. If I could have only moved my position, however slightly, it would have been relief unspeakable. But the hot rays of a southern sun, beating all the long summer day on my bare head, produced not half the suffering I experienced from my aching limbs. My wrists and ankles, and the cords of my legs and arms began to swell, burying the rope that bound them into the swollen flesh. (86)

Northup literally cannot move an inch because he is bound so tightly. Unable to move even slightly, he is completely under the control of his owners, one of whom, to Northup's good fortune, does not want him killed. He is forced to endure a version of hell, so hot that his flesh is burned. In fact, he is bound so tightly that he is physically disfigured, for the ropes apparently cut off the blood to his limbs and cause them to swell, increasing the pressure of his fetters. At this point of his most restrictive bondage, Northup thinks of the freedom of movement that he enjoyed in the North but lost when kidnapped. Describing his thoughts as the sun moved slowly through the heavens, he writes, "Suffice it to say, during the whole long day I came not to the conclusion, even once, that the southern slave, fed, clothed, whipped and protected by his master, is happier than the free colored citizen of the North" (88). "To that conclusion," he adds, "I have never since arrived" (88). Thus, when he is bound most tightly, his thoughts turn to the freedom of movement he enjoyed as a citizen of the republic, when his travels were determined by no one but himself and his family. After this incident, however, when he is finally released from his bondage, Northup is unable move on his own. "I attempted to walk," he explains, "but staggered like a drunken man, and fell partially to the ground" (88). Northup feels the effects of his enslavement even after being relieved of its immediate restraints.

After being freed from the immediate bondage of the ropes with which Tibeats has attempted to lynch him, Northup's thoughts again turn to the freedom to travel denied to all but the white man in the United States. He is, he points out, not a slave but a free citizen of New York, but he is unable to travel freely because he is enslaved. While he does have this "true" identity to console him, knowing as he does that he is actually a free citizen of New York, this knowledge offers him comfort but no protection, for his identity as a black man has outweighed his identity as an American. "I sighed for liberty," he explains, "but the bondman's chain was round me, and could not be shaken off. I could only gaze wistfully towards the North, and think of the thousands of miles that stretched between me and the soil of freedom, over which a *black* freeman may not pass" (92). Interestingly, Northup here describes freedom both as a place—"the soil of freedom"—and a right to travel—"over which a black freeman may not pass." In his account, as in Douglass's, the meaning of freedom frequently signifies both space and travel, the North and the right to go there. Thus, the fundamental American right, the freedom to travel wherever one pleases, is denied Northup, he argues, because he is black.

The bondage of slavery is also explicitly contrasted with the freedom to travel when Northup is later owned by Master Epps. Told by another slave that Epps is going to sell him, Northup expresses happiness that he will finally find some relief from Epps's harsh treatment. Epps finds out about Northup's response, however, when his wife overhears the conversation and reports it to her husband. The following day, Epps, who has refused to part with his slave, approaches Northup as he is working in the cotton field. "So, Platt, you're tired of scraping cotton, are you?" he demands (193). "You would like to change your master, eh? You're fond of moving round—traveler—ain't ye? Ah, yes—like to travel for your health, may be? Feel above cotton-scraping, I 'spose," he continues (193). Hoping to be sold to a tanner, Northup is instead given a severe "tanning" by his master. Such is the punishment for expressing a desire to leave his master's service and "travel" to another owner. It is certainly significant that Epps taunts Northup with the word "traveler," for both Northup and Epps know that slaves are not supposed to travel on their own, or even to desire such travel. Epps's punishment is harsh because Northup's expression that he desires to move according to his own wishes directly contradicts one of the fundamental aspects of slavery, that slaves move only according to their master's wishes. Slaves are not even allowed to desire self-willed movement, for desire is itself a sign of subjectivity.

Like Douglass, Northup does manage to move, both in accordance with the dictates of slavery and in direct contrast to those dictates. His expertise with the fiddle provides him numerous opportunities, especially during the holiday season, when his skills are in high demand at neighboring plantations. Furthermore, he visits distant plantations on several occasions in order to earn money for his master by working in another planter's fields. Much of the movement described by Northup, however, does not correspond to the demands of his various masters. Like Douglass's momentous fight with Covey, Northup's battle with Tibeats is the most obvious example of self-directed movement. Ordered to strip for a beating, Northup refuses and fights with Tibeats, after which he is almost lynched, as described above. On another occasion, Tibeats flies at Northup with a hatchet, intending to kill him, Northup believes. As is often the case for Northup the slave, he does not know at that instant whether to stand still or to flee, for either action may cause his death: "If I stood still, my doom was certain; if I fled, ten chances to one the hatchet, flying from his hand with a too-deadly and unerring aim, would strike me in the back. There was but one course to take. Springing towards him with all my power, and meeting him full halfway, before he could bring down the blow, with one hand I caught his uplifted arm, with the other seized him by the throat" (98). After struggling for some time, Northup decides that he must flee the scene in order to save his life. He writes, "A voice within whispered me to fly. To be a wanderer among the swamps, a fugitive and a vagabond on the face of the earth, was preferable to the life that I was leading" (100). Faced with a wilderness in front of him and a murderous master behind, Northup asks himself what is perhaps the slave's central question: "Whither should I fly?" (100). Unable to free himself physically from slavery but equally unable to move solely in accordance with the demands of his master, Northup must hover, circulate, and wander between realms, neither fully a traveler nor a slave. Not free to escape *from* slavery, he attempts to escape *within* it. In fact, his previous experiences with travel save him from being attacked by the dogs sent to chase after him. Although most slaves do not know how to swim because they are not allowed to learn, Northup had learned in his youth. As a result, he can travel in a different direction than most escaping slaves, who are unable to travel through the water and are forced instead to run on the small amount of solid land the bayou provides. Even when they are fleeing slavery, then, the movements of slaves are frequently determined by their masters.

In addition to the representations of Northup's direct confrontations with Tibeats, there are numerous cases cited in the narrative when Northup and the other slaves manage to subvert their master's authority by surreptitiously moving against his orders. Both Douglass and Northup realize that physical movement in its numerous aspects is perhaps the primary way to subvert the ideology of slavery. For instance, hired for a period to Peter Tanner, Northup is given charge of keeping in the stocks three slaves who had been caught stealing watermelons from Tanner's patch. Northup describes the scene as follows:

> Handing me the key [to the stocks], himself, Myers, Mistress Tanner, and the children entered the carriage and drove away to church at Cheneyville. When they were gone, the boys begged me to let them out. I felt sorry to see them sitting on the hot ground, and remembered my own sufferings in the sun. Upon their promise to return to the stocks at any moment they were required to do so, I consented to release them. Grateful for the lenity shown them, and in order in some measure to repay it, they could do no less, of course, than pilot me to the melon-patch. Shortly before Tanner's return, they were in the stocks again. Finally he drove up, and looking at the boys, said, with a chuckle,—
>
> "Aha! ye haven't been strolling about much to-day, any way. *I'll* teach you what's what." (95–96)

Although their movements were to be held in tight check, the three slaves and Northup were all able to enjoy relatively unfettered movement during Tanner's absence because of their cooperation with each other. Travel, it seems, is more easily accomplished in a community than on one's own, a conclusion directly contradicting the representations of travel described in Douglass's *Narrative*.[35]

Although in this case travel, as well as the temporary freedom of movement Northup and the three other slaves experience, is emancipatory, Northup well understands the dangers associated with slave travel, as does Frederick Douglass. Unlike Douglass, however, Northup is living in a region that is hundreds of miles distant from the nearest free state, so the dangers he faces are even more severe than those that Douglass and his friends confronted as he planned his escape. According to Northup,

> There was not a day throughout the ten years I belonged to Epps that I did not con-
> sult with myself upon the prospect of escape. I laid many plans, which at the time
> I considered excellent ones, but one after the other they were all abandoned. No
> man who has never been placed in such a situation, can comprehend the thousand
> obstacles thrown in the way of the flying slave. Every white man's hand is raised
> against him—the patrollers are watching for him—the hounds are ready to follow
> on his track, and the nature of the country is such as renders it impossible to pass
> through it with any safety. (183)

The manifold dangers are too overwhelming to encourage Northup to attempt an escape, but he does work as he can to counter obstacles he might meet. For instance, he beats Epps's dogs whenever he is alone with them so that they will become afraid of him and will not bite him if they are ever sent to catch him. But neighboring planters also have hounds, and Northup cannot intimidate all of them. In the end, the obstacles are too great, for Northup cannot make self-directed travel safe, despite his best attempts.

In addition to explaining the particular difficulties of escape from the "Deep South," Northup's descriptions of slavery in the Red River country show a marked distinction from those Douglass provides of plantation life in Maryland. Of course, the two men are describing different regions of the country, so their descriptions of the landscape and the plantations obviously differ. But Northup's descriptions illustrate a certain detachment from the scene that Douglass's do not, and Northup always seems aware of his outsider status when detailing the realities of life on a Louisiana plantation. In his autobiography, Frederick Douglass is describing the scenes of his childhood and the environment in which he matured, but Northup, captured when he was an educated adult, becomes in a way the ultimate "participant observer" during his years of captivity. His knowledge of his former life in New York seems to serve him as a psychological safety net, securing his identity as "Solomon Northup" despite the innumerable degradations he faces as "Platt." Because only he was aware of his background, the other slaves and the slave owners accept him as a member of slave society—he was, of course, a fully functioning member of the slave system—but his background also encourages a certain distance from the culture and society in which he participated for twelve years. After all, slavery was not an institution to which he was accustomed. Throughout the text Northup seems to be describing a region and a culture other than his own, so his narrative has a certain ethnographic feel to it. While Douglass transforms himself into a traveler, Northup's identity as a citizen of New York, and thus as a traveler in the South, is always available to him, at least rhetorically. The narrator, then, can view slavery from the perspective of Northup, the fully formed traveler, rather than from that of "Platt," the slave. For instance, when he is initially taken to William Ford's plantation, where he first works as a slave, Northup provides a detailed description of the natural landscape through which he passes. "On our route we passed the Grand Coteau or prairie," he writes,

> a vast space of level, monotonous country, without a tree, except an occasional one which had been transplanted near some dilapidated dwelling. It was once thickly populated, and under cultivation, but for some cause had been abandoned. The business of the scattered inhabitants that now dwell upon it is principally raising cattle. Immense herds were feeding upon it as we passed. In the centre of the Grand Coteau one feels as if he were on the ocean, out of sight of land. As far as the eye can see, in all directions, it is but a ruined and deserted waste. (147)

In excerpts such as this, Northup provides both an account of the southern environment and a description of the customs and occupations of the inhabitants.[36] This perspective was available to Northup because he had *already* traveled, prior to his enslavement, unlike Douglass, who only traveled after being a slave. In order to contrast their actions with those of the people of the North, Northup even describes the manner in which southerners perform particular acts, especially those related to farming. For instance, prior to an extended description of the cultivation of cotton, Northup writes, "[I]n as much as some may read this book who have never seen a cotton field, a description of the manner of its culture may not be out of place" (123). Here Northup recognizes that he may, in fact, be more widely traveled than many of his readers, so he provides a detailed description of the customs of the people among whom he is living.

As in more traditional ethnographic texts, Northup often describes as barbaric the customs of the people among whom he is living compared to the civilized society from which he has been taken. Describing a feud between his master Epps and a neighbor, Northup writes, "Such occurrences, which would bring upon the parties concerned in them merited and condign punishment in the Northern States, are frequent on the bayou, and pass without notice, and almost without comment. Every man carries his bowie knife, and when two fall out, they set to work hacking and thrusting at each other, more like savages than civilized and enlightened beings" (157). Northup clearly views himself as a member of northern society, and he cannot but condemn the actions of these two men, despite their later reconciliation. Furthermore, by reversing the roles and placing himself in a position of moral and textual authority over his putative master, Northup subverts the southern ideology that represents slaves as savages and the culture of the southern whites as the pinnacle of civilization and enlightenment. Like the traditional traveler, Northup uses the uncivilized behavior of the southern, barbaric "other" in order to bolster the civilized identity of his own (northern and "American") community and thus reaffirm his identity as Solomon Northup, the American citizen.

Whereas Douglass often focuses primarily on himself and his personal experiences with slavery, Northup provides the reader with numerous descriptions like this one of the society, environment, and culture of the region in which he is a slave. Of course his narrative, too, revolves around his own travels and those aspects of southern society that he encounters firsthand, but Northup's vision is more frequently turned outward. Unlike Douglass, Northup does not have to come to the realization that he is worthy of citizenship and full membership in society, for he has possessed these rights and had them taken from him. For Northup, citizenship is the basis, not the goal, of the narrative, so he does not feel the same need to earn the right to freedom. He is seeking to recover, not create, his identity as a traveler. Douglass, on the other hand, is born into slavery and must come to the realization that he is not inherently a slave before he can find the determination to escape from slavery. As a result, Douglass's autobiography is necessarily more egocentric than is Northup's, whose narrative focuses more readily on the experiences of the slaves (and slave owners) around him.

One of the conclusions Northup reaches about the people among whom he is living is that they are products of their environment, like everyone else. For instance, on his trip to New Orleans aboard the transport ship, Northup plans with two other slaves to take control of the boat and sail to New York.[37] They do not include any of the other slaves in their plans, even though there are far more slaves than free whites on board, for they fear that they will be betrayed: "There was not another slave we dared to trust," Northup explains. "Brought up in fear and ignorance as they are, it can scarcely be conceived how servilely they will cringe before a white man's look" (44). Because Northup and his fellow conspirators were raised as free citizens, they do not feel the fear of their white captors the other slaves do, who have not known anything but slavery under white masters. These slaves, argues Northup, are like Mary, a slave he has met previously in the holding cell in Washington, D.C. "Brought up in the ignorance of a brute," he argues, "she possessed but little more than a brute's intelligence. She was one of those, and there are very many, who fear nothing but their master's lash, and know no further duty than to obey his voice" (39). Had Mary or the slaves on the ship been brought up under different circumstances, they would have very different qualities, even identities, suggests Northup.

Not only slaves are affected by their environment, however, for Northup believes most of the cruelty by slave owners not to be the result of singularly evil personalities but one of the consequences of slavery. He frequently argues that slave owners are cruel because slavery is part of the culture, writing, for instance,

> It is true there are many kind-hearted and good men in the parish of Avoyelles—such men as William Ford—who can look with pity upon the sufferings of a slave, just as there are, over all the world, sensitive and sympathetic spirits, who cannot look with indifference upon the sufferings of any creature which the Almighty has endowed with life. It is not the fault of the slaveholder that he is cruel, so much as it is the fault of the system under which he lives. He cannot withstand the influence of habit and associations that surround him. Taught from earliest childhood, by all that he sees and hears, that the rod is for the slave's back, he will not be apt to change his opinions in maturer years. (157–58)

In passages such as this, Northup expresses a certain compassion for slaveholders, not simply the one or two who have shown him personal kindness. Like everyone, Northup explains, slaveholders are products of their social and cultural environments, so they do not know better than to treat slaves without mercy. Again describing William Ford, Northup argues, "The influences and associations that had always surrounded him, blinded him to the inherent wrong at the bottom of the system of Slavery. He never doubted the moral right of one man holding another in subjection. Looking through the same medium with his fathers before him, he saw things in the same light. Brought up under other circumstances and other influences, his notions would undoubtedly have been different" (62). Because they are not worldly enough—have not traveled as widely as has Northup—these slave owners are represented as acting as they do because they know no alternative. Unlike Northup, who has lived in a variety of communities, they understand only slave society. Thus, slave owners, like the slaves themselves, are created by their surroundings, Northup argues, and the communities to which they belong in large part determine who they are and what they believe.

For Worley, this argument is one of Northup's primary contributions to the literature of slavery, and he believes Northup's text unique in its espousal of such a philosophy. Northup's descriptions of the impact environment has on the individual slave owner are significant, argues Worley, because of what they further suggest about personal identity. As Worley recognizes, *Twelve Years a Slave* illustrates that the individual's identity—whether that individual be a slave owner or a slave, in the South or in the North—is determined by his or her community. Accordingly, Northup describes his community in some detail, always providing the reader with the names of his fellow slaves (which Douglass does only occasionally), and the text plainly illustrates the dependence he and his fellow slaves feel on the community as a whole. More important, however, Northup's ability to regain his liberty and his former status depends on the cooperation of the community of which he was a part before being kidnapped. As I've stated, Northup was far too distant from a free state to attempt to escape to freedom by himself, for the dangers posed by the patrols, the neighboring plantations, and even the natural environment itself were simply too great to be surmounted alone. Instead, Northup realizes, he must contact his family and depend on the assistance they can provide if he is ever to enjoy his freedom. In addition, because he realizes that Epps would send him away to Texas were he to discover that Northup was hoping to procure his freedom in this manner, Northup must be particularly cautious in his attempts to contact family or friends in the North. During his entire enslavement in Louisiana, he discloses his former status as a free man and the circumstances surrounding his kidnapping to one person only, the man who agrees to post Northup's letter for him. Only after hearing this man, Mr. Bass, argue about slavery with Epps does Northup begin to trust him. Significantly, the two points Bass consistently makes in his arguments with Epps revolve around the freedom to travel and the rights due to citizens of the United States. "Are all men created free and equal as the Declaration of Independence holds they are?" Bass asks Northup's owner (206). Bass later remarks, "You have books and papers, and can go where you please, and gather intelligence in a thousand ways. But your slaves have no privileges. You'd whip one of them if caught reading a book. They are held in bondage, generation after generation, deprived of mental improvement, and who can expect them to possess much knowledge?" (206–7), further supporting the argument that identity is determined by environment and that freedom is based on the right to travel.

Not only does a member of Northup's community come to rescue him from his enslavement on Epps's plantation, but Northup's participation in that community also serves as proof of his former identity and of his identity as a traveler in Louisiana and not as a slave. Because Northup's name had been changed to Platt shortly after his kidnapping, Henry Northup is unable to locate his friend when he reaches Marksville, the town nearest Epps's plantation. Accidentally learning that Northup's name had been changed, Henry Northup immediately convinces the sheriff to help him free his friend from the enforced "fiction" of his life as "Platt" the slave. Upon reaching Epps's plantation, the sheriff questions Northup in order to verify that he is indeed a free man who has various roles in his family and community in New York. For example, he asks Northup what other names he has, if he has a family in New York, what his wife's name is, and who married them. Thus, Northup verifies his "true" identity by describing his relationships with his wife and children, his minister, and his friend Henry Northup.

If these personal relationships verify his identity as "Northup" instead of "Platt," they also serve to guarantee his right to travel freely within the state of New York, where he will be recognized as the free citizen he is. His freedom and his rights thus depend on the community or communities of which he is a part. Unfortunately, Northup realizes, the national community neither guarantees nor supports his right to self-directed travel, for those rights are easily undermined, as he had learned twelve years earlier. Because he is a black man, Northup argues, he is not as free to travel as he ought to be as a citizen of the United States, for not all citizens enjoy the same level or degree of freedom. In fact, finally liberated after twelve years in slavery, there are few guarantees that Northup will not be kidnapped again and sold into slavery if he again travels too far from his home and depends on the national community to protect his rights. Because he is a black citizen, Northup concludes, he will never fully be an American traveler, for his right to self-directed movement will always be open to negotiation and retraction. Unlike Frederick Douglass in his 1845 autobiography, then, Northup does not finally become the free traveler but remains one whose movements, free as they may seem, will always be directed to some extent by the ideology of southern slavery.

Frederick Douglass, too, comes to qualify his optimism when he republishes his autobiography in 1855. The 1845 autobiography seems to suggest that Douglass has completed his transformation from slave to traveler by the end of the narrative, for once he has overcome his doubts and personal fears and begun to work for abolition, Douglass seems to believe he is free to travel almost anywhere he desires. Douglass's second autobiography, however, written ten years later, qualifies the optimism of this early text, for it describes Douglass's forced trip to England to escape the danger of his recapture by slave hunters in the North. In *My Bondage and My Freedom*, Douglass writes that after the details of his slave life had been made public with the publication in 1845 of his *Narrative of the Life of Frederick Douglass, an American Slave*, he was forced to flee to England in order to avoid the recapture made more likely by the success of his book. "A rude, uncultivated fugitive slave," he writes, "was driven, by stern necessity, to that country to which young American gentlemen go to increase their stock of knowledge, to seek pleasure, to have their rough, democratic manners softened with English aristocratic refinement" (370). While many young

Americans, particularly men, traveled to Europe during the late eighteenth and early nineteenth centuries in order to expand their intellectual and social horizons, "fugitive slaves" such as Douglass were forced to travel internationally—most frequently to Canada—in order to escape recapture, especially after the enactment of the Fugitive Slave Law in 1850. Like other Americans at that time, Douglass explains, he went abroad, but the travel in which he participated was of a different sort entirely than that enjoyed by white Americans.[38] Despite the freedom he has attained in the North, Douglass explains in this second text, he is still susceptible to recapture and is therefore not a truly free citizen of the United States. Unlike American citizens, Douglass explains, his freedom to travel has been transformed once again into forced movement, determined by the need to avoid recapture. Once again, then, the institution of slavery, not American democracy, determines how, when, and where Douglass must move.

Interestingly, the New York act that helped secure Northup's freedom, "An act more effectually to protect the free citizens of this State from being kidnapped, or reduced to Slavery," explicitly forbade the transportation of free persons out of the state by anyone other than those persons themselves. Reprinted as appendix A after Northup's narrative, it states,

> Whenever the Governor of this State shall receive information satisfactory to him that any free citizen or any inhabitant of this State has been kidnapped or transported away out of this State, into any other State or Territory of the United States, for the purpose of being there held in slavery; or that such free citizen or inhabitant is wrongfully seized; imprisoned or held in slavery in any of the States or Territories of the United States, on the allegation or pretence that such a person is a slave, or by color of any usuage or rule of law prevailing in such State or Territory, is deemed or taken to be a slave, or not entitled of right to the personal liberty belonging to a citizen; it shall be the duty of the said Governor to take such measures as he shall deem necessary to procure such person to be restored to his liberty, and returned to this State. (254)

It is illegal, this act proclaims, to transport citizens of New York out of the state for the purpose of being enslaved; in addition, the governor has a legal responsibility to resecure the freedom of any New York citizen wrongfully enslaved. This act thus becomes almost the antithesis of the Fugitive Slave Law, for it seeks to convert slaves into citizens, rather than converting citizens into slaves. Furthermore, the act reaches southward into slave "territory" to reclaim its citizens and return them to freedom, in contrast to the Fugitive Slave Law, which reaches northward and claims free (or freed) citizens as slaves. As in Northup's narrative, one of the primary issues in both the act and the law is travel, not only the movement of slaves or citizens out of their "home" states but also the lack of free movement that slavery entails. Ironically, the act was passed in 1846, the same year that Dred and Harriet Scott filed their initial petition in Missouri. Unfortunately for Dred Scott, the act did not forbid New York citizens from owning or transporting slaves in other areas of the country. As a result, John Sandford, Scott's owner from New York, could do with Scott as he pleased even before Justice Taney ruled in his favor, ten years after Scott's first petition. Because the scope of the New York act was limited to that state's citizens, the redefinition of movement and space that it engendered did not have the national significance of the Dred Scott decision or the Fugitive Slave Law. Unlike the New York act that freed Solomon Northup, both the ruling by the Supreme Court and the law passed by Congress essentially identified southern slave interests with national interests on the question of slave travel and the meaning of that travel to the nation as a whole. As Solomon Northup argued in his text, and as Frederick Douglass came to understand in his 1855 autobiography, until slavery was eradicated completely from the South, the entire country was bound to the institution and enslaved by its ideology.

CHAPTER THREE

Domestic Travel

The Narratives of Fanny Kemble
and Harriet Jacobs

A house divided against itself cannot stand.

ABRAHAM LINCOLN

Although travel during the early years of the nineteenth century may have provided male travelers, both free and slave, the occasion to fashion versions of a representative national identity, travel gave women the opportunity to step outside of their normal domestic routines and to investigate from a new perspective the household space constructed around them. According to Ann Romines, the house provides both protection and confinement; this dual character was particularly true as the "house" evolved into the "home" throughout the course of the nineteenth century and came to be seen as the special domain and dominion of women. For many female travel writers, moving outside of this paradoxical space allowed them not only to view their own domestic situations in a new light but also to address topics usually forbidden to women. According to Mary Schriber in *Writing Home: American Women Abroad, 1830–1920*, "Women's travel writing extends 'the beaten track' to include domestic spheres from which women were released when they traveled—as well as the propriety that would keep women close to home" (8). Freed from their own domestic space and the cultural norms that defined their boundaries in and through the home, however, many women travelers used their writings to investigate the domestic spaces of the society and region to which they traveled, which often offered them an alternative to their own model of the household. So while nineteenth-century American women left their domestic spaces when they traveled, they situated themselves both in relation to their original ideal of "home" and to their new, temporary domestic situations wherever they were traveling.

While many readers of travel narratives by both men and women have recognized the importance of the idea or ideal of "home," that idea has been particularly relevant to women's travel writing, explains Schriber: "Although travel writing by both genders is ostensibly about other lands but paradoxically about home, travel writing by women carries a special relationship to 'home' because by cultural assignment, women are 'about' home in a particular way" (9). But "home" can be construed to be a particularly broad concept, not only a building, such as a cottage, but also a region, a state, or an entire nation. In addition, for nineteenth-century Americans, home carried with it an especially broad array of cultural meanings; for instance, as Ken Egan Jr. has pointed out, "the American home increasingly carried the weight of yearning for social order in a turbulent, conflicted social scene" (14). "Home" is especially significant in accounts of intranational travel, for women travelers exploring their own nation could, even more directly than in those accounts of European journeys discussed by Schriber, participate in the construction of an ideal national domestic space. Describing a region, a society, and a culture paradoxically both their own and "other," northern travelers to the American South were thus simultaneously both home and abroad, both within and outside of their own "homeland."

If, as Dolores Hayden argues in *Redesigning the American Dream*, the antebellum United States created an ideal based on the household rather than the city or the nation, that ideal was initially based for most, as it was for Thomas Jefferson, on the model of the family farm, in which both men and women shared the responsibilities of the household and contributed to its upkeep. As the two regions on either side of the Mason-Dixon Line developed, however, this model gave way to new, competing ideals. In the South, the family farm evolved into the plantation, another type of household in which both social and economic functions were combined. In the North, the family farm gave way to the urban or suburban "home," which was designed allegedly to exclude the world of the marketplace and the economy from the domestic sphere.[1] This new ideal home was to act not as the seat of economic production and reproduction, as were the plantation and the family farm, but was to serve as a haven from the chaos of the market. The home was to be a special feminine world in which a wife and mother could nurture her husband and children apart from the competitive, masculine worlds of politics and economics.

The two spheres, public and private, are not so easily separated, however. As Elizabeth Fox-Genovese argues, households may be viewed as "the primary mediating units between the individual and society" (83), and Marilyn Chandler suggests that houses are "the locus of the central conflicts of American life" (6).[2] Given the central role of domestic space in the life of a society, the development of two distinct domestic ideals in the North and the South constituted a serious barrier to the development of a unified national culture.[3] This is exactly the barrier addressed by the travel writer Fanny Kemble, who seeks, through her *Journal of a Residence on a Georgian Plantation in 1838–1839*, to establish the basis for a national domestic space, founded on the ideal of the home then becoming common in the northern United States. Harriet Jacobs, too, in her *Incidents in the Life of a Slave Girl*, confronts the differences between the home and the household, arguing that the southern household can never be a home as long as slavery maintains the power of the master. Thus, while not generally viewed as a travel narrative, Jacobs's account both incorporates many of the issues prevalent in a more traditional travel account such as Kemble's and extends the critique offered by these accounts by allowing the reader a glimpse into the very center of the "domestic institution."

While travel books and articles by male travelers have traditionally focused on such topics as geography, geology, politics, economics, and social institutions, women have generally been restricted in the types of subject matter "properly" addressed in their writings. The titles of popular nineteenth-century travel texts on America express this difference clearly. Many men wrote and published books entitled simply *Travels in North America*, as did both Basil Hall in 1829 and Charles Augustus Murray in 1839, or *American Notes*, Charles Dickens's book. Women, on the other hand, expressed interest in the "interior" life and moral character of Americans, publishing books on *The Homes of the New World*, by Fredrika Bremer, *Society in America*, by Harriet Martineau, or *Domestic Manners of the Americans*, by Frances Trollope (whose son's book, in contrast, was entitled simply *North America*). Fanny Kemble's *Journal of a Residence on a Georgian Plantation in 1838–1839* and Harriet Jacobs's *Incidents in the Life of a Slave Girl* are also exemplary.

In "Scratches on the Face of the Country; or, What Mr. Barrow Saw in the Land of the Bushmen," Mary Louise Pratt divides nineteenth-century travel narratives into two categories. For Pratt, the distinction does not arise primarily from gender but from the type of narrator used, subject matter addressed, and language employed, all of which are, however, also significant for an analysis of gender differences. The first type, which Pratt terms "informational," focuses on landscapes and generally incorporates an impersonal, absent narrator. The inhabitants of a region, whose actions are represented as enumerations of ahistorical traits, are frequently described outside the main body of the text (123). The second, which she calls the "sentimental" travel narrative, foregrounds the narrator and derives its validity from its experiential, rather than its "objective," basis.[4] This second type has been the form generally chosen by women travelers; the validity of the text is based on the private life of an individual author.[5] In addition to using different types of narrators, the two forms include language that is likewise quite different. Many women writers, Pratt argues in *Imperial Eyes*, "avoided specialized statistical languages anchored in expertise, and instead called upon novelistic practice to express their findings" (161). Thus, the journals or series of letters in which women described their movement often read like confessional or epistolary novels. Significantly, women's travel texts are frequently "prefaced with a disclaimer which denies any scientific, academic, or other merit" (Mills 83), further distancing these narratives from those of men that purport to confront historical reality or ahistorical truth. Fanny Kemble feels it necessary to explain, for example, "I shall furnish you with no details but those which come under my own immediate observations" (55), asserting her authority within the household while calling into question her text's broader relevance. In addition, Kemble contrasts her book, based firmly on her own observations, with those other travel texts, such as the one by Harriet Martineau, which depended too heavily on hearsay and secondhand information.

In *Discourses of Difference: An Analysis of Women's Travel Writing and Colonialism*, Sara Mills argues that women writers typically focus their attention on individuals rather than on races, peoples, or classes, in contrast to many male travel writers. This focus is readily apparent in Fanny Kemble's narrative, for much of her book is a description of individual slaves who ask her for favors. As Diane Roberts argues, "After a while, the slaves are not 'them,' a multiple Other, but a series of characters" (111).[6] Kemble herself explains that once she has become accustomed to the slaves' complexion, "I now perceive all the variety among these black countenances that there is among our own race" (78), illustrating clearly a common prejudice of the time but expressing also her desire to individuate the slaves she encounters. While she does not identify herself completely with any of these slaves, she clearly sympathizes with them and desires to represent them as individual human beings with at least some concerns in common with herself, particularly motherhood.[7]

One of the most significant aspects of women's travel writing that critics have increasingly recognized is the attempt to incorporate dialogism into their texts, exemplified by Kemble's desire to include the voices of the female slaves in her journal or by Jacobs's incorporation of voices in conflict with southern authority. Pratt states that "sentimental" texts "are characteristically dialogic in the Bakhtinian sense: they represent the Other's voices in dialogue with the voices of the self and often tender the Other some credibility and equality" ("Scratches" 132), rather than representing themselves as sources of complete authority as is so common in men's travel writing. For instance, Kemble frequently includes in her narrative direct quotations from slaves, particularly the women who have had or are preparing to have children and are complaining of their working conditions and lack of adequate recovery time, and she does not always portray herself in a purely positive light in her interactions with the slaves and as the object of slaves' gazes.[8] In Pratt's terms, "the self sees, it sees itself seeing, it sees itself being seen" ("Scratches" 132).[9] Of course, Kemble and Jacobs maintain control of these voices, but alternative voices are not included in their texts solely for comic purposes or as examples of degradation and ignorance. The female author, like Jacobs, Kemble, or the women Pratt is describing, "seeks out and exploits heteroglossia" ("Scratches" 162).

But these travel texts do not only include a variety of individual voices. Nineteenth-century travel accounts can also be seen as "virtual compendia" of the discourses and discursive practices that were circulating in the United States at that time, according to Schriber, including republicanism, abolition, technological development, and the "woman question" (5). Because of their movement across so many geographical, racial, class, and gender boundaries, and because of their keen insight and ability to deconstruct the various discourses supporting slavery, both Jacobs's and Kemble's narratives are especially rich in this way. Jacobs directly questions the laws that force her to remain enclosed within her grandmother's crawl space while her "owner" is free to move about town. Kemble confronts the legal discourse of the southern states by questioning the need for laws banning marriage between the races even though, according to proslavery speakers, slaves are naturally repugnant to white people. Likewise, she asks, if slaves are incapable of learning, what is the need for a law forbidding the teaching of slaves to read? In this way Jacobs and Kemble use one discourse supporting slavery in order to question another and illuminate the contradictions inherent in southern ideology.

This desire to include more than one voice and to place the narrator within a social context frequently determined the form of female narratives as well. Women's travels were often published as a series of letters to a close friend, reflecting in their epistolary form the unique intersection of private and public that domestic space represents. Fanny Kemble's *Journal* follows this pattern; the text published in 1863 consists of a series of letters written by Kemble to her friend Elizabeth Dwight Sedgwick. Accordingly, each "chapter" begins "Dear E" or "My Dear E." These letters, however, were never sent to Sedgwick, so perhaps Kemble's use of the word "journal" in her title is appropriate. Like letters, domestic rituals such as journals also exist on the border of public and private worlds, as Romines argues. While a woman could supposedly place her most private, individual thoughts into her journal, the form of that journal, like the very fact of keeping a journal in the first place, was determined by those social forces that suggested that women belonged in the home, that women should focus on the domestic sphere, and that women's writings should be private, even secret, instead of public and open, as was men's writing. While these journals do often seem to be written in order to be shared, they were often shared not in a public forum but with a few close friends.

However, as with the usage of the letter format, the journal form was often simply a convention that served to make a woman's writing acceptable and, perhaps, more believable. Many authors never intended to send the letters and simply adopted the epistolary or journal format in order to make the writing more welcome to a wide audience, for this type of writing was expected by both the publishers and the public. When a woman's journal or series of letters was published, the author could (and generally did) protest that the work had not been written with an eye to publication. Even Jacobs, who is clearly writing her autobiography with an eye toward publication, explains that she would have preferred to remain unpublished, but her desire to help other female slaves has encouraged her literary endeavors. "I have not written my experiences in order to attract attention to myself," she explains in her preface; "on the contrary, it would have been more pleasant to me to have been silent about my own history" (1). This confessional tone may have served to draw the reader farther into the writer's confidences, thereby creating the image of a close community between reader and writer. In addition, however, as Romines points out, women may have used this form because they had few literary models on which to base their work.[10] These writers produced their works in the midst of an especially paradoxical situation, particularly if they were interested in reaching as wide an audience as Kemble and Jacobs plainly were. In the subject matter they addressed, in the form they used, in the narrative persona they created, and in numerous other ways, Kemble, Jacobs, and other women writers were forced to construct their narratives on the very borders of their personal and public lives.[11]

However, as Mary Jean Corbett explains, "Those who write autobiography do not necessarily disturb the ideological distinction between the public, masculine world and the private, feminine sphere" (108). Women who produced accounts of their travels, though, did confront this distinction even if they did not "disturb" it, for descriptions of movement within and among different domestic spheres necessarily foreground the difficulties of distinguishing between the public and the private. Unlike women writers who construct identities within a single domestic situation, those female travel writers who travel outside of their "home" environment must generally define themselves in relation to at least two distinct models of the household. Most chose to accomplish this by constructing a discursive self in and through a variety of domestic arrangements that serve not only as their primary subject matter but also as the organizing principle of their entire texts.

Describing two accounts written by Marie Callcott Graham and Flora Tristan, Pratt argues that for these women, traveling in South America in 1824 and 1833 respectively, "the indoor world is the seat of the self" (*Imperial Eyes* 159). Their two accounts "are emplotted in a centripetal fashion around places of residence from which the protagonist sallies forth and to which she returns" (157–59). Thus, it is this "initial fixed positioning that organizes the narrative" (159). In a travel narrative, however, this positioning intrinsically must take place both after and prior to travel, so a residence is always fixed in contrast to the movement that has already taken place or that will occur in the future. The "fixed positioning" Pratt describes, then, is a temporary stasis that occurs within a context of movement and travel.

This particular method of fashioning the self and structuring the account is not, however, simply a reflection of women's interests or skills but an indication of different methods of constructing knowledge and personal identity. "If the man's job was to collect and possess everything else," Pratt continues, "these women travelers sought first and foremost to collect and possess themselves. Their territorial claim was to private space, a personal, room-sized empire. From these private seats of selfhood, Graham and Tristan depict themselves emerging to explore the world in circular expeditions that take them out into the public and new, then back to the familiar and enclosed" (159–60). Places of residence provide these "exploratrices sociales" with solitary spaces that they can control, from which they can explore, and to which they can retreat.[12] For Jacobs, of course, her "place of residence" in her grandmother's house served primarily as a "loophole of retreat" through which she could assert her own subjectivity, although the space also provided her the opportunity to monitor her children and to maintain her relationship with her grandmother and other family members. For Kemble, on the other hand, the indoor world did mean family and domestic life, but it remained the site in which she could most effectively create herself as a discursive and political subject and from which she could venture in order to explore a wider social, geographical, and cultural world.[13] For example, Kemble explains to her correspondent that she hates the word "Missis" and has instructed the slaves not to call her by that title. She has explained to the slaves, Kemble writes, "and they appeared to comprehend me well, that I had no ownership over them, for that I held such ownership sinful, and that, though I was the wife of the man who pretends to own them, I was, in truth, no more their mistress than they were mine" (60). Kemble thus refuses to accept an identity as the mistress of a slave plantation and fashions herself instead as a woman who will not demand obedience but will rather seek to educate her dependents and assist them in any way that she can.

Unlike the conquering, exploratory impulse that sent so many men in search of dramatic vistas, the social concerns of many women travelers determined their movement outside of their households. When women did "sally forth" from their domestic spaces, the institutions visited reflect, not surprisingly, the activities and concerns of nineteenth-century women. Hospitals, prisons, orphanages, poorhouses, and schools were the primary sites for female travelers to investigate, as they were the principal concern of female reformers at this time.[14] Since the vast majority of women who wrote and published travel accounts were either middle or upper class, visits to these institutions reflect their responses both as women of privilege and as women subject to men's dominance. Thus, as Mary Schriber points out, women's representations of "others" frequently oscillated between empathy or compassion and arrogance or disdain (81). This combination of "ethnographic detachment" and "psychological attachment," or "doubling together with difference," Schriber argues, "sometimes inaugurates a schizophrenic identification with the other that, in its instability, amounts to an identity crisis" (85). Furthermore, the concern shown by these travelers, as Mills suggests, expressed not simply a gesture of solidarity but represented part of a larger "discourse of philanthropy which circulated through the nineteenth century and involved middle- and upper-class women" (96). Jacobs, for instance, seeks to address those women who might participate in philanthropic activities and to incite them to act on behalf of enslaved women. Kemble, too, clearly hoped to help the slaves on her plantation, and at times she seems to identify herself with the slaves, but Kemble did maintain a number of the prejudices of her time and her class.[15] Thus, despite her occasional identification with the slave others and her concern for their plight, Kemble did not envision herself as part of a transracial association of women. As Elizabeth Fox-Genovese argues, "Women were bound to each other in the household, not in sisterhood, but by their specific and different relations to its master" (101).

The subject matter of much women's writing, as well as the epistolary and/or confessional form and tone, has traditionally determined its critical and popular reception as well. Female narratives are often described as trivial because they contain descriptions of relationships and domestic details. Similarly, the supposedly private nature of the writing has undercut the subversive possibilities of many texts because of the perception of the author and her experiences as unique. Furthermore, as Sara Mills points out, although these texts show women in roles different from their representations in novels, plays, or poems of the time, these representations are often undermined by the description of the travelers as eccentric or abnormal (119). [16] Women's writing is also frequently described as having historical but not artistic value. Women's texts are seen as worthy of study for the light they shed on a particular historical juncture rather than for the creative and artistic qualities they exemplify. That is, while men's texts are traditionally valued as crafted products of an individual genius, women's narratives are seen as "merely" autobiographical or confessional, suggesting that their texts are simply the products of the outpouring of emotion (Mills 109). According to Mills, this critical stance encourages reading these texts as relating only to the individuals and not to the colonial contexts in which they were written (109). So, ironically, women's travel writing has traditionally been devalued for being too individual but also disregarded for not being individual enough.

More recently, however, critics have begun to value women's travel texts and fiction as both stylistically impressive and culturally significant. Many literary or cultural critics and historians now view the form and content of these works not as inherently deficient but as constituting an alternative to more masculine, patriarchal types of writing. Like many contemporary political reformers, these critics now realize, female travel writers and sentimental novelists hoped to use domestic space as a site from which to analyze and critique the patriarchal spheres of politics and the economy. [17] Paradoxically, the construction of a domestic space secured women opportunities to travel, and various types of movement (social, geographical, spiritual, etc.) constituted an integral facet of the domestic environment. Therefore, while the home offered these women an alternative to the worlds of industry and commercialization, women took advantage of the safety of the domestic sphere in order to move themselves and their concerns outside of that space and reinterpret the central political issues of the day as moral and religious ones.

This attempt was perhaps most explicit in the nonfiction work by Harriet Beecher Stowe and her sister Catharine Beecher, particularly in Beecher's early *A Treatise on Domestic Economy*, published in 1841 and revised and reissued by the two sisters in 1869 as *The American Woman's Home: or, Principles of Domestic Science*. The later volume is dedicated, "To the Women of America, in whose hands rest the real destinies of the republic, as moulded by the early training and preserved amid the maturer influences of home, this volume is affectionately inscribed." The "destinies of the republic" rest in the hands of American women because they can guarantee a promising future by maintaining an orderly home and by focusing on the moral, religious, and social education of their children, the future leaders of the nation. [18]

The masculine spheres needed the feminizing touch of a woman's hand in order to counter the amoral influence of the market and the political system.

Thus, the home should enter politics, although neither politics nor economics should ever enter the home. This is the argument that Harriet Beecher Stowe made in her revolutionary novel, *Uncle Tom's Cabin*. The primary problem with slavery, Stowe's novel suggests, is that it imports the economy into the household; the peace of the home is thus disrupted by the chaos of the marketplace. Because of the market's presence in the household, argues Stowe, the woman is no longer in control of the home environment. Women are thus unable to maintain order through the practice and application of domestic ritual, which in a properly functioning household keeps disorder at bay. So *Uncle Tom's Cabin*, argues Ann Romines, "is not a novel of domestic ritual" but instead "chronicles the repeated violation of domestic ritual occasioned by slavery. Again and again, patriarchy interrupts housekeeping" (19).[19]

But, argues Jane Tompkins, "The enterprise of domestic fiction, as Stowe's novel attests, is anything but domestic, in the sense of being limited to purely personal concerns. Its mission, on the contrary, is global and its interests identical with the interests of the race" ("Sentimental Power" 287). While Stowe hoped to keep the patriarchal worlds of politics and economics out of the home, she did not believe the matriarchal world of the home had nothing to offer these masculine spheres.[20] According to antebellum writers, however, this reformist agenda cannot proceed throughout the nation while slavery survives as a legal institution and disrupts the functioning of southern households. Instead, Stowe's model suggests, the women of the United States must wrest control of the domestic space of southern households and recreate these spaces as "homes," as discrete domestic institutions that stand outside of the worlds of politics and economics and can serve, therefore, as a space from which to reform these worlds. Women should regain this control because they alone have the moral and religious understanding to direct the household (and the society) in a Christian manner.[21] As Stowe explains, men are not sufficiently oriented to Christian ideals to appreciate fully their duty to God in the operation of the nation. By serving as a model of correct behavior in the home, and by expanding the domestic sphere to include the country as a whole, women can assist men in the proper leadership of the nation and its economy.

There was, then, a double movement occurring. Women were increasingly being relegated to the domestic sphere and instructed to live according to the emerging "Cult of True Womanhood," which demanded that they practice, according to Barbara Welter, "four cardinal virtues—piety, purity, submissiveness and domesticity" (21). At the same time, however, some women, such as sentimental novelists, were reinterpreting the nation as a home, thus guaranteeing

the need for their movement outside of the domestic sphere and their participation, albeit indirectly, in the operations of the country. "The very perfec-
tion of True Womanhood," suggests Barbara Welter, "carried within itself the
seeds of its own destruction. For if woman was so little less than the angels,
she should surely take a more active part in running the world, especially since
men were making such a hash of things" (41). Female travel writers exemplified
this paradoxical movement, for through their travels outside of their domestic
environments, they could interrogate the domestic space and use it in order
to move themselves into spheres to which they had traditionally been denied
access. According to Lora Romero,

> The increasing conventionality of claims for women's domestic identity would
> seem to circumscribe their lives completely within that home, but, ironically,
> making domesticity into an identity gave middle-class women a surprising
> amount of mobility. As an identity rather than simply a fixed location for women's
> lives, domesticity could—and did—travel. Women could argue that they contin-
> ued to embody domesticity even when they left home. And domesticity's opposi-
> tional origins, its status as a discourse about oppression and resistance, deter-
> mined that middle-class women's itineraries would include sites of social conflict
> and political struggle. (25)

In fact, domesticity had to travel, since for these women domesticity and
movement were integrally tied to each other. So while domesticity engendered
movement of various types—particularly social, cultural, and ideological—the
physical and discursive travel performed by many women provided the opportunity to focus on the domestic environment while simultaneously including
within that vision traditionally masculine spheres.

Therefore, the home space constructed by and around nineteenth-century
women was mutually dependent on ideas of travel and freedom of movement.
Travel constituted the major component that situated women so that they could
confront questions of nation and domesticity. And, of course, representations
(of women, of slaves, of the home, of the nation) also traveled, for representations are not stable phenomena but move easily from the discursive worlds of
travel texts and sentimental fiction to the broader arenas of politics, culture, and
economics.[22] Likewise, if the nation is the home writ large, then women must be
involved in the decision making that will determine the future of the country,
and if slavery is a spiritual and not an economic or political issue, then women
must involve themselves in its eradication. Thus the movement performed by
women travel writers within and outside of the home paralleled the movement

of the representations they produced within and between textual and extratextual traditions, institutions, and cultural formations.

On June 7, 1834, Fanny Kemble, a famous English actress traveling in the United States on a two-year tour, married Pierce Butler, a member of one of Philadelphia's wealthiest families. Unbeknownst to Kemble, a woman with confirmed abolitionist sympathies, Butler's fortune derived from his stake in the family's slave plantations on the Sea Islands of coastal Georgia. Together with his brother, Pierce was one of the wealthiest planters in the region, owning over six hundred slaves on two different rice and cotton plantations. During a nearly four-month trip to these plantations, Kemble kept a journal, not published until 1863, which has become one of the most important travel documents concerning the antebellum era, describing firsthand the conditions on two of the most extensive plantations in the South. As a member of a plantation household who was simultaneously opposed to the institution of slavery, Kemble was in a unique position to observe the day-to-day operations of the plantation and the scenes of domesticity not readily available to travelers visiting only briefly. Because of her status both as an internationally known actress and as the mistress of two large plantations, Kemble enjoyed a freedom of movement rarely described in accounts of southern travel.

Kemble took advantage of her unique position not only to travel throughout her husband's islands but also to visit neighboring plantations. She had carried with her from the North and from England convictions that she believed were incompatible with the ideology of the South, and she introduced and disseminated these subversive ideas by traveling broadly within her own household and around the region as a whole. So she spent much of her time exploring her husband's plantations, walking through the slave quarters, and visiting her neighbors, thereby spreading her "gospel" everywhere she traveled. In fact, for Kemble travel was a defining component of her personal identity. Before journeying South with her husband, she had traveled extensively throughout Europe and the United States, and she continued to take advantage of a freedom to travel widely denied to many during the nineteenth century. In addition, however, her narrative identity is quite fluid, for although she frequently describes herself, for example, as an Englishwoman "in whom the absence of such a prejudice [against slavery] would be disgraceful" (11), she also represents herself as an American who has married the owner of two slave plantations and apparently committed herself to a future in the United States. Thus, the households described by Kemble, as well as the ideal home she attempts to construct, are always represented both through and against her identity as a traveling woman.

As a result, Kemble's *Journal* is both an unprecedented analysis of slaveholding households and a text representative of much female travel writing.

Kemble seizes the opportunity of traveling in and through the South to move outside of her usual habits and habitations and to analyze both a new domestic situation and the region's patriarchal culture. In fact, by using her travels to analyze southern domestic ideology, she further creates her own personal independence, struggling against her husband in a household now under his control. She refuses to act like other southern women, who, according to Fox-Genovese, "lived their lives within and interpreted their identities through the prism of specific households" (81). Instead, Kemble defines herself as a traveler, for whom movement between and within various households determined identity. Travel thus serves as both a sign of and a means to Kemble's freedom. Her movement both reflects and promotes freedom, for the opportunity to travel that she enjoys as a wealthy white woman engenders the freedom to criticize that is a product of her explorations. As Diane Roberts suggests, "[I]t is 'down there,' the scandalous region of America, that Kemble became intimate with a range of behaviours unacknowledged, repressed or forbidden to someone of her gender, her race and her class. She wrote explicitly of sexuality and violence on her husband's estates, transgressing the role of the mistress of the plantation whose function was, in Mary Chesnut's words, to 'play the ostrich-game' " (104). However, it is not simply her presence "down there," but her travel from one region, sphere, and culture to another, that permits and promotes this intimacy. It is also, however, her travel within one nation that encourages her attempt to create a national domestic space, a "home" that could serve as a model not only for her northern urban readers but, more important, for the slaves whom she was, in her own way, attempting to free.

Kemble quickly recognized that one of the primary distinctions between the North and the South, as well as between the South and England, involved differences in domestic space. Through her description of her southern journey, Kemble investigated these differences and analyzed the impact that the institution of chattel slavery had on the southern household. Contrasting her personal experiences with the most common representations of life in the antebellum South, Kemble not only described the surface features, such as the ruined state of most slave owners' houses or scarcity of many consumer goods, but also searched for the underlying causes, focusing particularly on the work ethic of both slaves and whites and the role of women in southern society.

One of the first differences Kemble notes after leaving the North is the dilapidated state of many southern houses. Even the residences of the region's more wealthy inhabitants do not compare favorably to the farmhouses of most

middle-class farmers in the North or in England. In a letter written while on
Butler Island to her friend Harriet St. Leger but not included in the original
edition of the *Journal*, Kemble described the habitation of a colonel with whom
her traveling party had stayed for a few hours while awaiting transportation.[23]
Despite the man's wealth and his service with George Washington, his house
was in a terrible state: "His residence (considering his rank) was quite the most
primitive imaginable—a rough brick-and-plank chamber, of considerable di-
mensions, not even whitewashed, with the great beams and rafters by which it
was supported displaying the skeleton of the building, to the complete satis-
faction of any one who might be curious in architecture. The windows could
close neither at the top, bottom, sides, nor middle, and were, besides, broken
so as to admit several delightful currents of air" (30). Despite, perhaps because
of, her strongly negative reaction, Kemble provides a fairly detailed description
of the interior of the colonel's house, as she frequently does when describing
her visits to other planters. Kemble learns as she travels to her new home on
St. Simon's Island and visits the plantations of her Georgia neighbors that the
colonel's house is not atypical for the region. For instance, she describes the
house of one wealthy woman, the daughter of a former governor of Georgia, as
"like all the planters' residences that I have seen, and such as a well-to-do English farmer would certainly not inhabit" (150). Despite the "occasional marks of
former elegance," Kemble primarily notes the "air of neglect, and dreary, careless untidiness, with which the dirty, barefooted Negro servants are in excellent
keeping" (150–51). Visiting another adjacent planter, Kemble explains,

> How impossible it would be for you to conceive, even if I could describe, the
> careless desolation which pervaded the whole place; the shaggy unkempt ground
> we passed through to approach the house; the ruinous, rackrent, tumble-down
> house itself; the untidy, slatternly, all but beggarly appearance of the mistress of
> the mansion herself. The smallest Yankee farmer has a tidier estate, a tidier house,
> and a tidier wife than this member of the proud Southern chivalry, who, however,
> inasmuch as he has slaves, is undoubtedly a much greater personage in his own
> estimation than those capital fellows W—— and B——, who walk in glory and
> joy behind their plows upon your mountain sides. (278–79)

Far from constituting an aristocratic ideal, as common representations of slave
owners suggest, plantation owners such as these neighbors live in relative
squalor. The occasional attempt at elegance Kemble views as ridiculous because
of the general lack of basic cleanliness and comfort. She seems to prefer by far
the tidy farmhouses of the North, in which all of the members participate in the

upkeep of the family, each person fulfilling a certain role. Plantation owners are superior only in their own minds, according to Kemble.

The house in which Kemble lives with her husband and children (as well as the overseer) is little better, as it possesses none of the charm or luxury to which she is obviously accustomed. The house, she writes,

> is certainly rather more devoid of the conveniences and adornments of modern existence than anything I ever took up my abode in before. It consists of three small rooms, and three still smaller, which would be more appropriately designated as closets, a wooden recess by way of pantry, and a kitchen detached from the dwelling. . . . Of our three apartments, one is our sitting, eating, and *living* room, and is sixteen feet by fifteen. The walls are plastered indeed, but neither painted nor papered; it is divided from our bedroom (a similarly elegant and comfortable chamber) by a dingy wooden partition covered all over with hooks, pegs, and nails, to which caps, keys, etc., etc., are suspended in graceful irregularity. The doors open by wooden latches, raised by means of small packthread—I imagine, the same primitive order of fastening celebrated in the touching chronicle of Red Riding Hood; how they shut I will not attempt to describe, as the shutting of a door is a process of extremely rare occurrence throughout the whole Southern country. . . . Such being our abode, I think you will allow there is little danger of my being dazzled by the luxurious splendors of a Southern slave residence. (63–64)

Not surprisingly, she doesn't criticize her husband's house as directly as she does the abodes of her neighbors, but it is clear that Kemble is "underwhelmed" by her new habitation. Her ironic use of words and phrases such as "celebrated," "graceful irregularity," and "similarly elegant," testify to her disappointment, as does her plain statement that the house is "more devoid of the conveniences and adornments of modern existence" than any in which she has previously lived (64). Nor is the house appropriately divided, for one room serves as a "sitting, eating, and *living* room." These three activities should instead be divided among several rooms specifically created for each. Furthermore, her description points out her distress at the lack of differentiation between personal and public space. She and her family are rarely alone, for the slaves are constantly watching them, and Kemble is unable even to ensure her privacy by shutting them out of a room, as no distinction exists between the house's public and private rooms. Because a closed door is an "extremely rare occurrence," Kemble is never allowed privacy at all, for the outside world is always in a sense invading her private domain. Because of the difficulty of closing off one room from another, as well as the outside from the inside of the house, private and public are uncomfortably, inappropriately, even dangerously confused and combined, Kemble argues.

In addition, to summon her attendants, she explains, she and her family must "raise the windows and our voices, and bring them by power of lungs" (64), further erasing the distinction between public and private space. Accordingly, the household in the South encompasses not only the structure but the surrounding yards. In fact, because slaves are always both at work and at home, even when they are not within the house itself, the household expands to include any space in which the slaves happen to be.[24] As a result of her inability to summon her servants when she needs them, and because she finds the slaves in general so dirty, Kemble usually finds it easier to wait on herself, which she does "more than I have ever done in my life before" (61).[25] This, she wants the reader to understand, describes life in the house of one of the wealthier planters in the region.

The quarters that house the slaves are obviously in far worse condition. During her stay on the two islands on which her husband has plantations, Butler and St. Simon's, Kemble makes a number of sojourns to the slave "settlements" and visits slaves in their huts. Not surprisingly, she is horrified by what she discovers there:

> Such of these dwellings as I visited today were filthy and wretched in the extreme, and exhibited that most deplorable consequence of ignorance and an abject condition, the inability of the inhabitants to secure and improve even such pitiful comfort as might yet be achieved by them. Instead of the order, neatness, and ingenuity which might convert even these miserable hovels into tolerable residences, there was the careless, reckless, filthy indolence which even the brutes do not exhibit in their lairs and nests, and which seemed incapable of applying to the uses of existence the few miserable means of comfort yet within their reach. (68)

The state of these quarters is due both to slaves and their owners. Kemble regularly chides the masters for not providing better living conditions for their slaves, pointing out repeatedly that the quarters are no improvement over stables or barns, but she also blames the slaves themselves for not attempting to improve their lot through tidiness and cleanliness. She frequently attempts to convince the slaves to clean up their houses and other buildings, particularly the hospital, a frequent destination of Kemble's tours of the plantation.[26] However, she realizes that slaves need to be taught the importance of cleanliness and cannot be expected to have the same standards as those women who have grown up in a more privileged setting.

Moving throughout her extended household, checking on the health of those she believes are under her care, Kemble seems to view the squalor of the slave quarters as not only a health issue but also a reflection of immorality, on the part of both the slaves and their masters. Her travels within her husband's plantation, as well as her visits to neighboring households, provide her with the opportunity to investigate personally the conditions of the slaves. Her status as an outsider seems to grant her the understanding and the authority to condemn what she finds in a way that would be impossible had she not experienced a change of perspective by traveling to and through the South. In fact, her very desire to understand slavery and to help alleviate the suffering of her husband's slaves is a result of her travels across so many geographical, social, cultural, and ideological boundaries.

Kemble believes her main obstacle to improving the lives of her husband's slaves is the widespread unwillingness on the part of both the free and the slave populations to perform meaningful labor. The problem, according to Kemble, is that nobody in the South actually works. White southerners believe labor the domain only of slaves. "The Northern farmer," Kemble writes, "thinks it no shame to work, the Southern planter does; and there begins and ends the difference. Industry, man's crown of honor elsewhere, is here his badge of utter degradation; and so comes all by which I am here surrounded—pride, profligacy, idleness, cruelty, cowardice, ignorance, squalor, dirt, and ineffable abasement" (291).[27] Similarly, slaves perform only as much labor as they must, and they generally only pretend to work. The problem is that their basic needs will be met regardless of the labor performed, as long as they look as if they're working. "The laziness seems to me," Kemble writes, "the necessary result of their primary wants being supplied, and all progress denied them" (322). As Blake Allmendinger argues, Kemble believed the slaves "responded to work by imitating, and hence trivializing, the act of labor" (510). In fact, even the masters whom the slaves are imitating do no real labor and are themselves simply pretending to work. Like the acting that she depended on but despised, slavery encouraged appearance over reality. Thus slaves, as well as their masters, seemed to Kemble simply to be performing roles rather than accomplishing true labor.[28]

In contrast, when the slaves are provided some incentive to work, they perform their tasks admirably. She discovers this change in work ethic by hiring with her own money a few slaves to clear a path for her so that she can stroll more easily. After telling her slave companion Jack that she is willing to pay some young men for their labor, Kemble quickly has as many workers as she needs, who are "zealous and energetic" (307). For Kemble, working for their wages is important because they can earn money but more important because she has instilled the idea that they ought to be rewarded for their labor. She is glad that "the novelty of the process pleases them almost as much as the money they earn" and believes "they quite deserve their small wages" (307). When she had earlier provided wages to some slaves for work performed, Kemble had stated to her correspondent, "[I]n short, very involuntarily no doubt, but, nevertheless, very effectually I am disseminating ideas among Mr. [Butler]'s dependents, the like of which have certainly never before visited their wool-thatched brains" (217). Thus, Kemble uses her position as a traveler and as a woman from outside of this ideological environment to spread new ideas and to bring the slaves types of knowledge that her different perspective has provided her. For Kemble, then, instilling in the slaves the knowledge of alternative economic, social, and cultural structures, such as an understanding of the theory of wages and capitalist economics, is as important as the exchanges of any particular transaction.

She is most indignant at the lack of wages or other rewards when she encounters slaves who are particularly skilled in a certain area, such as carpentry. For instance, the rice mill machinery is "under the intelligent and reliable supervision of engineer Ned" (187), but he is treated the same as any other slave. He receives no special favor, and his family does not benefit from his expertise:

> Now E[lizabeth], here is another instance of the horrible injustice of this system of slavery. In my country or in yours, a man endowed with sufficient knowledge and capacity to be an engineer would, of course, be in the receipt of considerable wages; his wife would, together with himself, reap the advantages of his ability, and share the well-being his labor earned; he would be able to procure for her comfort in sickness or in health, and beyond the necessary household work, which the wives of most artisans are inured to, she would have no labor to encounter. (188)

In the North, Kemble suggests, Ned's knowledge and skills would bring him a wage sufficient to provide for himself and his wife, who would have "no labor to encounter." Ned, his wife, and their children would have a home. However, rather than having the opportunity to maintain a home environment for herself and her husband, as she would be able to do were they to live in the North, Ned's wife must work in the fields and reap nothing from her husband's skills.[29]

Under the institution of slavery, slave families must labor for free, for no matter how hard they work or how much expertise they gain, they never personally benefit. According to Kemble, their owners reap all of the gain without expending any labor, which makes these white families also suffer from their inability to complete satisfying labor and receive their just reward. White men spend their time disciplining their slaves, argues Kemble, and white women have absolutely nothing to do. As a result of this complete lack of occupation, Kemble pities southern women "for the stupid sameness of their most vapid existence, which would deaden any amount of intelligence, obliterate any amount of instruction, and render torpid and stagnant any amount of natural energy and vivacity" (192). Kemble has previously told her friend Elizabeth that southern ladies are "extremely sickly in their appearance" and "languid in their deportment and speech" (101). They "seem to give themselves up . . . to the enervating effect of their warm climate" instead of meeting the southern climate with "energetic and invigorating habits both of body and mind," as she does (102). Kemble suggests that because of slavery, as well as the fertility and climate of the region, the lives of the inhabitants are too easy and do not demand the labor that is necessary for a healthy lifestyle and happy home.[30]

In a properly functioning household, every member has a specific role to play, and everybody works toward a common goal: a peaceful, stable domestic environment. In a "home," believes Kemble, the man participates in the outside world of business and politics while the woman keeps the interior space in order. Other members, such as servants, cooperate and seek to assist the woman maintain the domestic space. In contrast, in a slave household the masters and the slaves work toward different goals. Rather than cooperating with each other, each of the members stays busy participating in "the most disgusting struggle which is going on the whole time, on the one hand to inflict, and on the other to evade oppression and injustice" (86). The members of a slave household, in other words, are not free to fulfill the roles to which they are most suited.[31]

As the matriarch of the household, Kemble should be responsible for the health and well-being of her family, both black and white. However, because she is not in control of her own domestic situation but answerable to her husband, she is not able to engage in those activities that are most suitable to her. In this way, the structure of slavery, in which all members of the household are under the authority of the patriarch, enters directly the domestic space and the family unit. While Kemble does spend much of her time and energy attempting to fulfill her role by visiting the hospitals, listening to the complaints of the slaves, and interceding on their behalf with Mr. Butler, she is ultimately helpless, for she, like the slaves, lives within her husband's jurisdiction. Unlike northerners at this time, argues Fox-Genovese, southerners "did not view either families or households as primarily female preserves, but as terrain that contained woman's sphere" (195). Because the economy is intimately involved in the daily functioning of the household, Kemble's husband is firmly in control. After listening to a woman's story of being tied and whipped while pregnant, Kemble exclaims, "And to all this I listen—I, an Englishwoman, the wife of the man who owns these wretches, and I cannot say: 'That thing shall not be done again; that cruel shame and villainy shall never be known here again' " (241). Kemble is, she realizes, practically powerless in her own household.[32] As Fox-Genovese explains, Fanny Kemble "grasped a central truth about plantation households: Missus was not Massa" (132).

But she is not entirely powerless. For one thing, she spends much time and energy serving as an intercessor for the slaves to her husband. Kemble seeks, for instance, to convince her husband and his overseer to improve the conditions in the plantation hospital, and on numerous occasions she speaks with her husband on behalf of individual slaves. In this way, she travels back and forth from the world of her husband to that of his slaves, listening to stories of hardship and retelling them to the slaves' master. In fact, she fulfills her role so well that the slaves begin to flood her with requests. "No time, no place, affords me a respite from my innumerable petitioners," she explains, "and whether I be asleep or awake, reading, eating, or walking—in the kitchen, my bedroom, or the parlor—they flock in with urgent entreaties and pitiful stories" (108). While she seems to regret the lack of privacy that results from these solicitations, she cannot refuse to hear them, for she believes she is fulfilling one of the few roles open to her, bridging the gap between the two groups that constitute her household and using her ability to travel between and within these two groups in order to deliver, interpret, and translate stories for the slaves.

She again travels outside of the bounds prescribed for white southern women when she tends to the sick slaves and assists in the cleaning not only of the hospitals but also the homes of individual slaves she visits. For example, when Kemble finds a slave in the hospital "suffering dreadfully from the earache," she removes the leaves that had been tied to the woman's head and washes her swollen face and neck, such an unusual operation, Kemble writes, "that I had to perform it for her myself" (98). According to Diane Roberts,

> Kemble repeats stories of pregnancy and labour, dropped wombs and backache, over and over again, as she reports the dirty conditions in which slaves lived, unhygienic medicine, overt bodily functions. All this was outside her sphere, yet she allows her "ladyhood" to be violated by smells, pain, filth and knowledge of a world of violence and sexuality officially forbidden to the plantation mistress. While it is true that the plantation ethic charges the mistress, as "mother" to the household, with nurture of everyone from her own children to slave babies, nursing of blacks was not allowed to pull the mistress off her pedestal. (110)

However, Roberts fails to appreciate fully that, while Kemble may be overstepping the bounds of the plantation mistress, her actions are perfectly in keeping with the behavior of a woman in charge of a home, who was responsible for all of the members of the family, however broadly construed. Even more important than the personal assistance Kemble provides, though, is the domestic ritual she attempts to introduce into the slaves' lives. She mentions at one point that as the slaves are petitioning her for summer clothes, she "conjured them to offer us some encouragement to better their condition by bettering it as much as they could themselves—enforced the virtue of washing themselves and all belonging to them" (88). At another point, she tells some slave girls who are spending their free time playing with each other to be more orderly and to use their time for cleaning, not playing (100).

Kemble hopes that she may transform these female slaves into homemakers and thus somehow make them other than slaves. Because slavery and the ideal of the home are mutually exclusive, Kemble suggests, she can eliminate slavery by recreating the slave huts as model homes. By transporting to the South the ideology of the "home" and reforming (or for slaves, by creating) a proper domestic space, Kemble hopes to be able to alter the political system of the region. Kemble attempts to proclaim this gospel of cleanliness and domesticity early in her stay on the plantation as she explores one of the slave quarters:

> Thus I traveled down the "street," in every dwelling endeavoring to awaken a new perception, that of cleanliness, sighing, as I went, over the futility of my own exertions, for how can slaves be improved? Nathless, thought I, let what can be done; for it may be that, the two being incompatible, improvement may yet expel slavery; and so it might, and surely would, if, instead of beginning at the end, I could but begin at the beginning of my task. If the mind and soul were awakened, instead of mere physical good attempted, the physical good would result, and the great curse vanish away; but my hands are tied fast, and this corner of the work is all that I may do. Yet it cannot be but, from my words and actions, some revelations should reach these poor people; and going in and out among them perpetually, I shall teach, and they learn involuntarily a thousand things of deepest import. (69)

Even though slavery was often referred to as the "domestic institution" by southerners, slavery and domesticity are antipathetic in Kemble's schema, so importing the latter will surely rid the region of the former. As she explains, her "hands are tied," because she does not have the power of the master of the household, but she can still accomplish her task by working within the space of the domestic sphere allowed her in this context. Although she is not fully in charge of her own domestic sphere while she is on her husband's plantation, she does attempt nonetheless to fulfill her matriarchal duties, primarily by moving herself outside of the domain prescribed by southern society and by educating the members of her extended family in the domestic rituals proper to a correctly functioning home.

Even these seemingly minor tasks are radical enough, however, to provoke her husband into forbidding her to continue them. Butler, Kemble sadly explains, "has declined receiving any of the people's petitions through me" (210). And her movement about the plantation and the region is often quite restricted, by the environment, social tradition, and ideas of propriety.[33] On Butler Island, she finds, "My walks are rather circumscribed, inasmuch as the dikes are the only promenades" (56).[34] In fact, any movement at all outside of the house itself is viewed as odd, she believes. Southern women do not traditionally walk about their plantations, so Kemble must have paths constructed and cleared for her peregrinations. Women in the South are so tightly confined within their households, Kemble suggests, that any travel outside of the close quarters of the plantation buildings must be preceded by the construction of pathways. She has become a frontierswoman, it seems, trailblazing her way through the moral wilderness of the South as she pursues her travels in areas previously unexplored by the region's women.

In addition, she must face the innumerable dangers that, she is told, await the unsuspecting woman wandering outside. For instance, her personal slave companion, Jack, tries to keep her from taking walks in the woods because of the snakes. "Today I walked out without Jack," she writes, "and, in spite of the terror of snakes with which he has contrived slightly to inoculate me, I did make a short exploring journey into the woods" (244). In another passage, she explains that she "compelled my slave Jack, all the rattlesnakes in creation to the contrary notwithstanding, to cut and clear a way for my chariot through the charming copse" (267). Jack, it seems, does not quite understand how to assist a plantation mistress who is constantly traveling, and he is apparently uncomfortable with her desire to move outside of the traditional bounds of southern womanhood. Likewise, her husband perhaps recognizes that Kemble's desire to explore the plantation and run the household will undermine his practically complete authority over all of the members of "his" household.[35] Given the extent of her husband's control, Kemble's actions and movements are, in many ways, revolutionary.

Kemble worries, on the other hand, that her husband's incorporation of economic issues into the running of the household will lessen her respect for him. Instead of laboring outside of the home as he should, Butler is spending his time on domestic affairs that would be better left to her control. Kemble finds, for instance, that she cannot listen to her husband command pregnant slave women to fulfill their allotted task work: "How honorable he would have appeared to

me begrimed with the sweat and soil of the coarsest manual labor, to what he
then seemed, setting forth to these wretched, ignorant women, as a duty, their
unpaid exacted labor! . . . I hope this sojourn among Mr. [Butler]'s slaves may
not lessen my respect for him, but I fear it; for the details of slaveholding are
so unmanly, letting alone every other consideration, that I know not how anyone with the spirit of a man can condescend to them" (114). The pregnant slave
worker is a particularly fertile symbol for Kemble and other writers, for this image exposes both the labor and the domestic conditions that underlay slavery,
reinforcing the status of the slave as the foundation of both production and reproduction within the plantation household. Slavery is perhaps "unmanly" for
Kemble because masters refuse to labor within their proper domain, outside
of the home in the world of business and economics. While he himself remains
within the domestic sphere, Kemble's husband commands slave women to leave
their houses and perform men's work in the fields. Slavery, it appears, turns men
into women and slave women into men.[36] Nor does slavery allow Kemble to
fulfill her proper function as the head of the household. In contrast, Kemble argued through her *Journal*, the home should be maintained as a separate sphere,
so that both men and women would be free to pursue their own proper labor.

Discursively, then, Kemble sets up the ideal of the home as a site from which
she can criticize southern patriarchal ideology and seek to remodel the southern household. For Kemble, it seems, the home is a nonideological textual space
from which she can venture into the ideologically determined masculine worlds
of politics and economics. She fails to recognize, however, that all space, both
public and private, is ideological, or, in the words of George Eliot, "There is
no private life which is not determined by a wider public life" (qtd. in Hayden,
Redesigning 61). According to Fox-Genovese, the impact of the American Revolution, developing capitalism, and industrialism resulted in the tendency "to
confine women and their labor to the household, increasingly represented as a
nurturing home rather than a productive unit, and to associate them explicitly
with motherhood and domesticity, viewed as specialized responsibilities" (59).
Thus, the ideal of the northern home grew out of a specific conjuncture of political and economic institutions. Far from providing a space separate from these
worlds, the "home" is a product of them, for without a certain type of capitalist
means of production and accompanying institutions and traditions, the ideal of
the home would not have developed in the first place. Gillian Brown explains,
"Domestic ideology with its discourse of personal life proliferates alongside
this economic development which removed women from the public realm of
production and redirected men to work arenas increasingly subject to market
contingencies" (3). Kemble therefore bases her critique of southern slavery and

patriarchy on a model of the home that is itself integrally and intimately linked
to a patriarchal system and that seeks to keep women out of public life and safely
silenced within the private domestic sphere.

However, Kemble herself does move outside of her own domestic space in
order to enter the public world of letters, through her published *Journal*.[37] Although, according to Judith Fryer, woman "has been denied, in our culture, the
possibility of dialectical movement between private spaces and open spaces"
(50), Kemble does travel, within and outside of the domestic and public spheres.
In fact, Kemble's *Journal* describes almost constant travel on her part, from England to the United States, from the North to the South, to neighboring plantations and towns, throughout her husband's island holdings, and into a variety of
natural settings, as well as the ideological, political, or social travel that takes her
to the houses of her slaves, inside the "filthy" environment of the plantation hospital, and into the confidences of the slave women. This travel is accomplished,
furthermore, in a geographical, social, and ideological environment that seems
to discourage almost any movement by women at all.

She does not, however, appear to use this movement as an opportunity to
analyze the "home" domestic sphere in the North from which she has temporarily escaped. Rather, Kemble uses the freedom to travel conferred on her
as a woman of means in order to focus her attentions on the domestic ideology
of the South. The North that she describes, in fact, offers comfort, security, and
freedom. At times she even compares herself to a slave and hopes to flee to the
North, writing in her *Journal*, "[W]e are to return as soon as possible now to the
North. We shall soon be free again" (287). Kemble thus feels bound by slavery
and seeks to attain further freedom by traveling North, even though she has
enjoyed an unusual degree of personal liberty and has frequently traveled outside of the boundaries of southern ideology. Travel is thus both an expression
of Kemble's freedom and, as in this instance, a means of attaining a degree of
freedom denied her in the South.

For Kemble, then, the freedom engendered by her travels outside of her home
space in Philadelphia (and England) provides her new perspectives and encourages her to question the ideological structures in which she is placed in
the South, but her travels do not stimulate her to focus on the domestic space
constructed around her prior to the journey to her husband's plantations. In
order to criticize the southern household, she always depends on the ideology
of the "home," so after one of her many excursions on her husband's islands, for
instance, she writes, "On my arrival at home—at the house—I cannot call any
place here my home!" (258). Although her personal history (for instance, as an
actress, a businesswoman, a travel writer, or the economic savior of her family)

consisted of almost constant work outside of the bounds of traditional female spheres, in her *Journal* she seems to subscribe wholeheartedly to the domestic ideology then being constructed in the North.

If movement from the North to the South encouraged Fanny Kemble to expand the freedoms she enjoyed and to develop further her discursive identity, for Harriet Jacobs, author of *Incidents in the Life of a Slave Girl*, travel was the determining factor in the creation of a textual and political subjectivity. While movement granted Jacobs a similar freedom from the domestic space to which she had been confined by her patriarchal society, her travel is of a different sort entirely than that of Fanny Kemble. Jacobs, after all, had to travel in order to escape slavery and thereby become a legally and socially recognized person. Kemble, on the contrary, had already established herself in the public arena through an international reputation as an actress and an account of her travels in the northern United States, so she visited the South as a person of some fame and, of course, as the wife of a well-established planter. Thus Kemble's travels, as I've argued, both produced and illustrated her freedom. While her journey provided her with experiences and perspectives to which she had not formerly had access, she traveled (and wrote) within a protected space in which her physical person, at the very least, was in little danger of assault. Harriet Jacobs enjoyed no such privilege. Born into slavery, Jacobs had to face extreme physical danger and mental anguish in order to establish herself as an individual not only in the domestic sphere but also in the public imagination. Like Frederick Douglass and Solomon Northup in their slave narratives, Jacobs is intensely interested in the definition of United States citizenship, seeking to expand the rights provided citizens to those millions then held in slavery. Unlike these two men, however, Jacobs centers her argument for political rights and her critique of slavery in the domestic spaces that she inhabits. Accordingly, her text describes several types of travel—not only the travel to political freedom in the North included in so many slave narratives but also her travel from a household in which she had no power to one of her own making. For Jacobs, travel is almost as much a social, cultural, or rhetorical phenomenon as it is geographical, for some of the narrator's most significant self-directed movement, in fact, comprises little physical progress. Like Douglass and Northup, then, the *geographical* travel described in Jacobs's text is necessary but not sufficient for complete freedom, for travel of other types must accompany this literal journey to freedom in the North.

Jacobs's *Incidents in the Life of a Slave Girl*, published in 1861, is in many ways a traditional work of travel literature, for like other women writers, Jacobs uses her travel narrative to describe first and foremost the domestic situations in which she finds herself. In addition, despite her cruel treatment by many white men and women, Jacobs refuses to generalize about any race or gender, another characteristic of much women's writing. Furthermore, Jacobs addresses her book to a specific audience, northern women, and works toward a certain intimacy between writer and readers. She begins by assuring the readers that her book is indeed true—"Reader, be assured this narrative is no fiction"—and, like many women (and slave) writers, worries that she is not talented enough to produce a worthy book—"I wish I were more competent to the task I have undertaken" (1). In addition, Jacobs structures her narrative around the experiences of a foregrounded narrator and protagonist, Linda Brent, so the text's validity derives from the experiences of this individual.[38] Around this central figure, however, revolves a great variety of voices and discourses, some supportive of slavery but most opposed to it, exemplifying the heteroglossia so often found in women's travel narratives. Even the book's reception marks it as a woman's work, for it has been dismissed as fictional for many of the 139 years since its publication. Thus, while Jacobs's book uses the strategies of a number of genres, including sentimental fiction, the male slave narrative, and the seduction novel, it rests firmly within the tradition of female travel writing.

The text particularly resonates with Fanny Kemble's narrative in its focus and in the criticisms of slavery it puts forth. Both Kemble and Jacobs conclude that slavery corrupts everyone involved, both slave and free. It undermines the institution of marriage, not only for the slaves but also for their owners, they argue, and it breaks apart families, primarily by not recognizing slave marriages and by selling members of a slave family to different owners, but also through the distrust and immorality bred in the family of the master. Both Kemble and Jacobs suggest that slavery is worse for women than for men. Kemble is shocked that slave women are required to complete as much physical labor as the men and must then work for their own families, which in turn are frequently torn apart by greed and lust. Jacobs, on the other hand, says little about the labor requirements of slavery but focuses instead on the physical, emotional, and spiritual costs associated with the sexual demands frequently placed on female slaves. Furthermore, both writers describe the majority of the slave mistresses they encounter as lazy and ineffectual housekeepers. Jacobs describes Mrs. Flint, for instance, as "totally deficient in energy" and writes that she "had not strength to superintend her household affairs" (12), a result, Jacobs argues, of Flint's corruption by slavery.

This corruption, each suggests, is not readily apparent to the traveler who only briefly visits a plantation, for the surface features of slavery may encourage a false interpretation in the observer if he or she is too easily led astray. For instance, Kemble admonishes Harriet Martineau for depending too readily on information supplied by others, and Jacobs reproaches clergymen who visit the South and are guided in their movements by slaveholders. When a traveling clergyman asks a slave if he is happy, the slave will naturally answer in the affirmative for fear of punishment, Jacobs explains. This clergyman then returns home, she writes, "to publish a 'South-Side View of Slavery' and to complain of the exaggerations of abolitionists" (74). Jacobs then wonders, "What does *he* know of the half-starved wretches toiling from dawn till dark on the plantations? of mothers shrieking for the children, torn from their arms by slave traders? of young girls dragged down into moral filth? of pools of blood around the whipping post? of hounds trained to tear human flesh? of men screwed into cotton gins to die? The slaveholder showed him none of these things, and the slaves dared not tell of them if he had asked them" (74). In order to garner an accurate portrait of slavery, Jacobs argues, one must not so readily accept the ideology presented by those in control, for evidently even within the United States not everyone enjoys freedom of speech. An accurate representation of the institution of slavery can only be provided by someone like her, Jacobs argues, who not only has faced the corruption that the system breeds but also has escaped to a space in which she can speak and write more freely. Only a slave can write about slavery truly, yet only an ex-slave can write about it at all. For example, only a slave could correct the impression Mrs. Flint presented when she shed a tear at the funeral of Aunt Nancy, her slave who, Jacobs believes, has been killed through the Flint family's cruelty, but only a former slave like herself would actually have the opportunity to do so. "We could have told them a different story," Jacobs explains, "a chapter of wrongs and sufferings" (147). In fact, once she has traveled outside of slavery and published her account, Jacobs does tell "a different story": her *Incidents in the Life of a Slave Girl*.

In another passage, Jacobs argues that she could easily correct the misunderstandings of the English traveler, Amelia Murray. As Jacobs writes, "A small portion of *my* experience would enable her to read her own pages with anointed eyes. If she were to lay aside her title, and, instead of visiting among the fashionable, become domesticated, as a poor governess, on some plantation in Louisiana or Alabama, she would see and hear things that would make her tell quite a different story" (185). In order to view slavery, Jacobs advises, Murray should not depend on those who benefit from slavery to portray accurately the institution but should enter the household of the slave and "become domesticated," not as a pampered guest but as one who would be dependent on the household. Jacobs also points here to the close ties between slavery and domesticity. From within the slave household, Jacobs argues, Murray could gain a truer insight into the realities of the "domestic institution." Rather than discover a safe, comfortable home, Murray would encounter a space infested by the concerns and the cruelties of the southern slave economy and would witness the extreme measures necessary to sustain the outward appearance of happiness and tranquility. That is, Murray should travel not only geographically but also socially, Jacobs seems to suggest. Thus, not all travel texts are equal, Jacobs and Kemble argue, for their journeys have given each access to scenes that few travelers have viewed.

Perhaps one of the similarities between Kemble's and Jacobs's texts most apparent to a nineteenth-century audience would have been the degree to which the seemingly incessant motion of the two writers allowed them to address topics generally forbidden to women. Kemble is particularly open about the children fathered by the former overseer on her husband's plantation, and she regularly discusses the "mulatto" offspring in the households she visits.[39] Jacobs is even more explicit than is Kemble about the sexuality that underlies slavery.[40] She describes her life as a young slave woman to be an unceasing assault on her virtue and her body; Dr. Flint, the father of the young girl who legally owns Linda Brent, frequently propositions her. Jacobs writes, "I now entered on my fifteenth year—a sad epoch in the life of a slave girl. My master began to whisper foul words in my ear. Young as I was, I could not remain ignorant of their import" (27). She describes herself during this period as having to remain almost constantly in motion in order to escape the clutches of Dr. Flint, already expressing her subjectivity through movement and thereby foreshadowing her later, more radical flight. Later, Brent resorts to physical confinement and concealment in order to save herself from Dr. Flint's demands. As Valerie Smith suggests, however, even though she may have been physically confined, she is not as rhetorically restrained as many female authors, for Jacobs is far more open about the sexual advances of her master than the sentimental tradition encouraged (38). Jacobs also makes it clear that her experiences are not unique, for she faces only what most would who were in her position. Dr. Flint is obviously not the sole master raping, or attempting to rape, his female slaves, and Brent is not the only one of his slaves confronting Dr. Flint's sexual demands. Thus, by relating her story so honestly and directly, Jacobs, more effectively than any other writer, represents slavery as institutionalized rape.[41]

One of the main results of these unfortunate relationships, argues Jacobs, is the dissolution of any family stability, particularly for the slaves but also for the families of the owners. Accordingly, these owners are not capable of maintaining a satisfactory home environment, and the members of the household are unable to fulfill their proper roles.[42] Jacobs tells her audience, "Reader, I draw no imaginary pictures of southern homes" (35). Northern girls who marry plantation owners, Jacobs argues, "have romantic notions of a sunny clime, and of the flowering vines that all the year round shade a happy home. To what disappointments are they destined!" (36). Jacobs is trying to counter the image of the southern plantation that, according to Mauri Skinfill, "took shape in the popular consciousness as tranquil home to both Southern planter and attendant slaves" (65). The truth, says Jacobs, is that the southern household is tranquil for neither.

According to Winifred Morgan, Jacobs's text illustrates that "[t]he institution of slavery is evil because it perverts all relationships between men and women, children and parents, slaves and free people" (85). Mrs. Flint is unable to construct a healthy or happy household because she is so jealous of her husband's liaisons with his slaves. As the matriarch of the family, she ought to serve as the one person to whom members of the household could confide their troubles; however, Brent learns soon enough that she cannot depend on Mrs. Flint in that capacity. Mrs. Flint represents instead a jealous fiend who is but one more danger for Brent to avoid. Jacobs writes, "The mistress, who ought to protect the helpless victim, has no other feelings towards her but those of jealousy and rage" (27–28). Because Mrs. Flint knew her husband's character, argues Jacobs, "She might have used this knowledge to counsel and to screen the young and innocent among her slaves; but for them she had no sympathy" (31).[43] Even if her mistress were sympathetic, however, Brent could gain no true protection, for in the slave household the master held all of the power. Through his interactions with both his wife and Brent, Dr. Flint illustrates, as Jacobs writes, "that I gained nothing by seeking the protection of my mistress; that the power was still all in his own hands" (34). As many writers, including Kemble, have shown, the slave mistress is ultimately powerless even in her own household, and Mrs. Flint, like Brent, is "compelled to live under the same roof with him—where I saw a man forty years my senior daily violating the most sacred commandments of nature" (27). Thus, the household in which Jacobs is forced to live is not a civilized home but a wilderness not subject to the dictates of society, a state of nature beyond law, order, and religion.

In contrast, Brent's grandmother, who has not only won her freedom but also earned a position of some respect in the community, furnishes her with almost everything she could want from a home. Because Brent is not provided for by the Flint family, she depends on her grandmother for her basic necessities: "I was indebted to *her* for all my comforts, spiritual or temporal. It was *her* labor that supplied my scanty wardrobe" (11). When Brent is upset, she frequently escapes to her grandmother's house for a brief time, and she depends on the food from that kitchen when she cannot get enough to eat from Dr. Flint's household. Thus, even as a child Brent depends on flight to battle the effects of slavery. Furthermore, in a move that prefigures her later escape, she uses the safety of her grandmother's domestic environment to travel outside of the spheres to which slavery tries to confine her. In fact, Brent is not the only slave who depends on the nurturing environment created in her grandmother's home, for, because of the neglect engendered by slavery, Brent's grandmother takes care of an extended group of her children, grandchildren, and other relatives with profits from the business she operates in her home.[44]

However, after her very early childhood, Brent is not allowed to remain with her grandmother for any extended length of time, for the family relationships of slaves are not respected. As Jacobs explains, "[M]y mistress, like many others, seemed to think that slaves had no right to any family ties of their own; that they were created merely to wait upon the family of the mistress" (38). Nor is Brent allowed to marry the man of her choice, since Dr. Flint would never grant them his permission. Even if this freeman whom Brent loves could obtain the necessary permission, Jacobs explains, "[T]he marriage could give him no power to protect me from my master" (42).[45] And if they had children, Jacobs continues, "[T]hey must 'follow the condition of the mother.' What a terrible blight that would be on the heart of a free, intelligent father," whose children could be sold at the whim of their owner (42). In this way, because it dissociates the paternal function from the biological father, slavery creates multiple fathers and, thus, multiple families. Brent, in fact, has been in this very situation her entire life, for neither her parents nor her free grandmother has been able to shield her effectively from the danger posed by Dr. Flint. As a result, while she remains a slave she must constantly move between her two households, Dr. Flint's and her grandmother's, and seek to create her personal identity out of her ceaseless travel.

For Jacobs, "home" comes to mean the nurturing relationships that sustain her in her difficulties. While she cherishes the idea of a house safe from intrusion and lust, she represents home both as a safe haven and as her ties with relatives and friends. As Jean Fagan Yellin argues, unlike most male narrators of slave texts, "Jacobs's Linda Brent locates herself firmly within a social matrix" (xxvii).[46] Jacobs's domesticity is primarily relational rather than structural or physical, so she focuses much of her text on the individuals to whom she is related through familial, social, or economic ties. For example, while Brent serves the Flint family, her grandmother is given her freedom and becomes the "mistress of a snug little home, surrounded with the necessaries of life" (17). Even though her children and grandchildren remain in slavery, this woman provides as much of a home as she can for them. Brent and her young uncle Benjamin believe everyone should have the same opportunity to provide for their families, and they "longed for a home like hers" (17). Jacobs writes, "There we always found sweet balsam for our troubles. She was so loving, so sympathizing! She always met us with a smile, and listened with patience to all our sorrows. She spoke so hopefully, that unconsciously the clouds gave place to sunshine" (17). Here "home" for Jacobs is more than simply a structure, for it represents her grandmother and the joy her grandmother offers. Home is where she can be happy, where she can be with her loving relatives, and where she can feel safe from assault.[47]

Once Brent has children of her own, she strives to provide them with an environment in which they will be happy and secure. This is impossible while she remains within the domestic situation provided her by southern society, she realizes, for both children will be open to abuse, neglect, and sale at their master's whim, and her daughter will grow up to be as vulnerable to sexual exploitation as she has been. Brent believes slavery much more difficult for women, so she is very upset when she learns that she has given birth to a daughter: "When they told me my new-born babe was a girl, my heart was heavier than it had ever been before. Slavery is terrible for men; but it is far more terrible for women. Superadded to the burden common to all, *they* have wrongs, and sufferings, and mortifications peculiarly their own" (77). In order to safeguard them from harm, Brent escapes from Dr. Flint's household, pretending to flee north, hiding in a succession of homes, and settling finally into a minuscule crawl space in the top of her grandmother's house.[48] While Dr. Flint unsuccessfully searches for her, she manages to arrange for the purchase of her children by their white father, a local lawyer whom Brent had chosen as a lover in order to counter the advances of her master.[49] The children then move to Brent's grandmother's house, although they do not know of their mother's hiding place. Brent thus creates a safe domestic space for her children by refusing to accept passively the situation at Dr. Flint's.[50] Instead, she travels outside of the domestic sphere forced on her by slavery and actively creates her own home that will more effectively secure her children's futures. While clearly not ideal, Brent's secret domestic situation above her grandmother's living space most effectively allows her to create a home for her children, for during the seven years she spends in the crawl space, she is able to arrange for her children's sale, observe them as they grow, and shield them from harm by Dr. Flint. Since "home" means to Jacobs primarily the maintenance of the relationships important to her, Brent's space in the attic provides her with the opportunity to establish a type of home, even though her children are unaware of her participation.

Of course, in order to secure her children's safety in this manner, Brent herself must undergo extreme hardship. Under the eaves she is hardly protected from the elements, for both the heat in the summer and the cold in the winter easily penetrate the roof of her grandmother's cottage. Furthermore, the space in which she survives for these seven years, which measures only nine by seven by three feet at its tallest point, does not provide her enough room to move. Insects and rodents constantly crawl across her, and she breathes her only fresh air from a one-inch hole she has bored in the overhang. Her sole companionship comes late at night when her grandmother or her uncle passes food up to her. During most of her seven years, she is unable to leave her solitary confinement at all. Yet, she writes, "I would have chosen this, rather than my lot as a slave, though white people considered it an easy one" (114). Jacobs thus prefers the active construction of a home, no matter how unorthodox or unbearable, to the passive acceptance of life within the corrupt household of her master. As Elizabeth Becker argues, "Through the home she creates for herself in the garret, Brent defines her own sense of true womanhood—an unshakable devotion to her children and commitment to their chance for a better life in freedom" (418).

Brent's confinement in the crawl space away from the direct control of Dr. Flint can be contrasted with the movement she performs outside of the legal and social structures of southern society, for even though she is physically inert, she has crossed a number of political and ideological boundaries.[51] Travel for Jacobs is thus as much a psychological and ideological activity as it is a geographical and physical one. Refusing to move according to the values of a slave society, Brent chooses one form of transgression, stasis, until a preferable form, travel to the North, is available to her. In this way, Brent essentially redefines travel to incorporate not only the physical movement to a region outside of the slave South but also the circumvention or transgression of slave ideology, despite her physical location within the geographical region. Unable to travel physically, Brent travels ideologically. In so doing, she is able to remove herself from the control of her master yet remain at the only home she has known in order to safeguard her children and, in a sense, author her own and her children's subjectivity. As Smith and other critics have recognized, the garret in her grandmother's house, small as it may be, offers Brent the opportunity to act in a positive manner, changing her confinement into what she calls a "loophole of retreat" (114). The succession of small spaces in which Brent hides, argues Smith, "are at once prisons and exits" (32). According to Smith, "Jacobs explicitly describes her escape as a progression from one small space to another" (31). By exploiting this "loophole" within the slave South, Jacobs is thus able to escape, despite remaining in the region. That is, because her master and others looking for Brent have assumed that "escape" would mean for Jacobs "physical movement to the North," Jacobs is able to determine her own movements by redefining travel as both a physical *and* an ideological activity. Her use of a "loophole" thus depends on her exploiting a definition of "travel" not recognized by her pursuers.

Thus, although Brent's physical movements are severely limited by her grandmother's crawl space, she is able to travel. In fact, she is even able to move physically somewhat, for, small as the space comprising her "loophole of retreat" is, it cannot limit her movements entirely. For instance, while she finds herself suffering from an inability to move freely and regularly, Brent does manage to reposition herself enough to prevent paralysis. As Jacobs explains, "It was impossible for me to move in an erect position, but I crawled about my den for exercise" (115). Brent's physical mobility is, clearly, hampered but not completely restricted by her environment.[52]

Ironically, Brent is able temporarily to switch roles with her master, Dr. Flint, for she manages to direct his movements in search of her. As Marilyn Wesley points out, "his mobility functions as a kind of imprisonment, whereas her immobility allows a measure of genuine control" (57). Dr. Flint makes several trips to New York in hopes of recapturing her, expending considerable time and money on these excursions, even borrowing five hundred dollars from a white woman who is temporarily hiding the narrator. Brent also fools him by writing letters, which she knows will fall into his hands, and arranging for them to be postmarked in New York. After receiving these letters, Flint tries to convince her uncle to travel to Boston in order to bring her home, and, when this scheme fails, the doctor writes to the mayor of Boston seeking assistance. Of course, he gets no reply, as Brent had anticipated.

In constant danger of detection and recapture while she remains in the South, however, Brent finally secures her physical freedom by traveling to the North. Unlike Frederick Douglass, who refuses to describe his escape in order to protect those who have helped him, thereby undercutting his own representation of himself as a self-made man, Jacobs provides a fairly detailed description of her journey north. She is especially clear about her dependence on a community of fellow conspirators, both black and white. Peter, a close friend of her family, arranges with a ship's captain to provide Brent with safe passage to Philadelphia. Although she initially backs out for fear of capture and gives her berth to her friend Fanny, another runaway hiding nearby, Brent finally decides to risk the trip after believing she is in danger of discovery in her garret. Pretending to be two women traveling north to join their husbands, Brent and her friend sail up the Chesapeake Bay and land finally in Philadelphia, where each secures assistance in traveling on to New York.

Like Douglass and Northup, Brent proves that she is no longer a slave by directing her own journey. Because she has already traveled into her garret and thus outside of southern society, however, Brent's escape northward is partly an extension of her previous travels, a physical manifestation of her earlier ideologically transgressive journeys. After all, as Smith explains, Brent "dates her emancipation from the time she entered her loophole, even though she did not cross into the free states until seven years later" (29). Of course, the physical journey is also far more significant, for in the North she is in a much better position to care for her children and secure her complete freedom from slavery. Her journey by sea to Philadelphia is, in a sense, a reverse Middle Passage, in which Brent is hidden below decks in tight quarters with her friend but taken to freedom rather than enslavement. The sea journey also prefigures her later trip to England, where Brent witnesses a society far freer from prejudice than what she has encountered in the United States. Only in Britain does she come to understand more fully what her freedom might entail. Although she had already subverted slave ideology by her travel into the garret, Brent's escape to Philadelphia, New York, and Boston becomes one of the central steps in her progression toward her dreams of traveling to freedom and of creating her own home environment for herself and her children.

Brent's journey to the North does not provide her with complete freedom, however, for she is still in danger of recapture and is subject to the prejudices and laws in the North that restrict or determine her travels. For instance, during her trip from Philadelphia to New York, Brent is unable to travel as she'd prefer, for, she learns, "They don't allow colored people to go in the first-class cars" (162). According to Jacobs, "This was the first chill to my enthusiasm about the Free States. Colored people were allowed to ride in a filthy box, behind white people, at the south, but there they were not required to pay for the privilege. It made me sad to find how the north aped the customs of slavery" (162–63). Even though she has gained relative freedom by traveling to the North, she is unable to move freely even here. So, rather than travel as a passenger, Jacobs explains, "We were stowed away in a large, rough car, with windows on each side, too high for us to look out without standing up. It was crowded with people, apparently of all nations" (163). Apparently, Brent's travels are far from complete, despite her recent escape.

Brent's freedom is further curtailed by her financial situation, for she is unable to provide herself with her own place to live. She must instead enter another person's home again, this time as a servant receiving wages rather than as a slave. While she certainly has a freedom as a paid worker she had not previously enjoyed under slavery, Brent is still not entirely free, for she is kept within this household by economic necessity. As Carolyn Porter has suggested, "In becoming free, male slaves become men; but Linda [Brent] never possesses herself. She can determine only who will possess her and her children" (362). In a sense, Brent simply remains a woman, still subject to the demands of a larger patriarchal society. Of course, these new demands placed on her do not invalidate her achievements, for Brent has managed to secure a degree of freedom unknown to enslaved women in the South. Although she is forced to find employment with a society that does not place a high economic value on women's labor, she does have some choice as to how or where she will seek the employment she needs in order to support herself and her children. Brent is fortunate in her employment, for she goes to work for a woman who shows herself to be sympathetic to Brent's plight.

Even though Mrs. Bruce, her new employer, is extremely kind to her, Brent remains uneasy about her new domestic situation, particularly because she is unable to live with her children. "The old feeling of insecurity, especially with regard to my children, often threw its dark shadow across my sunshine," she writes (169). Neither Brent nor her children are yet free enough from the dangers posed by slavery to act as they might wish. Jacobs writes, "Mrs. Bruce offered me a home for Ellen; but pleasant as it would have been, I did not dare to accept it, for fear of offending the Hobbs family. Their knowledge of my precarious situation placed me in their power; and I felt that it was important for me to keep on the right side of them, till, by dint of labor and economy, I could make a home for my children" (169). Furthermore, on several occasions she is forced to flee New York when she learns that Dr. Flint or his son-in-law has come to the city to recapture her. However, her ability to travel at these times in order to escape from her pursuers is perhaps the truest sign of her freedom, for even though her movements have, in a way, been provoked by Dr. Flint, she here exerts control over her journey and her destination. Thus, her travel is both the sign and the cause of her political subjectivity and freedom.

Her happiest arrangement comes after she has narrowly escaped recapture; she manages to wrest her daughter from her harsh situation in the house of Mrs. Hobbs and flees to Boston, where she meets her son. "The day after my arrival was one of the happiest of my life," she explains. "I felt as if I was beyond the reach of the bloodhounds; and, for the first time during many years, I had both my children together with me" (182). She is finally able, albeit briefly, to establish a home for her children. "The winter passed pleasantly," she explains, "while I was busy with my needle, and my children with their books" (182). Before the passage of the Fugitive Slave Law, Brent is safe in Massachusetts, for she knows her pursuers will not attempt to catch her in that abolitionist state.

The home she has begun to establish in Boston is disrupted, however, by economic necessity and by the death of her former employer, Mrs. Bruce. In order to make more money so that in the future she can establish a domestic situation more economically secure, Brent agrees to travel to England to care for the daughter of Mr. Bruce. Although she is again separated from her children, this journey offers her a view of a society that she argues is not corrupted by the institution of slavery. She notices the extreme poverty of the peasant class in England, but these families, she notes, enjoy a degree of security about which she has only dreamed. The people she encounters are indeed "among the poorest poor," she explains, but she believes "the condition of even the meanest and most ignorant among them was vastly superior to the condition of the most favored slaves in America" (184). The peasants may have to toil in the fields, but their homes are secure and their families intact, she argues, so they are neither forced to flee nor snatched from their homes:

> Their homes were very humble; but they were protected by law. No insolent patrols could come, in the dead of night, and flog them at their pleasure. The father, when he closed his cottage door, felt safe with his family around him. No master or overseer could come and take from him his wife, or his daughter. They must separate to earn their living; but the parents knew where their children were going, and could communicate with them by letters. The relations of husband and wife, parent and child, were too sacred for the richest noble in the land to violate with impunity. (184)

Unlike slaves, the peasants of England were able to maintain their families and live in safety. Their lives may have been difficult, Jacobs explained, but they were able to create and maintain their own homes, the single most important right that Jacobs notes, for all other freedoms seem to derive from that of constructing a secure domestic space.

As with her travel to the North, Jacobs's travel abroad not only provides her with new perspectives on freedom and movement but also produces that freedom; thus, Jacobs finds freedom both *in* and *as* self-directed movement. As many writers have explained of their journeys, travel has given Jacobs expanded knowledge of both herself and her nation, for she appreciates even more fully after her trip to England what "freedom" might be or what a "home" safe from violence might entail. Like Northup and other travelers, Jacobs thus uses her journeys to expand her own knowledge and to explain her new perspective to readers who are not as widely traveled as she—whether travel be defined geographically, physically, socially, or ideologically.

The possession of a safe domestic space is Brent's constant goal, and she returns to the United States with some dread, for she will not be able to rest as securely in this country. Upon her return she remarks, "It is a sad feeling to be afraid of one's native country" (186). Even though she is in the North, she will have to resume her periodic escapes from the city when she believes herself in danger of recapture. This process becomes particularly difficult after the passage of the Fugitive Slave Law. Working again as a domestic servant in the home of the newly remarried Mr. Bruce, Brent is confronted yet again with the prospect of fleeing to safety. The second Mrs. Bruce informs Brent that she should again make her escape from New York, and, while Brent appreciates her employer's kindness, she is disheartened by the prospect of continued travel. She explains, "I was weary of flying from pillar to post. I had been chased during half my life, and it seemed as if the chase was never to end" (198). Having been prevented when in the South from freedom of movement, Jacobs is now faced with the prospect of not having the freedom to remain stationary, since she must continually travel in order to maintain her freedom. Denied the freedom *to* travel as a slave, Jacobs the fugitive is denied the freedom *from* travel.

Even after her freedom has been purchased and she is no longer a fugitive slave, Jacobs feels enslaved by her situation. She will be truly free, Jacobs realizes, only when she is able to settle down in one place and construct a safe, secure home environment for her children. According to Yellin, even though Brent does not have her own home, she does achieve her main objective, freedom: "While Linda Brent's secondary goal—a home—remains elusive, *Incidents*, like all slave narratives, ends with the achievement of freedom, the narrator's primary goal" (xxix). Yellin fails to appreciate, however, that for Jacobs freedom is ultimately the possession of a home. Home is, thus, not separate from but one part of Jacobs's primary goal, for only by living in her own home will Jacobs and her children truly be free. Furthermore, like her readers, "whose homes are protected by law" (54), Jacobs wants to be free not only from the danger of recapture and physical enslavement but also from the economic enslavement of poverty. As Claudia Tate argues, "Freedom in *Incidents* is less a region—North—than a place that sustains an opportunity for Jacobs to grant herself the authority of personal inviolability, in short, black female self-authority" (27). Thus, though Jacobs and her children have gained independence from her former master, her narrative does not end with her peace, for her travels have been unable to provide her with her ultimate goal, the establishment of her own home. Contrasting her story with those of the heroines of popular sentimental novels, Jacobs writes, "Reader, my story ends with freedom; not in the usual way, with marriage. I and my children are now free! We are as free from the power of slaveholders as are the white people of the north; and though that, according to my ideas, is not saying a great deal, it is a vast improvement in *my* condition. The dream of my life is not yet realized. I do not sit with my children in a home of my own. I still long for a hearthstone of my own, however humble" (201). Ironically, freedom is imagined by Jacobs as both movement and stasis, represented both by the journey and the hearthstone. While travel has provided Jacobs with some freedoms, particularly the freedom to write, and has given her the opportunity to fashion a personal identity, stasis is her ultimate goal, for she seeks above all else the freedom and comfort of a peaceful domestic environment.

By rejecting her objectification as the sexualized object of another's desire, by traveling to political freedom in the North, and by creating a narrative space in which she can tell her own story, Jacobs recreates herself as a discursive subject. Furthermore, by describing her ongoing attempts to create a satisfactory domestic space in which she would be free to raise her children, Jacobs creates herself as a political identity-in-progress, freed from the tyranny of slavery but still subject to the prejudices and biases directed to one of her race, gender, and class. According to Mauri Skinfill, "The particular way Jacobs' existence remains problematic in the North suggests the degree to which the Southern economy and its attendant ideologies were not singularly Southern but were embedded, rather, in a more general national character" (75). Jacobs's attempt to create a domestic space is, therefore, an attempt to fashion a national domestic ideology in which everybody would be free to construct her own home.[53] Thus, although travel has produced a freedom previously denied to Harriet Jacobs, this travel has not granted her the same degree of freedom enjoyed by other travel writers such as Fanny Kemble, who was free not only to write, to describe, and to criticize but also to live without the economic necessity of attaching herself to the household of another in order to enjoy a stable and secure domestic space.

CHAPTER FOUR

Frederick Law Olmsted and the Consolidation of the American Economy and Culture

> The spirit of capitalism . . . had to fight its way
> to supremacy against a whole world of hostile forces.
>
> MAX WEBER

In a brief letter to his younger brother, John, Frederick Law Olmsted once wrote, "I believe that our farmers are, and have cause to be, the most contented men in the world" (qtd. in Fein 12). For a man who regularly left his own farm in the hands of other family members or various tenants, this statement seems rather ironic, for Frederick Law Olmsted was anything but content on the 185-acre Staten Island farm his father had purchased for him in 1847. Initially interested in "scientific farming," Frederick had hoped to create a model farm that could serve as a beacon to the independent yeomen of the region, and he did spend several productive years at this employment, growing prize-winning fruits and vegetables, helping to establish a county agricultural society, and introducing a number of innovations to the traditional farming techniques employed in the area.[1] After his initial excitement dissipated, however, Olmsted's restless energy and curious mind failed to provide him with the patience to stay on his farm for any extended period of time. Instead, he followed a number of other pursuits, beginning in 1850 with a trip to England with his brother, John, and a friend, Charles Loring Brace. Upon his return, Olmsted wrote and published *Walks and Talks of an American Farmer in England*, a book whose title is indicative both of Olmsted's peripatetic nature and his definition of himself. Like Crèvecoeur, Olmsted pictured himself as an American farmer, even though his almost constant travels tended to undermine this self-representation.

Using the little fame he had garnered from the publication of this first book, in 1852 Olmsted won a position with the *New York Times* as a traveling correspondent in the southern United States.[2] He departed for the South in

December, traveling down the seaboard states and along the Gulf of Mexico to New Orleans, returning to New York in April 1853. A second trip took him and his brother through Kentucky and Tennessee to New Orleans, on horseback to Texas, and back to New Orleans, after which John sailed for home while Frederick covered much of the territory in the "back country" he had already seen, arriving in New York in early August 1854.[3] Olmsted originally went South, he explained in a letter to Frederick Kingsbury in October 1852, "mainly with the idea that I could make a valuable book of observations on Southern Agriculture & general economy as affected by Slavery; the condition of the slaves— prospects—tendencies—& reliable understanding of the sentiments and hopes & fears of sensible planters & gentlemen that I should meet. Matter of fact matter to come after the deluge of spoony fancy pictures now at its height shall be spent" (*Slavery and the South* 82).[4] His primary interest, he states, is agriculture and the economy. While he will certainly investigate slavery, he had assured his editor that he would not argue from a deeply partisan position. Unlike his friend Brace, Olmsted was no abolitionist, and his fairly conservative opinions on slavery and abolition arise throughout his private letters and published works. His primary goal with the newspaper series, he explains here and in the first article published in the *New-York Daily Times*, was to observe firsthand the customs and condition of the inhabitants of the South, white and black, and to report his findings "with candor and fidelity" (*SS* 86).

Upon returning to New York in 1854 from his second southern trip, Olmsted began immediately to revise his letters for book publication. He revised slowly, for he wanted to include additional material discovered during his extensive research in New York libraries and his wide reading of newspapers, journals, and pamphlets. The three books that grew out of his collections of newspaper articles, *A Journey in the Seaboard Slave States*, *A Journey through Texas*, and *A Journey in the Back Country*, were published in 1856, 1857, and 1860 respectively. *The Cotton Kingdom*, a consolidation of these three, appeared in 1861. In addition to revising his articles, during this period Olmsted also became involved in the New York literary establishment, as an editor of *Putnam's Magazine* and as a part owner of Dix, Edwards, and Company, the publishing house that brought out his first two books of southern travel. Olmsted was deeply involved in all aspects of publishing—editing, marketing, and acquisitions— and he worked with a number of the day's most influential writers, including Emerson, Thoreau, Melville, Longfellow, and Stowe.[5]

He was finally becoming the literary figure he had desired to be more than ten years earlier, for when Olmsted had returned from England in 1850, he had explained to his father (upon whom his ambitions depended financially) that he hoped to gain access, in his words, to "a sort of literary republic which it is not merely pleasant & gratifying to my ambition to be recognized in, but also profitable" (qtd. in Powell xiii). Olmsted, it seems, had been ready to move beyond his local environment and to become a figure on the national stage. For him, that national stage meant involvement in the burgeoning print culture of the United States. If, as Benedict Anderson argues, the modern nation is founded on the production and distribution of print materials, then Olmsted chose wisely as he sought to become a figure of national importance.[6] Olmsted's reputation in this "republic of letters" was confirmed by his dispatches from the South, so for Olmsted personally, southern travel, writing, and the nation were united in a particularly significant manner. Travel through the American republic in a sense served Olmsted as a passport into the literary republic; this literary republic, in turn, worked to bolster and assure Olmsted's position and reputation in the American republic.

Olmsted did not simply want to become famous, however, for he continued to believe in the importance of social work and reform.[7] According to Charles Beveridge, Olmsted had inherited from his Puritan forefathers a belief that "the chief purpose of life was to be of service to other members of society" (7). Earlier hoping to serve as a model farmer for those around him, Olmsted planned through his travels in the South to reform an entire region and to bring about the development of a national economy and culture. The nation could not continue as two distinct regions, with one slave and one free, Olmsted believed. "The mountain ranges, the valleys, and the great waters of America all trend north and south, not east and west. An arbitrary political line may divide the north part from the south part, but there is no such line in nature; there can be none, socially," he argued in his introduction to *The Cotton Kingdom* (3). Of course, while such a line may have been primarily political rather than natural, it was anything but arbitrary, as Olmsted's work surely illustrated. Olmsted's job, as he saw it, was to help bring about the changes in the South necessary to eradicate the political, economic, social, and cultural boundaries that served to separate the two regions. "One system or the other is to thrive and extend, and eventually possess and govern this whole land," he argued (4). He wanted to ensure that the right system thrived, extended, possessed, and governed.

As he had earlier on Staten Island, he turned again to the farming ideal, arguing through his travel books that the South should model itself on New England and hoping that the plantation owners and poorer folk of the South would transform themselves into yeoman farmers. Olmsted claims throughout his work that he is interested primarily in farming, but if he hoped to reform the southern "culture" of agricultural production, he was also attempting to alter southern "culture" in that term's broadest sense. Focusing on the economics of southern agriculture and slavery, and arguing against the institution of slavery primarily on the grounds that it was inefficient, Olmsted sought to reconfigure southern society entirely and to re-form the nation as a whole in the image of his native New England. For Olmsted, this image is both agricultural and industrial, a complex combination of a yeoman ideal and a belief in the efficiency and value of the burgeoning industrial capitalism of the Northeast.

In a note added to the text of *Masters of Small Worlds: Yeoman Households, Gender Relations, and the Political Culture of the Antebellum South Carolina Low Country*, Stephanie McCurry argues, "Bourgeois travel literature on the antebellum South bears striking resemblance to that analyzed by Edward Said on the Near East, or 'Orient.' Similar dichotomies were employed to distinguish slave from free-labor society: passion/reason, laziness/industry, despotism/democracy. In this sense the discursive construction of the Low Country registered power relations between observers and observed similar to those at work in the Near East, except of course that the South was not a colony" (38). Nowhere are these dichotomies more exploited than in Olmsted's works. The South, he believed, was being ruined by the institution of slavery, which not only relied on a dependent, lazy, and inferior class of slaves but also hindered the creation of a productive, energetic class of free laborers. The wealth of the region was concentrated, he explained, in the hands of a small minority of slave owners, who ruled their domains as despots rather than rational men. Because of slavery, the South had become a "cotton kingdom" rather than an agricultural democracy, Olmsted believed, more reminiscent of European values than American ideals and, therefore, a region tied more to the past than to the future, unlike the American North. Thus, while the South was not exactly a northern colony, Olmsted did hope to expand the culture of the North and to effect an economic and social transformation of the region in order to produce, eventually, a unified national economy and culture.

Like Crèvecoeur seventy years earlier, who had depended on a paradigm of farming to define his ideal national culture, Olmsted also ignored the centrality of travel in his own life and in the life of the nation. He insisted on defining himself as a farmer, signing his southern pieces "Yeoman" throughout his time as a traveling correspondent, even after an absence of several years from his Staten Island farm. Likewise, he defines the one group in the South with whom he identifies, the German immigrants of Texas, as free-soil farmers, even though their lives have also been determined by their status as travelers and immigrants. Olmsted deplores the lack of movement in the South and constantly complains about the absence of a southern infrastructure that would enable the free and easy movement of people and goods. What movement there is in the South Olmsted condemns as indicative of a "frontier" state of civilization, which he contrasts with the "settled" society of the North. Thus, Olmsted the traveler depends on the ideal of a stationary, independent yeoman farmer at the same time that he criticizes the inhabitants of the South for remaining too settled and for refusing to travel in appropriate ways. He condemns the travel he does encounter in the South because it is not controlled by the needs and demands of the market economy he ultimately serves.

Olmsted also hoped to serve as a representative figure, and he is in many ways just that. If he is finally representative of the national identity, however, he becomes such because of his status as the exemplary representative of the emerging middle class of the industrializing North.[8] Thus, as a representative of the northern bourgeoisie, Olmsted illustrates the attempt to reconfigure the nation in order to support the northern capitalist economy, serving as a member of what Mary Louise Pratt calls the "capitalist vanguard" as he strives to define and develop a national economy and corresponding culture. After all, as interested as he was in reform, Olmsted did not seek to alter the basic structure of what he defined as American society as much as he did expand that society and assist in the consolidation of a nation built on its ideals and ideology.

Since the time of its publication, perhaps the single most widely known narrative of travel through the antebellum South has been Olmsted's *The Cotton Kingdom*, which grew out of a request from his London publisher to condense his three books on southern travel into a single volume. Deeply involved in the Central Park project at the time, Olmsted convinced Daniel Goodloe to direct the condensation of his previous works—*A Journey in the Seaboard Slave States*, *A Journey through Texas*, and *A Journey in the Back Country*.[9] Ironically, despite the participation of Goodloe, *The Cotton Kingdom* is in many ways Olmsted's most paradigmatic work. In addition to incorporating significant portions of his other books and describing his travels through many of the various regions of the South, *The Cotton Kingdom* more than any other of his books addresses most directly the issue of slavery and his arguments concerning the causes and results of the "peculiar institution." Publishing this text just as the Civil War was getting underway, Olmsted was less concerned with expressing the conciliatory tone he had employed in his previous works than he was with solidifying public opinion, both in England and in the North, against the newly forming Confederacy, as the introduction he wrote for the volume verifies. With his first three books of travel in the South, Olmsted had hoped to dissuade his southern countrymen from pursuing a course that he believed made little economic sense, but his tone had hardened by the time *The Cotton Kingdom* was published. While he might have hoped earlier to avoid a war with the South, by the time *The Cotton Kingdom* came out in November 1861, Olmsted had realized that the two sides were irrevocably at odds.

The Cotton Kingdom was originally published in London, where it was "widely reviewed in the British press and sold quickly enough that it was reprinted two years later," according to Witold Rybczynski (196). In fact, Rybczynski argues, "It undoubtedly had a small role in hardening some British attitudes against the Confederacy, which was never formally recognized by Great Britain" (196). Since its initial publication, Olmsted's book has been prized for its supposed objectivity. For instance, John Stuart Mill, to whom Olmsted had dedicated the book, wrote that Olmsted was "calm and dispassionate" (qtd. in Wilson 221). Despite its original place of publication, however, *The Cotton Kingdom* also "had in its time a good deal of influence on the Northern point of view toward the South," as Edmund Wilson points out (220).[10] The book was generally well received in the North, though not widely reviewed (Roper 180).[11] James Russell Lowell stated, "I have learned more about the South from your books than from all others put together" (qtd. in Wilson 221), and United States Senator Charles Sumner called it "a positive contribution to civilization" (qtd. in Roper 180).

While the book did, then, exert some influence at the time of its publication, perhaps a more important impact has been its effect on later attitudes toward the antebellum South. For several generations of historians and other readers interested in the South prior to the Civil War, *The Cotton Kingdom* has been one of the primary sources for learning about the region and its people during this time. As Dana White has pointed out, "For the founding generation of Southern studies, Olmsted's was 'the outside view of that society' " (25). Lawrence Powell agrees, writing in his introduction to a recent edition of *The Cotton Kingdom*, "The descriptive portions of the book have established it as a classic among historians, including those who disagree with its conclusions" (ix). Olmsted presented himself in all of his books as an impartial recorder of events and attitudes, and this self-representation has been accepted by most readers of his books, many of whom have essentially transformed Olmsted into an early ethnographer, describing him as a traveler who views objectively but refuses to become too deeply involved in the culture that he studies. Broadus Mitchell, writing in 1924, exclaimed, "If any adventurer upon the South possessed open-mindedness, Olmsted did" (69), and J. Saunders Redding argues that Olmsted was "as objective an observer as ever took a journey" (qtd. in

White 11). In the second volume of his magisterial series *The Americans*, Daniel Boorstin commends Olmsted's "full-bodied travel books, which are judicious without being dull, colorful without being lurid; they restore the reader's faith in the human capacity for precise and reliable observation, when few others seem capable of it. . . . There is no better introduction to Southern life on the brink of the War, and there are few comparable travel books in all American history" (466). For much of *The Cotton Kingdom*'s history, few readers would have disagreed with Boorstin's assessment of Olmsted's objectivity and keen eye for factual detail.[12] In fact, according to Carolyn Porter, Olmsted "continues to be described in *The Oxford Companion to American Literature* as a man 'noted for his unbiased travel books' " (363).

However, some recent critics, such as Powell, White, and Porter, have begun to question Olmsted's impartiality and to analyze his texts more critically.[13] For instance, Powell writes in his introduction, "The idea of writing a special series of articles about the South, the use of the term 'the Slave States' in the title, even Olmsted's pseudonym, 'Yeoman,' all suggest that he was not simply a neutral, disinterested observer" (xix). *The Cotton Kingdom*, Powell argues, "advertises itself as a travel account and a book of reportage, which it assuredly is. But it is also an ideological treatise verging at times on the polemical, and it must be read on these two levels, bifocally as it were" (ix). While Mitchell had written in 1924 that Olmsted "sought not to vindicate a partisan premise" (114), Porter has analyzed the ideological use to which Olmsted put his observations: "Olmsted's 'investigations' were vast and various, but they served always to demonstrate that the conjunction of cotton and slavery bred poverty—economic, social, and cultural" (363). Thus, while Mitchell may have been correct that Olmsted sought "to accomplish the prosperity of the South and the nation" (114), this concern did not prohibit him from expressing his deep partisanship and his beliefs in the superiority of the New England ideal.

Despite this recent critical willingness to view Olmsted's writings in a more ideological light, however, most recent work on Olmsted's southern travel texts has viewed them primarily in terms of their importance to his later work as a landscape architect. For example, in his biography of Olmsted, Rybczynski, an architect himself, investigates most thoroughly Olmsted's influence on the American landscape. George Scheper is also typical of recent Olmsted critics when he writes, "We can see within the framework of Olmsted's journalistic project regarding slavery the germ of his public parks idea, both growing out of the same reformist soil" (383). Even Powell concludes by viewing Olmsted's southern travels as primarily a step toward his later vocation, arguing, "[F]or

Olmsted the most lasting result of his involvement in the slavery debate was his discovery of the vocation he had long been searching for. His Southern travels deepened the reform commitments that led to his work as a landscape architect and urban reformer" (xxxi). Thus, Olmsted's later impact on the landscape of the nation, especially as the architect and superintendent of the Central Park project, has served many critics as the lens through which to view all of Olmsted's work.

Of course, Olmsted's journeys in the South and his published accounts of those travels can usefully be interpreted in this manner, but they are also important cultural documents in their own right and should be read as such. As Porter's remarks especially suggest, the ideological power of these works lies not only in their eventual manifestation in New York's Central Park, Boston's Prospect Park, or the numerous neighborhoods and universities Olmsted helped design and create. Rather, their power and their importance lie more fully in the way in which Olmsted's southern texts, especially *The Cotton Kingdom*, gave voice to a reform-minded, capitalist ideology that came eventually to be identified not only with New England and the rest of the North but with the United States as a whole. According to Powell, "As both a travel account and an ideological treatise, both a rich source of historical evidence and a fount of sectional stereotypes, *The Cotton Kingdom* reveals as much about the antislavery mind of the North as it does about the slave society of the South" (xi). Even more important, Porter argues, "Perhaps more decisively than any other single book, *The Cotton Kingdom* registers the voice of the dominant white North that would prevail after the war" (363). Because most of those who read Olmsted's texts have been sympathetic with his overall theme—"the defense of a democratic, commercial, and urban society dependent on free labor in contrast to an aristocratic, fundamentally agrarian order based on slave labor," in the words of Dana White (xix)—the biases and prejudices in his texts have frequently been missed, dismissed, or ignored. Thus, perhaps the widespread use of Olmsted's works by historians and the reception of those works as objective testimonies are indicative of the almost universal adoption of this reform-minded, capitalist perspective within the United States since the end of the Civil War.[14]

The argument of that perspective in *The Cotton Kingdom* appears fairly simple and straightforward. Slavery, Olmsted believes, is not primarily a moral issue but an economic one, and the South should give up slavery because it is inefficient.[15] For Olmsted, many of the problems of southern society can be traced through slavery to the region's underlying economic structure. He focuses especially on the uneven distribution of wealth in the South, explaining that the advantages of large plantations "accrue only to their owners and to the buyers of cotton" (478). In the introduction written for the publication of *The Cotton Kingdom*, Olmsted argues,

> [I]f all the wealth produced in a certain district is concentrated in the hands of a few men living remote from each other, it may possibly bring to the district comfortable houses, good servants, fine wines, food and furniture, tutors and governesses, horses and carriages, for these few men, but it will not bring thither good roads and bridges, it will not bring thither such means of education and of civilized comfort as are to be drawn from libraries, churches, museums, gardens, theatres, and assembly rooms; it will not bring thither local newspapers, telegraphs, and so on. (17–18)

In the space of twenty years, Olmsted continues, wealth in the North would be invested in "improvements," such as roads, schools, and mills, but in the South would be reinvested entirely in slaves. Thus, wealth in the North is shared by the entire community, but only the individual slave owner enjoys the fruits of the surplus in the South. Because these individual slave owners are reticent to spend their money on projects that will not directly benefit themselves, the concentration of wealth in just a few hands discourages the development of an infrastructure that would benefit the entire population.

Furthermore, the practice of reinvesting surplus solely in more slaves prohibits the development of commerce with other regions. Rather than importing slaves, Olmsted asks, what would be the benefit to a region if the same number of energetic free white workers were encouraged to immigrate instead? Contrasting a group of slaves recently bought from Virginia with a "steamboat load of the same material—bone and muscle" of German immigrants bound for Iowa or Wisconsin, Olmsted wonders, "In ten years' time, how many mills, and bridges, and schoolhouses, and miles of railroad, will the Germans have built? And how much cloth and fish will they want from Massachusetts, iron from Pennsylvania, and tin from Banka, hemp from Russia, tea from China, and coffee from Brazil, fruit from Spain, wine from Ohio, and oil and gold from the Pacific, silk from France, sugar from Louisiana, cotton from Texas, and rags from Italy, lead from Illinois, notions from Connecticut, and machines from New Jersey, and intelligence from everywhere?" (230). Instead, Louisiana or Texas imports twenty thousand dollars of slave "bone and muscle" and carries on little trade with any other state or country but Virginia, from which new slaves are generally bought. Broader trade and commerce, Olmsted suggests, would lead to the development of a more advanced system of roads, which would encourage further trade. Roads thus become for Olmsted both the sign and the symbol of larger modes and methods of exchange and circulation. At present,

however, except for the trade in slaves and cotton, the South lacks almost completely a developed system of commerce and, accordingly, an adequate system
of public roads.

Southern cities, too, suffer from a shocking absence of public institutions,
argues Olmsted. Norfolk, for instance, "is a dirty, low, ill-arranged town, nearly
divided by a morass" and has only "a single creditable public building," although
it boasts "a number of fine private residences" (111). Olmsted writes, "It has all
the immoral and disagreeable characteristics of a large seaport, with very few
of the advantages that we should expect to find as relief to them. No lyceum or
public libraries, no public gardens, no galleries of art, and though there are two
'Bethels,' no 'home' for its seamen; no public resorts of healthful amusement; no
place better than a filthy, tobacco-impregnated bar-room or a licentious dance-
cellar, so far as I have been able to learn, for the stranger of high or low degree
to pass the hours unoccupied by business" (111). Almost every southern city
Olmsted visits compares to Norfolk in its complete lack of "creditable" public
institutions. Obviously, the rural districts are even worse.

In addition to allowing an uneven distribution of wealth and discourag-
ing the construction of public institutions, the effects of slavery are manifested
mainly in two other areas: the environment and the personal life of the people,
both black and white. While Olmsted explains that he will focus primarily on
the economy, he clearly recognizes that this economy is integrally connected
to the natural environment and to the customs and beliefs of the people.[16] And
the habits of the people, argues Olmsted, are determined by their participation
in slavery. As Olmsted himself explained in his seventh letter to the *New-York
Daily Times*, "I did not intend when I commenced writing these letters to give
much attention to the subject of Slavery; but the truth is, the character of the
whole agriculture of the country depends upon it. In every department of industry I see its influence, vitally affecting the question of profit, and I must add
that everywhere, and constantly, the conviction is forced upon me, to a degree
entirely unanticipated, that its effect is universally ruinous" (*SS* 103). Initially,
he explains, he wanted to direct his attention to the habits of the people and the
agricultural productions of the region and thereby avoid discussions of slavery, but he soon realized that he simply could not describe the region without
directly confronting slavery and its effects.

Slavery (as well as the cotton industry that depends on it) wears out and
ruins the land, argues Olmsted. His most frequent comment on the environment throughout his two trips seems to be "the soil worn out in cultivation"
(69). Traveling in Louisiana and Mississippi, for instance, Olmsted writes, "I
passed during the day four or five large plantations, the hillsides worn, cleft,

and channelled like icebergs; stables and negro quarters all abandoned, and everything given up to nature and decay" (410).[17] Although he finds the soil in
Virginia of a poor quality, in much of the South the land that he sees is extremely
fertile but has been ruined by the poor agricultural practices encouraged by the
commitment to cotton. "In its natural state the virgin soil appears the richest I
have ever seen," Olmsted remarks of some land in Mississippi, but, because of
the plantation owners' carelessness, "its productiveness rapidly decreases" (411).
In contrast, Olmsted suggests, "If these slopes were thrown into permanent ter-
races, with turfed or stone-faced escarpments, the fertility of the soil might be
preserved, even with constant tillage. In this way the hills would continue for
ages to produce annual crops of greater value than those which are at present
obtained from them at such destructive expense—from ten to twenty crops of
cotton rendering them absolute deserts" (411). Much the same is true throughout the South, Olmsted argues, for cotton production and slavery encourage
the abandonment of plantations in favor of richer, virgin soil further west. "If
you ask, where are the people that once occupied these," Olmsted writes of the
abandoned plantations he passes in Louisiana, "the universal reply is, 'Gone to
Texas' " (287–88).

Along with the abandoned land go any improvements the owners had made,
so southerners are always starting from the beginning. As Olmsted explains of
western Louisiana, "The improvements which the inhabitants have succeeded
in making in the way of clearing the forest, fencing and tilling the land, building
dwellings, barns, and machinery, making roads and bridges, and introducing
the institutions of civilization, not compensating in value the deterioration in
the productiveness of the soil, the exhausted land reverts to wilderness" (288–
89). In fact, as he travels through this region, much of which has only fairly
recently been cleared for the first time, Olmsted notes, "[A] larger area had
been abandoned, we thought, than remained under cultivation" (287). "With
the land," Olmsted continues, "many cabins have, of course, also been deserted,
giving the road a desolate air" (287). Thus, throughout the South, Olmsted verifies what he had learned upon entering Virginia at the beginning of his trip, that
"the natural resources of the land were strangely unused, or were used with poor
economy" (8).

The slave owners' tendency to wear out the soil and emigrate westward draws
from Olmsted some of his most violent opposition to slavery. He is adamantly
opposed to the expansion of slavery into the new territories and, in fact, even
helped supply money, a printing press, and weaponry to some free-soil activists
in Texas. According to Broadus Mitchell, "No one understood better than Olmsted, with his constant harping on the evils of the South's extensive system of

agriculture, that slavery was not only a system for the government of slaves under individual masters, but a system of colonization as well. He found the process of exhaustion of soils and consequent removal to new ones going on in the rich southwest as well as in the older planting districts" (137). Perhaps what most bothers Olmsted about this movement westward is its inherent suggestion of inefficiency and restlessness; these emigrating plantation owners are too inefficient to be yeomen and too aimless to be true travelers. According to Olmsted, travel should be purposeful and productive, and it should contribute to the civilization and economy of the nation as a whole, both North and South. In contrast, the movement practiced by these slave owners resembles drift more than travel and suggests to Olmsted surrender and defeat, for these slave owners are moving *from* rather than traveling *to*.

However, the land and soil ruined through wasteful agricultural practices can be redeemed, Olmsted suggests, by the immigration of workers with a northern work ethic. In contrast to those slave owners heading to Texas, these immigrants would epitomize useful and structured travel, for they would be entering a region in order to redeem and improve it, *im*migrating as much as *e*migrating. In order to use fully "the immense natural privileges and advantages possessed by the South," Olmsted claims, "the general enterprise and close application, the industry and skill which is used at the North" is required, instead of the inefficient and wasteful methods of the native inhabitants of the South (*SS* 258). "[W]ithin twenty miles of Washington," states Olmsted, land abandoned by slave owners may be purchased very cheaply, and, as "[s]everal New Yorkers" had recently shown, may be made quite productive once again (29). When he sees land that is productive, Olmsted frequently suggests that northern industry is responsible, even if those working the land are southern, slave or free. For instance, Olmsted notes that one particularly well-kept field was being plowed by men using "a light, New-York-made plough" (189). Furthermore, northern industry seems not only to make abandoned land productive again but even to improve the appearance and quality of the landscape itself. One of the very few examples Olmsted describes of beautiful landscape he views from the window of a stagecoach built in Pennsylvania and operated by northerners in North Carolina. Only through the frame provided by a stagecoach window produced in the North can Olmsted see any beauty in the southern landscape. The northern ideology manifested here in the stagecoach and epitomized by the efficiency of its operators becomes the literal window through which Olmsted views the environment, as Olmsted transforms this stagecoach into both a frame of reference and a vehicle of perception.

The northern work ethic not only can redeem abandoned land but is generally responsible, in Olmsted's view, for any of the improvements or luxuries he discovers in the South. In North Carolina, he notes, "The locomotives that I saw were all made in Philadelphia; the cars were all from the Hartford, Conn., and Worcester, Mass., manufactories, and invariably, elegant and comfortable" (168).[18] What is produced in the South is the product of shoddy workmanship, as he understands when he sees carts that "look as if they were made by their owners, in the woods, with no better tools than axes and jack-knives," except their wheels, "which come from the North" (179). And in east Texas, the only butter Olmsted can buy is from New York, despite the abundance of nearby land that is excellent for grazing cattle (295).

Thus, more significant than the ruinous impact slavery has on the land is its disastrous effect on the inhabitants of the South, both black and white. Most noticeably, Olmsted observes, slaves are practically incapable of meaningful work. Upon first encountering slaves in Washington, D.C., Olmsted notes "that they must be difficult to direct efficiently, and that it must be irksome and trying to one's patience to have to superintend their labour" (28). One northern laborer can perform as much work as at least four slaves, he writes (105). "[T]he great mass, as they are seen at work, under overseers, in the fields," Olmsted states, "appear very dull, idiotic, and brute-like; and it requires an effort to appreciate that they are, very much more than the beasts they drive, our brethren—a part of ourselves" (32). One group of slaves, containing both men and women, Olmsted describes in the following terms: "Clumsy, awkward, gross, elephantine in all their movements; pouting, grinning, and leering at us; sly, sensual, and shameless, in all their expressions and demeanour; I never before had witnessed, I thought, anything more revolting than the whole scene" (162).[19] While Olmsted does believe in the superiority of the white race and often acts according to his belief in "the child-like quality common in the negroes" (266), he argues that slavery, not an inherent racial deficit, is responsible for many of the negative qualities that slaves possess.[20] In short, Olmsted claims, "A man forced to labour under their system is morally driven to indolence, carelessness, indifference to the results of skill, heedlessness, inconstancy of purpose, improvidence, and extravagance" (104). On the other hand, he continues, "Precisely the opposite qualities are those which are encouraged, and inevitably developed in a man who has to make his living, and earn all his comfort by his voluntarily-directed labour" (104).[21] Slaves who have an interest in the outcome of their work show the truth of this belief, Olmsted argues, and "Men of sense have discovered that when they desire to get extraordinary exertions from their slaves, it is better to offer them rewards than to whip them; to encourage them, rather than to drive them" (255–56). Unfortunately, there are apparently few "men of sense" in the South, for most slave owners try to work their slaves by threats and punishments, and slaves generally are lazy, indolent, and careless.

According to Olmsted, most white workers in the South also possess these same qualities. Because southerners equate manual labor with slavery, most white southerners refuse to do much work at all, according to Olmsted. Because they so frequently interact with slaves, whites who do perform manual labor adopt the habits and poor work ethic of their enslaved coworkers. According to Olmsted, "It is not wonderful that the habits of the whole community should be influenced by, and be made to accommodate to these habits of its [slave] labourers. It irresistibly affects the whole industrial character of the people. You may see it in the habits and manners of the free white mechanics and trades-people. All of these must have dealings or be in competition with slaves, and so have their standard of excellence made low, and become accustomed to, until they are content with slight, false, unsound workmanship" (103). Thus, argues Olmsted, the slave work ethic infects the entire community. In one of his letters to the *Times*, Olmsted writes, "[T]he non-slaveholders are unambitious, indolent, degraded and illiterate;—are a dead peasantry so far as they affect the industrial position of the South" (qtd. in Beveridge 15).[22] Poor whites, Olmsted explains, "almost all appear excessively apathetic, sleepy, and stupid, if you see them at home" (327), and, he writes, "This was as much the case with the women as the men" (327). In addition, slavery has caused the poor whites of the South to become cowardly and weak. In short, "white labour cannot live in competition with slave-labour" (90). Slavery not only causes white laborers to be lazy and ignorant, but it actually creates the class as a whole. "[N]o slave country, new or old, is free from this exasperating pest of poor whites," Olmsted claims (290).

All of these problems, Olmsted suggests are caused by the institution of slavery and the presence of large numbers of slaves. As he writes toward the end of *The Cotton Kingdom*, "The field-hand negro is, on an average, a very poor and very bad creature, much worse than I had supposed before I had seen him and grown familiar with his stupidity, indolence, duplicity, and sensuality. He seems to be but an imperfect man, incapable of taking care of himself in a civilized manner, and his presence in large numbers must be considered a dangerous circumstance to a civilized people" (564–65). Thus, rather than simply constituting a danger to those who are enslaved, slavery actually retards, even prohibits, the development of a civilized society. "In other words," argues Olmsted, "if the slaves must not be elevated, it would seem to be a necessity that the citizens should steadily degenerate" (475). For this reason, Olmsted is particularly angered by the possibility of the expansion of slavery into new territories in the West, for if it is not gradually abolished, he argues, slavery will cause the downfall of the South and the entire nation. For Olmsted, it seems, the cultural and economic degeneracy of slavery is every bit as important as the moral.[23]

Olmsted's overall argument concerning slavery and its effects on the landscape, agriculture, work ethic, and morality of the South are illustrated most clearly when he spends two consecutive nights with families in northeastern Tennessee, the first night in the house of a slave owner and the second in one without slaves. "Night before last I spent at the residence of a man who had six slaves; last night, at the home of a farmer without slaves. Both houses were of the best class common in this region" (401–2).[24] The slave owner, Olmsted writes, was "much the wealthier of the two, and his house originally was the finer, but he lived in much less comfort than the other" (402). His house was "in great need of repair," was "disordered," and was "dirty" (402). The man and his wife acted very piously but were not as Christian as they tried to appear, for they "were very morose or sadly silent, when not scolding and re-ordering their servants" (402). Their son, who constantly cried and bullied his mother, cursed a slave girl "with a shocking volubility of filthy blackguardism" and whispered obscenities with another boy until falling asleep (402). Even worse, in Olmsted's view, "The white women of the house were very negligent and sluttish in their attire" (402). Finally, the food provided to Olmsted was not only "badly cooked" but also "badly served by negroes" (402).

"The house of the farmer without slaves," in contrast, "though not in good repair, was much neater, and everything within was well-ordered and unusually comfortable" (402). The women were not only "cheerful and kind" but were "clean and neatly dressed" (402). And the food was the best he had eaten in months. "The table was abundantly supplied with the most wholesome food— I might almost say the first wholesome food—I have had set before me since I was at the hotel at Natchez" (402). "All the work, both within and without the house," Olmsted concludes, "was carried on regularly and easily, and it was well done, because done by parties interested in the result," not simply by slaves "interested only to escape reproof or punishment" (402). For Olmsted, the moral is clear: slavery causes laziness, filthy habits, and immorality, while free labor encourages people to be clean, kind, hardworking, healthy, and moral.

Of course, what Olmsted is doing in this passage, as he is in much of the book, is contrasting the slave household with an ideal based on his vision of the yeomen of his native New England. According to Lee Hall, "yeoman" symbolized for Olmsted "integrity, versatility of skill and mind, and purity of spirit" (10). Furthermore, Hall argues, "yeoman" signified "the basic ingredient of

American civilization, the ideal democratic citizen who exercised his rights and responsibilities to himself, his family, and his community" (10). It is this ideal that underlies everything Olmsted sees, for this yeoman ideal is the "vehicle" with which and through which Olmsted views the entire South. Not surprisingly, the South fails to live up to Olmsted's vision, since for Olmsted, a "civilized community" must "resemble New England," as Powell argues: "It should be settled in compact villages and small towns populated by artisans, tradesmen, and modest-sized manufacturers, linked by ties of trade to small commercial farmers on tidy homesteads in the surrounding countryside" (xx).

For Olmsted, the yeoman is everything the southerner is not: hardworking, intelligent, curious, and aware of the outside world. Few people he meets in the South, except immigrants from the North or Europe, possess any of these qualities.[25] Almost by definition, then, if people whom Olmsted describes possess these qualities, they are not really southerners; in fact, in Olmsted's view, these people cannot be southerners, for they would then subvert his entire structural schema. Therefore, when Olmsted observes independent farmers in the South who are working according to his ideal, he immediately describes them in terms of his native New England. For instance, describing in his initial letter to the *Times* some northerners who had settled near Washington, D.C., Olmsted writes, "They are usually small farmers, occupying from fifty to one hundred and fifty acres of land, and tilling it mainly by their own labor and that of their families, in the old New-England way. They are said to have greatly improved the character of the county" (*SS* 89). Learning that working the land only with one's own family was "the old New-England way" would have come as a surprise to the large number of small, independent southern farmers who did not own slaves. When Olmsted views "the patriarchal institution . . . under its most favourable aspects," he describes the positive qualities of the plantation as due to its owner's "practical talent for organization and administration, gained among the rugged fields, the complicated looms, and the exact and comprehensive counting-houses of New England, which directs the labour" (183). Thus, any positive aspects Olmsted encounters are almost always, in his texts, directly traceable to the influence of a northern work ethic and an adherence to the ideal of the yeoman farmer.

Of course, there were countless farm families in the South who did not own slaves and managed to support themselves, but Olmsted refuses to recognize these people as in any way admirable. According to McCurry, "The obviously nonelite whites glimpsed off the beaten track could, then, only be 'poor whites,' no matter how much land or how many slaves they owned" (41). For instance, after Olmsted overtakes on the road "three young men of the poorest class" who, despite their belief that he is a fellow southerner, express strong antislavery sentiment, Olmsted warns the reader not to trust their claims: "But let the reader not be deceived by these expressions; they indicate simply the weakness and cowardice of the class represented by these men. It is not slavery they detest; it is simply the negro competition, and the monopoly of the opportunities to make money by negro owners, which they feel and but dimly comprehend" (400). For Olmsted, nonslaveholding whites in the South are, by definition, lazy, stupid, practically worthless, and poor. Olmsted thus manages to indict both groups of southern whites: those who own slaves and those who don't. Some, he argues, are vagabonds and move too much, while others are shiftless and don't move enough.

It is significant that Olmsted meets these young men on the road, for it is on the roads and railroads that Olmsted initially encounters many with whom he speaks.[26] The road, after all, has long been the space where members of different communities, races, cultures, or classes have most frequently interacted with each other. This space is even more significant for Olmsted, because he places such an emphasis on travel and on the infrastructure (or lack thereof) designed to encourage the movement of people, goods, and ideas. According to Olmsted's ideal, this movement of people, goods, and ideas should follow a fairly strict order. A well-built system of transportation, notably roads and railroads, should serve as a network to connect the various members of a community or a nation, each of whom shares equally in the benefits provided by that network. Were the South a "civilized" region, the largely independent yeoman farmers would use the transportation system to move their surplus to markets and to receive goods and information from the wider world. Especially important for Olmsted is the movement of printed material, particularly books, newspapers, and other periodicals, for these play an essential role in the distribution of important information and serve to facilitate the correction of a community's most pressing problems. A well-developed transportation infrastructure is integral to Olmsted's vision, "not only to facilitate local commerce but also to carry on the widening trade with distant markets," argues Powell (xx). Olmsted further believed, continues Powell, that the access to these markets provided by this system of transportation in New England "had made possible both rising standards of living and 'civilization'" (xx). In addition, good roads are essential to American democracy because the citizen of the republic is, for Olmsted, fundamentally a traveler, a figure in motion along with the goods and ideas constantly circulating throughout the nation.

The South, according to Olmsted, essentially has no developed system of transportation, for what roads the South does possess are practically impass-able, and the railroads are so poorly managed as to be extremely difficult to use. The region, he believes, is intrinsically hostile to the free and easy circu-lation of people, especially slaves, and of goods. According to Olmsted, society in the South has been structured so that movement is either severely restricted or not appropriately channeled, as in the North where a well-developed system of transportation efficiently moves people, goods, and ideas according to larger economic and cultural values. This theme, the extreme difficulty of southern travel, informs Olmsted's writing from the very beginning of his journeys. In his first letter to the *Times*, Olmsted complains about the railroads immediately after the three paragraphs that introduce his new series. Describing his initial trip to Washington, D.C., Olmsted writes,

> Twelve hours of travel over exceedingly mismanaged railroads, changing cars four times; a few miles by omnibus, and a few more of horse-draft; no chance to dine or sup, only to snatch a poor mouthful in a ferryboat; left, nevertheless, half an hour at one point, with no one to direct you or explain the delay; obliged to run at another to save your passage; no fires in New-Jersey; roasting ones in Maryland;— so you come from the metropolis to the capital of the United States. Fares high, and speed low. It is too shameful to be passed without grumbling. (*SS* 86)

When Olmsted is traveling by stagecoach in the South, he frequently gets out and walks, generally arriving at his destination long before the coach, much to his disgust. For instance, in North Carolina, Olmsted leaves a stagecoach and walks toward his destination, initially expecting to be picked up once the stage catches him. However, "In about an hour after I left the coach," he explains, "the driver, mounted on [a horse named] Bob, overtook me: he was going on to get fresh horses" (138). Although he does have some difficulty following the road, Olmsted eventually reaches his inn by eight o'clock at night. The stagecoach, however, does not arrive until much later, for, "At three o'clock in the morning, the three gentlemen that I had left ten miles back at four o'clock the previous day were dragged, shivering in the stagecoach, to the door" (139).

Of course, Olmsted fails to realize that he is judging southern transportation by his standards and according to his needs. Because much of the commerce in the South depended on rivers to transport the cotton and other produce to market, perhaps the region did not have the same needs for a well-constructed system of roads and railroads as did the North. Furthermore, if southerners gen-erally travel only within their immediate vicinity, as Olmsted regularly suggests, then it should not be surprising that the South is not prepared for travelers, a frequent complaint. He often seems to be condemning southern society for not catering more fully to his personal needs. While Olmsted may be frustrated, for instance, that "[t]he road was a mere opening through a forest of long-leafed pine" (138), such a road may have served perfectly the travel needs of the local inhabitants.

For Olmsted, the poor roads and transportation system in the South serve both as a sign and a symptom of the undeveloped economy and the uncivilized society he finds there: "There is nothing that is more closely connected, both as cause and effect, with the prosperity and wealth of a country, than its means and modes of travelling, and of transportation of the necessities and luxuries of life" (141). Southern roads, he believes, are indicative not of a developed civilization but of a society in a frontier state. Rather than adhering to a yeoman ideal, Olmsted argues, the South has remained in a constant frontier state because of its reliance on slavery and dedication to an inefficient economic system. "[T]he frontier condition of the South," Olmsted states, "is everywhere permanent" (554). Robert Lewis argues that, according to Olmsted, "Slavery made the temporary disadvantages of the frontier stage perpetual" (390). According to Lewis, the "frontier condition" implied for Olmsted "certain features which were the antitheses of 'civilization.' It presumed no clear division of labor . . . [and] an unsettled population of 'wanderers.' . . . [I]nherited institutions and established standards were lacking. . . . Lastly, the pioneers demonstrated the traits of 'individualism' attending freedom from external controls" (389). This "frontier condition" seems to be marked primarily by purposeless or nondirected movement. The people are "wanderers," and they do not move or act according to the rules of civilized behavior but are, instead, too individualistic. Of course, Olmsted regularly berates southerners for not moving at all or for having no conception of distance. He finds, "It is rare to find in the plantation districts a man, white or black, who can give you any clear information about the roads or the distances between places in his vicinity" (SS 309). When southerners do travel, however, Olmsted suggests that their movement does not serve any worthy goal. According to Olmsted, for example, the inhabitants of the region surrounding Natchitoches, Louisiana, are practically wild: "These are often handsome people, but vagabonds, almost to a man. Scarcely any of them have an regular occupation, unless it be that of herding cattle; but they raise a little maize, and fish a little, and hunt a little, and smoke and lounge a great deal, and are very regular in their attendance on divine worship, at the cathedral" (279). Despite these men's occupation as herders, Olmsted claims they do little that is recognizable as work, perhaps because they are not as acquisitive as Olmsted believes "civilized" people should be. He seems not to recognize herding as an occupation, even suggesting of some men he meets in eastern Texas, who "were chiefly herdsmen," that their condition "appeared to incline decidedly to barbarism" (312). Elsewhere, he describes "the restless, almost nomadic, small proprietors of the South" (296). According to Olmsted, in the South people are not "travelers" but, rather, "nomads" or "barbarians." True travel, suggests Olmsted, is teleological, but southerners move without any clear goals.

In the South it is not only physical movement but motion of many kinds that Olmsted deplores. Many of the boundaries strictly enforced in the North are frequently crossed or ignored in the South. Of course, travel inherently possesses at least the potential for transgression, but Olmsted doesn't seem to recognize this potential, at least not in his own travels. For Olmsted, travel is so rigidly defined by his ideological concerns that he does not see the irony of his critique; apparently, if the movement of a group is transgressive, then that group does not consist of "travelers" but of "nomads" or "vagabonds." Thus, Olmsted does not believe his travels are truly comparable to the movements of southerners.

Ironically, Olmsted is particularly upset by southerners' failure to adhere properly to racial boundaries. He is frequently "struck with the close cohabitation and association of black and white" in the houses of both rich and poor white southerners (31). He is equally appalled, however, by the close association of men and women. Of the "habitations" (not "homes") of poor white people, Olmsted notes, "Swine, hounds, and black and white children, are commonly lying very promiscuously together on the ground about the doors" (31). In these groups, not only are racial and sexual boundaries crossed, but even those that separate the human from the animal. Finally, social boundaries are blurred, as Olmsted is often frustrated in his attempts to categorize socially the people whom he meets. He notes disapprovingly, for instance, "Every white Southerner is a person of importance" and thus "must be treated with deference" (555). Elsewhere Olmsted writes, "I found that, more than any people I had ever seen, they were unrateable by dress, taste, forms, and expenditures. I was perplexed by finding, apparently united in the same individual, the self-possession, confidence, and the use of expressions of deference, of the well-equipped gentleman, and the coarseness and low tastes of the uncivilized boor—frankness and reserve, recklessness and self-restraint, extravagance, and penuriousness" (216). Not only are individuals difficult to place within the social hierarchy from their dress, speech, or habits, but perhaps these individuals do not consistently inhabit one stationary place within that hierarchy. Unlike Olmsted the New Englander, whose travels actually serve to consolidate his subjectivity and position within a social hierarchy, southerners come to seem fragmented, hybrid, even grotesque, and their movements subvert, rather than define, a stable identity in Olmsted's texts. Thus, Olmsted's vocabulary seems insufficient to the task of defining or describing the class of most southerners. As he explains, "The difficulty of giving anything like an intelligent and exact estimate of the breeding of any people or of any class of people is almost insurmountable, owing to the vagueness of the terms which must be used, or rather to the quite different ideas which different readers will attach to these terms" (553). By not acting or dressing according to the rules of the social hierarchy recognized in the North, these individuals call the very hierarchy into question by means of their ease of movement throughout the various levels.[27] Of course, Olmsted is clearly contrasting these individuals with himself, a stable, noncontradictory, and easily identifiable individual subjectivity, despite his almost constant travels, he suggests.

Rather than participate in unhindered travel, Olmsted believes, individuals should move (or be moved) geographically and socially according to the needs and demands of a society based on a free-market economy. Olmsted apparently hopes for maximum economic fluidity with minimum social movement. Ironically, Olmsted the traveler discovers that movement is at least potentially threatening to an established order. Of course, not all movement is transgressive, for the type of travel that Olmsted is demanding the South incorporate would serve to bolster rather than subvert a northern capitalist culture and ideology. Olmsted finds motion by southerners distressing because it does not correspond to his idea of proper movement; that is, while it does generally support a slave economy, it does not assist in the construction of the free-market system he hoped to see established there. According to Powell, "He observed a homespun economy and considered it impoverished. He observed a premodern work ethic and condemned it as laziness. He observed farmers living on the margins of the cash economy and mistook their situation for 'barbarism'" (xxvii). Thus, according to Powell, Olmsted finds most disturbing not poor southerners' lack of ambition or work ethic but their lack of desire to participate in a market economy. As Mary Louise Pratt argues, "Subsistence lifeways, non-monetary exchange systems, and self-sustaining regional economies are anathema to expansive capitalism" (*Imperial Eyes* 154–55). This, finally, is what Olmsted is most concerned with, and it is this, participation in a market, that underlies his idealization of the yeomanry.

It is an economy and society based on the values and needs of the middle class then emerging in the North that Olmsted finally desires for the South, so all movement should be in the service of this economy and society. Olmsted defines slave society as inferior because slaves frequently move (or work) in ways that Olmsted takes to be nonessential or too costly. Because slaves have no choice, they must work wherever they are placed by their owners.[28] On the other hand, free laborers can move to wherever the work is the most financially rewarding, so supposedly only those projects that are most important will be able to hire the adequate number of workers. The market thus determines where workers are most needed and makes certain that they move accordingly, despite the suggestion that these laborers are "free."[29] This law of the market seems most relevant when Olmsted questions the value of draining the swamps of Louisiana. He writes,

> I must confess that there seems to me room for grave doubt if the capital, labour, and especially the human life, which have been and which continue to be spent in converting the swamps of Louisiana into sugar plantations, and in defending them against the annual assaults of the river, and the fever and the cholera, could not have been better employed somewhere else. It is claimed as a great advantage of Slavery, as well as of Protection, that what has been done for this purpose never would have been done without it. It if would not, the obvious reason is, that the wages, or prospect of profit would not have been sufficient to induce free men to undergo the inconveniences and the danger incident to the enterprise. There is now great wealth in Louisiana; but I question if greater wealth would not have been obtained by the same expenditure of human labour, and happiness, and life, in very many other directions. (253)[30]

Only in a society that is based on slave labor does Olmsted have to ask this question, for in the North, he suggests, where the market not only directs movement but also provides its purpose and meaning, only profitable projects would be funded and would be able to acquire adequate labor resources.

Furthermore, according to Olmsted, only a free-market economy and the promise of individual reward will produce the efficiency necessary to a civilized society. Unlike free laborers, whose very freedom allows, even encourages, them to seek out the place where they are most needed and will thus earn the highest wages, slaves have no incentive to perform work but spend time instead seeking to avoid it. "[T]he constantly-occurring delays, and the waste of time and labour that you encounter everywhere," writes Olmsted, "are most annoying and provoking to a stranger" (102). Everywhere Olmsted notes a "want of system and order" (102), and, he claims, "You notice in all classes, vagueness in ideas of cost and value, and injudicious and unnecessary expenditure of labour by a thoughtless manner of setting about work" (103). "[C]ommercially speaking," Olmsted argues, southerners are "but in a very small part a civilized people"

(509), making explicit his equation of civilization with a well-developed free-labor economy.

One of the questions with which Olmsted seems most obsessed—"How do the middle classes of the two regions compare?"—highlights his prejudice. In fact, the question demands an answer favorable to northern society, for the very terms of the question presuppose the type of economy on which that society is built. Because he was prepared to see a largely aristocratic society in the South, Olmsted viewed nonslaveholders as "peasants," while the poor in the industrialized North he seems to have viewed as simply future members of the middle class. The only class in the North comparable to Virginia's lowest class would be the European peasant immigrants, argues Olmsted. However, he explains, in the North this group is "a transient class, somewhat seldom including two generations, and, on an average, I trust, not one. It is therefore practically not an additional class, but, overlooking the aged and diseased, a supplement to our lowest normal class" (557).[31] Thus, the movement taking place within the social hierarchy serves to eradicate poverty and improve the entire society.

For this reason, European immigrants seem to be more "American" than do inhabitants of the southern states, so the one group in the South that Olmsted admires are the German immigrants of Texas.[32] The Germans seem to provide the only hope for the establishment of a civilized society in Texas; in fact, Olmsted actively participated in the struggle by these German immigrants to make Texas a free state. "[I]f the Germans continued to flock into the country," Olmsted explains to a farmer he meets,

it would rapidly acquire all the characteristic features of a free-labour community, including an abundance and variety of skilled labour, a home market for a variety of crops, denser settlements, and more numerous social, educational, and commercial conveniences. There would soon be a large body of small proprietors, not so wealthy that the stimulus to personal and active industry would have been lost, but yet able to indulge in a good many luxuries, to found churches, schools, and railroads, and to attract thither tradesmen, mechanics, professional men, and artists. Moreover, the labourers who were not landholders would be intimately blended with them in all their interests; the two classes not living dissociated from each other, as was the case generally at the South, but engaged in a constant fulfillment of reciprocal obligations. I told him that if such a character of society could once be firmly and extensively established before the country was partitioned out into these little independent negro kingdoms, which had existed from the beginning in every other part of the South, I did not think any laws would be necessary to prevent slavery. It might be a slave State, but it would be a free people. (373–74)

This seems to be the course Olmsted desires for the South as a whole, with northern yeomen generally serving the role of the German immigrants here in Texas. Slavery would eventually die out, Olmsted believed, if the development of a free-labor economy were encouraged in the South. Because free labor is so much more efficient (and profitable) than a slave system, slave owners should gladly undergo the change from a slave to a free-labor economy, with slaves slowly earning their freedom once they had proven their ability to accept the responsibilities of freedom.

Slowly, then, the southern economy should be incorporated into the northern, and the development of a true civilization in the South could commence. Northern capitalism, then, would expand across the South (and the West as new territories joined the Union), and a national economy and culture would be established. Olmsted, then, is a prophet of a new economic order, a member, in Pratt's terms, of the "capitalist vanguard." Describing the colonization of South America by the nations of Europe, Pratt writes, "Ideologically, the vanguard's task is to reinvent América as backward and neglected, to encode its non-capitalist landscapes and societies as manifestly in need of the rationalized exploitation the Europeans bring" (*Imperial Eyes* 152). Within the United States, Olmsted's task was much the same, as he sought to connect the two primary regions of the nation and to bring about a consolidation of their economies, cultures, and societies.

Travel is essential to this project. To begin with, as Olmsted suggests throughout his journeys in the South, the American citizen is first and foremost a traveler. Unlike the inhabitants of the South, who either are unable to travel freely because they are enslaved or are forced by their inefficiency to drift without purpose across the southern landscape, the true member of the American republic would travel with purpose and direction, aiding the development of the nation by contributing to the circulation of ideas and values. Thus, travel is also integral to Olmsted's project because, as his texts illustrate, the ideology he represents enters the South through travelers like himself or the Texas immigrants whom he so admires. Olmsted and these immigrants thus become vehicles for the transportation of northern bourgeois ideology into the "cotton kingdom" he is trying to reform. Of course, the hallmark of this reformed society, Olmsted believes, will be the free and easy circulation of goods, ideas, and people. In a truly civilized and united American nation, Olmsted concludes, travel will not be determined by individual greed or aristocratic values but will support and define the very democratic ideals that inhabit these American travelers and citizens.

CHAPTER FIVE

Tourists with Guns (and Pens)

Union Soldiers and the Civil War South

What is an expeditionary force without guns? Tourists.

DEAN MACCANNELL

By far, the four years that witnessed the largest movement of travelers through various parts of the South were those between 1861 and 1865. During these years, approximately two million northern visitors, most members of the Union Army, traveled to or through at least one of the southern states. During this same period, many southerners, too—approximately 750,000 Confederate soldiers—traveled through the region and also visited briefly parts of Pennsylvania and other northern states. A surprising number of these soldiers wrote narratives or kept diaries describing their travels. E. Merton Coulter emphasizes this vast number of travelers and written accounts in the preface to his bibliography, arguing, "Not again until the twentieth century, if then, were there as many travelers in the South or in any other part of America as during the Civil War; for soldiers, who made up the vast majority, were travelers even though they did not have the opportunities for observation nor the viewpoints which charac-terize peacetime visitors. And never have as many travel accounts been written dealing with so short a period of American life as appeared on the Confederacy" (x). Only rarely had most of these visitors, the overwhelming majority of whom were young or middle-aged men, traveled outside of the vicinities immediately surrounding their birthplaces. Their beliefs about the American nation, and about the cultures, environments, and populations of regions other than their own, depended largely on newspapers, travel books and other texts, and the stories and stereotypes circulated within and among their communities. Even those who had been raised in one of the North's metropolitan areas had often had only limited exposure to people whose lifestyles were dramatically different from their own. These were frequently tourists with little prior experience of interregional or intercultural travel.

According to Shelby Foote, the simple fact of movement dramatically altered the ways in which many of these soldiers, Union and Confederate, thought about themselves and their larger communities. As Foote writes, "Whatever else the veterans brought or failed to bring home with them, and whether they returned to snugness or dilapidation, with or without back pay, bonuses, and pensions, they had acquired a sense of nationhood, of nationality. . . . They knew now they had a nation, for they had seen it; they had been there, they had touched it, climbed its mountains, crossed its rivers, hiked its roads; their comrades lay buried in its soil, along with many thousands of their own arms and legs" (1042). The travel most southerners experienced during these years encouraged in them a stronger sense of their regional identity, even creating a sectional patriotism where there had been little before the Civil War, according to Foote.[1] On the other hand, Foote explains, the Union soldiers who traveled through the South during this period emerged from the war with a transformed sense of the nation as a whole. Having engaged in a four-year war in order to keep their nation unified, these soldiers discovered through their movement across the entire country both the vastness and the diversity contained within its borders. Like the numerous travelers to the South before them, these soldiers shifted and enlarged their perspectives on their nation and their national identity, expanding their views of what the United States was and should be. Thus, one of the most significant aspects of the American Civil War was simply this movement of an unprecedented number of individual travelers, as well as the incontrovertible result that the movement of the Union Army had on the land and society through which it passed.

Like the numerous travelers before them who had visited the South and written about their experiences, Union soldiers confronted a region quite unlike their own. Through their writings they addressed many of the same themes, and used many of the same strategies, as had earlier travel writers. Many found the natural environment of the South surprisingly beautiful, describing it as a tropical Eden. Like Bartram, though, many thought nature in the South also dangerous, marveling at the fertility of the land while worrying about the disease, innumerable insects, and unbelievable heat. In addition, like Douglass and Northup, Union soldiers wondered about the rights of the slaves, many seeing the expansion of American citizenship as the primary goal of the entire war but others viewing the freed or escaped slaves merely as burdensome contraband. While few writers addressed the importance of the domestic situation as directly as did both Kemble and Jacobs, "home" was a particularly significant concept for almost all of these writers, for "home" came to mean not only the specific household from which these soldiers had traveled but also expanded to include their community, their state, the North, and the nation. Finally, many of the writers saw a different economy and work ethic in the South, describing much of what they encountered in terms that Olmsted had used in his newspaper series and books only a few years earlier.[2]

Despite confronting a number of the same themes and incorporating many similar descriptions, however, these Civil War soldier-authors reached dramatically different conclusions. Earlier writers traveled to the South to confront what they saw as the nation's internal "other," concluding that the region needed to be transformed in order to become sufficiently "American." These Union soldiers, on the other hand, frequently concluded that the South was (and should remain) part of the same nation, regardless of the differences they saw. In fact, the Union's basic position was that the South *was* part of the nation and should not be allowed to become "other." Most important for these travelers were the numerous connections and continuities between North and South. Confronted with the breakup of their nation, Union soldiers used their narratives to seek the reincorporation of the South into the national community and to identify and celebrate those aspects of the region that they found most "American." For instance, they frequently encountered cultural sites that spoke of a common national history, and many argued that the two regions shared both racial and cultural ancestries. In addition, the war was frequently defined as one between a particular group of southerners and the rest of the country rather than between North and South; for instance, many soldiers described their enemy as "secessionists" rather than as "southerners." Most narrators also included descriptions of the large number of "Unionists" in the South, many of whom were even members of the Confederate Army. The South was not so different that it should not be unified with the North, these authors concluded. Only a few rebellious members of southern society were irredeemably "other," so the war to preserve the Union was both justified and worthwhile.

Beneath the surface differences they encountered in the South, argued these writers, lay essentially the same values and goals. In order for them to conclude finally that the South was indeed part of the same nation as the North, however, many of these writers had to revise their ideas of the basic characteristics of their nation. Travel gave them that opportunity, as they confronted qualities clearly not their own and attempted to reconcile these qualities with the values and goals that they saw as forming the core of the American nation. In addition to giving these Union soldiers a broader sense of "America" and demanding from them a new definition of their nation, their wartime travel also made them more fully American, for they participated in one of the most basic of the country's freedoms, the right to travel. Of course, soldiers were frequently not in complete control of their movements, and their individual "travels" were not the only significant movement occurring during this time, for the overall movement of the Union Army was of supreme importance during the war. As much as the travels of these individual writers who sought to reincorporate the South into the country, the movement of the Union Army as a whole recreated the nation, as the land over which it passed and the society through which it traveled were both reconstituted as unconditionally American. If the movement of the army unified the nation militarily, then the travels of the individual soldiers solidified that union in their own minds and in the minds of those who read about their travels.

As Shelby Foote points out, perhaps the most telling marker of the shift toward a newly unified national identity was the change from the plural to the singular verb in relation to the subject "the United States." Before the war, Foote notes, in both this country and abroad, general usage demanded the plural verb: "the United States *are.*" After the war, on the other hand, the singular verb came into general use: "the United States *is*" (1042). This shift, I argue, came about largely because of the travel of the almost three million men and women who participated in the war, as well as the impact their travel had on countless Americans who experienced the consequences of the war directly but traveled primarily through the stories and descriptions provided by these many individual soldier-tourists. Essential, then, to the belief in a newly reunited American nation that became so prevalent after the Civil War was the simple fact of travel and the mass of literature that that travel produced.

Movement, of course, is one of the primary actions of armies, so the letters, diaries, and narratives written by Union soldiers during the Civil War record almost constant movement. Many of the accounts are finally little more than records of the almost innumerable villages, towns, and rivers these soldiers pass by or through. For instance, although his account is frequently rich in narrative detail, Elisha Hunt Rhodes twice provides long lists of the towns he has visited with the Union army. Under the heading "List of towns visited by the 2nd R.I. Vols since June 5th, 1861," on New Year's Eve of that year, Rhodes listed seventy-three towns in New York, New Jersey, Pennsylvania, Maryland, and Virginia, adding that they had also seen "many other towns whose names I have forgotten" (86). Rhodes later includes a list of sixty-three towns visited by his regiment between June 13 and August 1, 1863, averaging more than one new town each day. Of course, these soldiers frequently moved over the same territory more than once, so lists of new towns visited or rivers encountered might not provide an accurate description of the army's movements. For instance, entering Virginia in August 1864, Rhodes writes, "This made twenty-five times that I have crossed the Potomac since I entered the Army" (169). Many entries in these diaries resemble that of George Stephens when he writes, "Our regiment has been on the move ever since our arrival in Beaufort" (241). In fact, soldiers moved so constantly that they often had no clear idea of their location. Rhodes writes at one point, "I do not know exactly where we are" (81), and George Whitman writes in a letter home, "I believe I last wrote home from Lowell, but a fellow has to change about so often in this country, its hard work to remember where he was two days ago" (93). Of course, the lower the rank of a soldier, the less likely he would know the reasons for or the destinations of his movements.[3] As Rhodes explains, "We do not know our destination and do not care if it only means an advance and the close of the war" (51). Although he rose through the ranks rapidly, early in the war Rhodes was not in a position to question the army's movements, even when he believed they were misguided.[4] "I am well," he writes to his family, "but do not like the appearance of things. We are moving in the wrong direction it seems to me. Well, I hope it will turn out all right" (69). The role of the soldiers, particularly the privates, was not to think but to move, and move they did. "As I look back I am bewildered when I think of the hundreds of miles I have tramped, the thousands of dead and wounded that I have seen, and the many strange sights that I have witnessed," Rhodes wrote later (85).

One of the first lessons Rhodes and other soldiers learn upon entering the army is that they no longer have the freedom of movement they have enjoyed as civilians. For example, after Rhodes and a few other men have signed up but have not actually reported for full-time duty, the desire they feel for this freedom clearly clashes with the expectations of the commanding officer. "At night I wanted to go home," Rhodes explains, "but the Captain said that I was a soldier and must sleep in the Armory. So I slept upon the floor with a lot of other fellows and howled most of the night, much to the disgust of the Captain. As we were still citizens we claimed the right to do about as we pleased" (6).[5] Once fully enlisted, however, Rhodes realizes he can no longer expect to travel so freely. His journal entry of June 6, 1861, reads: "Went back to Providence and resumed drill in the Armory. No more could I control my own movements, and we were kept shut up in the Armory most of the day" (8). Unlike the previous night, Rhodes explains, "We did not howl all night either, for we found that as we were now soldiers regularly mustered into the U.S. Service we couldn't do as we pleased" (9). So, a few days later, when Rhodes attempts "to get a pass to

go to Pawtuxet," where his family lives, he fails to receive permission to travel
to his home and must instead stay with his regiment (10).

The army attempts to determine almost all aspects of a soldier's life by maintaining control over his or her physical movements. Soldiers are told not only
when and where to go, but also how they should move. Rhodes explains in one
entry, "Here we were ordered to reduce our baggage to the least amount possible
to get along with. We are to travel light hereafter" (105). In fact, the army claims
the right to control every action a soldier makes, as Rhodes comes to realize
when he is later in a position of command. After a soldier from a New Jersey
regiment is convicted of desertion, Rhodes attempts to be excused from attending the man's execution but does not succeed. In fact, Rhodes is commanded to
march his company past the dead man so that each soldier will learn the penalty
of desertion. "[A]s each Company approached the grave," Rhodes writes, "the
Captain gave the command 'Eyes right,' and each soldier was obliged to look at
the body" (199). The army cannot, however, control completely the response to
these orders, as Rhodes illustrates when he admits, "I was glad when it was over"
(199). Of course, the army has managed to curtail the further movements of the
soldier executed; his attempt to determine completely his own movements demanded that he desert the army entirely, but since he was recaptured, the army
did bring him back under its authority.

Nonetheless, the army does not always succeed in its attempts to control its
members. Like slaves, soldiers are frequently moved rather than provided opportunities to travel; also like slaves, however, soldiers regularly use their forced
movements for their own ends. While soldiers may be expected to move in a
certain manner, they frequently decide to travel according to their own priori-
ties or wills. The soldier from the New Jersey regiment disobeyed his orders and
traveled away from the scene of fighting. Because self-directed movement is so
threatening to military discipline, the punishment for such travel is generally
swift and severe. Desertion, the most extreme form of individual travel in which
a soldier can engage, has therefore traditionally brought about the execution
of those who are caught. However, severe punishment becomes difficult when
more than one soldier decides to travel, as when a company retreats in disregard
of direct orders. For example, describing the Union Army's advance on Richmond, Virginia, Rhodes writes, "The Rebels came into our rear and fired into
us from three sides of a square. The way we did leave! Everybody travelled as fast
as possible. Many were captured, but I came out all right" (139). Of course, an
army does sometimes command soldiers to retreat, but it seems clear here that
Rhodes and his fellow soldiers have their own safety foremost in their minds.

Soldiers do not travel (rather than move) only when they act in direct contra-
diction to their orders.[6] Nonetheless, because much of the movement in which
they participate is not determined by their individual wills, soldiers are rarely
viewed as tourists. The Union Army did allow a certain freedom of movement,
however, and many soldiers spent their free time traveling throughout the regions in which they found themselves. At least during their free time, soldiers
regularly acted the part of tourists. Even when they were moving as a unit,
though, many soldiers took notice of the surrounding countryside or stopped to
speak with people they met. As Thomas Clark argues in his foreword to *Travels
in the Confederate States*, "Soldiers did not necessarily give up their powers of
observation just because they were being moved about as involuntary travelers
under the dictates of military discipline" (vii). In a sense, these northern men
were travelers any time their full attention was not directed toward the goal the
army had given them. That is, travel was at times simply an attitude toward
their surroundings as much as a separate journey for their own pleasure. During the Civil War, then, soldiers participated in a complex, constantly shifting
combination of movement and travel, both as individual soldiers and as members of companies, regiments, and battalions. Because they were tourists who
observed their environment carefully, at least on occasion, the writings they
created provide rich illustrations of the search for answers to those questions of
most importance to the distressed nation, as narratives by travelers through the
South have done since before the founding of the American republic.

As Clark suggests, many Union soldiers paid close attention to their surroundings, for they were frequently moving through territory new to them. On
route to his training outside of Washington, D.C., for instance, Rhodes takes advantage of the journey to look at the new scenery he is passing. "We arrived this
morning in New York," Rhodes explains, "and as I had only visited New York
once before I enjoyed the sail up to the city" (11). George Whitman does not receive as much pleasure from his movements, but he, too, observes with interest
the surrounding environment. "Well[,] Walt," Whitman writes to his brother,
"We had rather a tedious journey way down there in Tenn (two weeks steady car
riding aint much fun I tell you) but then we saw considerable of that part of the
Country" (115). In fact, away from the fighting, many troop movements seem
to take on the appearance of travel tours, particularly in the early months of the
war when the people of the North believed the war would be over quickly. "The
weather is warm and the scene is delightful," Rhodes exclaimed. "The ships are
gaily decorated with flags, and it looks more like a pleasure excursion than an
army looking for the enemy" (53).

Even when the army itself was not advancing or otherwise moving to a new location, soldiers were regularly allowed to wander through their surroundings on their own. Near the nation's capital, Rhodes writes, "Orders have been issued to allow the soldiers in camp to visit Washington often. This order will be popular" (46). Rhodes explains, "We have time to visit the interesting points in the city, and I have a horse that I can use at pleasure: I often take rides out to the camps and begin to feel quite at home upon an Army horse" (41–42). On their way back to Washington, D.C., after the surrender of the Confederate Army three years later, Rhodes and his men are given the opportunity to visit the former Confederate capital: "One fourth of our men are allowed to visit Richmond daily, and in this way all of the soldiers will have a chance to see the late Rebel Capital" (233). Rhodes believes his men deserve the freedom to travel through the Confederate city, since their bravery had contributed to its downfall as the capital of the rebellious region: "I think that this is right for the boys have earned the right to see the city captured by their valor" (253). In a sense, they have fought for their own freedom as well as that of the slaves. Because they have performed particularly well as soldiers, they are rewarded with increased freedom of movement.

Rhodes himself spends much of his spare time during his four years in the Union Army traveling out of his camp and visiting friends in neighboring regiments. In fact, Rhodes seems to become impatient when he is forced to remain in one location for an extended period. He especially dislikes marching, when he is required to move but not able to draw nearer the enemy. In addition, when he stays in one locale, he often becomes bored with the surrounding countryside because it offers no novel sights, as he explains in October 1861: "I am getting weary of marching orders and wish that we could move, for we have been in Camp Brightwood for two months, and I know every tree within two miles of camp" (36).[7] In fact, Rhodes takes such pleasure from his short journeys that he welcomes one promotion partly because it provides him more freedom to travel. Even though he generally refuses to ride in an ambulance because, he says, "I prefer to walk with my men" (121), Rhodes has no reservations when offered the opportunity to acquire a couple of horses. "The Colonel offered to make me Adjutant or Captain just as I pleased. As an Adjutant is allowed two horses and is a member of the Regimental Staff I decided in favor of the horses. So good bye sore feet for sometime to come," he rejoices (123). Once he has his two horses, Rhodes takes every chance he can find to ride about the countryside. After buying "a fine bay horse with a white mark on his face," that can "run like a deer" (124), for instance, Rhodes enjoys "a fine ride today in search of flowers" (134). A year later, Rhodes is still taking pleasure excursions, although he has acquired a new horse. "My mare Katie is a beauty," he writes, "and I enjoy the rides both on duty and for pleasure which I take every day" (174). Throughout his remaining time in the Union Army, Rhodes seems to spend as much time as possible in the saddle exploring the countryside around his various camps. Thus, although he has an increasing amount of responsibility as he is promoted through the ranks, Rhodes values his ability to travel through these regions and observe the natural and cultural environments in which he finds himself. After all, with the increased responsibility Rhodes faces as an officer comes a certain increase in the amount of travel, in contrast to movement, he is allowed. Like all Union soldiers, enlisted and officer, Rhodes moves according to the commands of his superiors but also takes opportunities to travel as frequently and as widely as he can. Like most soldiers, Rhodes travels within the confines of the Union Army's regulations, so he does not travel with complete freedom. Still, travel he does.

Not surprisingly, the texts that grow out of the travels made by Union soldiers describe a countryside, a society, and a culture quite different than the ones from which these soldiers came. Many of the distinctions noticed speak positively of the region these travelers are encountering. Camped outside of Savannah, Georgia, for instance, George Pepper remarks that the cemeteries "merit the particular notice of the traveler" (287). Several pages later, Pepper again interrupts his descriptions of the battles he has witnessed to discuss at more length the positive qualities he has discovered in this southern city. He writes, "Savannah is indeed a most captivating city, and its attractions have left imprints on the mind which are seldom forgotten. Let us give a hasty glance at a few of the public and private characters" (293). Several full pages of description follow in which Pepper elaborates on what he finds most admirable about the architecture and society of Savannah.

Elsewhere in the region, Elisha Rhodes was discovering the charms of Virginia, noting, "I enjoyed the trip to Manassas Gap very much. It is the most romantic place I ever saw" (112). Some of the positive characteristics Rhodes describes, however, have been eradicated by the war, so the beauty is more in the past than the present. For example, Rhodes explains, "The plantations as a rule are deserted but show that this was before the war a delightful country" (59). Even those parts of the South that are not as beautiful as others hold a fascination for Rhodes and others because of the insight they can provide into the culture of the region prior to the war. After the end of the war, for example, Rhodes remains in Virginia for a short period to help settle disputes and take care of other war-related matters. He finds the time quite interesting, suggesting, "This life reminds me of *Uncle Tom's Cabin.* Many of the ex-slaves are at work, and this gives us a chance to watch plantation life. I cannot say that I admire it very much, for it seems to be a lazy sort of living. The ladies dress in old styles but seem to be educated" (231). Again, Rhodes finds the beauty or the interesting qualities more historical than contemporary. Of course, the beauty of some areas has been destroyed by Rhodes and his men themselves. Of one city in Virginia, Rhodes remarks, "When we reached Ream's station we found quite a village with a good depot, fair dwellings, work shops and well cultivated gardens and fields fenced in. When we left nothing remained but smoking ruins, trampled fields and a rail road useless for some days" (158). In a sense, then, Rhodes seems to be romanticizing somewhat the past of the region as he is in the process of destroying that past and reconfiguring its present and its future, or writing an elegy for the Old South as he works to incorporate a new South into the society of the entire nation.

Robert Shaw, too, finds much of interest in the South, although, like many writers on the war, he tempers his positive descriptions with more negative ones. "There are a great many fine places between here & Charlestown," he writes, "but the houses generally seem shabby inside" (16). Like Fanny Kemble, Shaw suggests that the appearance of southern wealth and beauty is only a surface feature of the society, for the attractive facades often hide "shabby" interiors. These are not homes, Shaw suggests, but only beautiful shells. Thus, while some travelers found much to admire in southern society, the majority qualified any positive descriptions with remarks of a more negative nature.

Most Union soldiers, in fact, found the differences they encountered far more negative than positive. Northern soldiers often agreed with Olmsted's analysis that the South was a backward, uncivilized society in need of economic reform.[8] Like Olmsted, for instance, Rhodes frequently complains that the roads, especially in Virginia, "are in a horrible condition" (148), and Thomas Wentworth Higginson concurs with Olmsted's assessment of the southern work ethic. He suggests, as does Olmsted, that most improvements in the South result from "northern enterprise." In Jacksonville, Higginson notes, "The wharves were capacious, and the blocks of brick warehouses along the lower street were utterly unlike anything we had yet seen in that region, as were the neatness and thrift everywhere visible. It had been built up by Northern enterprise, and much of the property was owned by loyal men" (105). The continued immigration of northern workers (and soldiers) into the South will only continue to improve southern society, Higginson and other writers suggest. George Pepper says of Nashville, for instance, "Since the war, the arrival of Northern energetic, enterprising business men has given to the city a fresh appearance, and has galvanized into more active life the citizens of this spasmodic city" (16). Northern immigrants not only better the city with their improvements but also serve as models to inspire the less energetic citizens native to the city.

In a passage that could have come directly from *The Cotton Kingdom*, Alonzo Quint argues, "Free labor and slave labor *cannot* flourish together. Where industry is considered menial, it loses its vitality" (46). In another passage reminiscent of Olmsted's text, Pepper argues that much of the population of the South lives in wretched poverty, writing, "The poor of this section are as ignorant, filthy, and wretched as can be found anywhere in the world. They are the dirtiest people I ever saw" (271). William Burson, who suggests that the land is "almost a garden of Eden," argues that the problem is not laziness but greed, agreeing with Olmsted that slavery destroys the land and corrupts the slaveholder. "The blighting curse of slavery was manifested everywhere," Burson writes. "Numerous were the farms one could see that had been worn out by avaricious slaveholders in trying to get the last cent's worth out of both land and slaves" (78). Because of the greed and inefficiency inherent to the institution of slavery, Burson adds, the South has not progressed as rapidly as the North: "How different, thought I, is the North from the South in point of improvement. The Southern people were using farming utensils that had been laid away by the North for fifty years" (78). For Burson, the South is a society of the past and is being left behind as the rest of the nation progresses and advances.

The poverty and lack of progress in the South is frequently represented as un-American, reminding some observers of Europe more than of their own nation. John William De Forest writes, for instance, "The poverty of the once flourishing city of New Orleans is astonishing. I have seen nothing like its desolation since I quitted the deserted streets of Venice, Ferrara and Pisa. Almost the only people visible are shabby roughs and ragged beggars. Many poor Irish and Germans hang about our regiments begging for the refuse of our rations" (qtd. in Masur 81). The few people De Forest does encounter must not be American but rather Irish or German, and the city reminds him of the desolation of aristocratic European cities rather than of the bustle of the democratic cities of the American North. George Whitman, who once suggests, "The Villages we have passed through are the most God forsaken places I ever saw" (73), finds that he is glad to arrive once again in Annapolis, where he writes, "I am very glad to get back to a civilized country" (112).

Higginson not only finds southern society and culture poverty stricken but is also generally unimpressed with the natural environment.[9] Having set up his camp on one of the Georgia Sea Islands, Higginson writes,

I look out from the broken windows of this forlorn plantation-house, through avenue of great live-oaks, with their hard, shining leaves, and their branches hung
with a universal drapery of soft, long moss, like fringe-trees struck with grayness.
Below, the sandy soil, scantily covered with coarse grass, bristles with sharp pal-
mettoes and aloes; all the vegetation is stiff, shining, semi-tropical, with nothing
soft or delicate in its texture. Numerous plantation-buildings totter around, all
slovenly and unattractive, while the interspaces are filled with all manner of wreck
and refuse, pigs, fowls, dogs, and omnipresent Ethiopian infancy. (8)

For Higginson, few aspects of the southern environment are comforting or alluring. Beyond the soft moss hanging on the trees, all of the flora is stiff, hard,
and coarse. The only color he mentions is the gray of the moss, hinting that even
that plant has a certain metallic quality, perhaps suggestive of both bayonets and
Confederate uniforms. An integral aspect of the natural environment for Higginson is also the dilapidation, filth, and excess he associates with the institution
of slavery—the tottering plantation, the animal refuse, and the countless slave
children.

George Stephens, also stationed on the southeastern coast, finds the landscape almost completely desolate. Morris Island, he writes, "is so barren that
you cannot find as much as a gypsum weed growing. Our situation is almost
unbearable. During the day the sun is intensely hot, and this makes the sand
hot; so we are sandwiched between the hot sun and the hot sand" (252). Still, the
evenings are pleasant, so at night, especially, Stephens believes "Morris Island
beach the most magnificent on the whole Atlantic coast" (252). For Stephens,
the South alternately becomes heaven and hell, in an inverted equation in which
light is punishing and darkness refreshing and restorative.

In contrast, De Forrest, encamped near New Orleans, never finds relief from
the heat. According to him, "There is no letup, no relenting, to the heat. Morning after morning the same brazen sun inflames the air till we go about with
mouths open like suffering dogs. Toward noon clouds appear, gusts of wind
struggle to overset our tents, and sheets of rain turn the camp into a marsh, but
bring no permanent coolness" (qtd. in Masur 85). In addition, he writes, "It is
a land moreover of vermin, at least in this season" (85). "Flies are thicker than
in Egypt," he continues, "and mosquitoes thicker than in Guilford" (89). Afterward stating that his regiment had not yet been under fire, De Forrest quickly
corrects himself: "No, I am mistaken: we did know what it was to suffer; to
wilt under a Southern sun, and be daubed with Louisiana mud; to be sick by
hundreds and die by scores" (90). Thus, for De Forrest, the unbearable climate

and the unrelenting assault by southern insects were enemies as dangerous as the Confederate Army itself.[10]

Most northern observers, however, found at least some aspects of the natural environment in the South beautiful. Before confronting the onslaught of vermin on shore, even De Forrest thought the landscape worthy of acclaim. Sailing to his post in the city, De Forrest writes, "We had a charming sail from Fort Jackson to New Orleans through scenery which surpasses the Connecticut River valley and is not inferior to that of the Hudson, though quite different in character" (80). Higginson, too, occasionally finds the lush southern flora appealing. He describes his experiences on St. Simon's Island as follows:

> When we afterwards landed the air had that peculiar Mediterranean translucency which Southern islands wear; and the plantation we visited had the loveliest garden, though tangled and desolate, which I have ever seen in the South. The deserted house was embowered in great blossoming shrubs, and filled with hyacinthine odors, among which predominated that of the little Chickasaw roses which everywhere bloomed and trailed around. There were fig-trees and date-palms, crape-myrtles and wax-myrtles, mexican agaves and English ivies, japonicas, bananas, oranges, lemons, oleanders, jonquils, great cactuses, and wild Florida lilies. (67)[11]

Both soldiers perhaps find the landscape most beautiful as they are first encountering it, for after having experienced the heat for several days, they seem to change their opinions of the environment. Thus, the same tropical climate that produces such unbearable heat and innumerable "vermin" can also provide benefits to the region. Much of the South, these writers acknowledge, contains a dazzling array of plant and animal life, a characteristic of southern nature that is both charming and threatening. As these men come to understand, much of the South, as Rhodes says of "a fine section of Virginia," is "very fertile" (230), a quality that can produce beauty of an almost tropical character but can also encourage an excess that seems to destroy as much as it creates.

The mountains of the South draw special comment from many of the soldiers who served in a theater of the war that provided them access to the Appalachians, and few feel as threatened by the environment as those who served further south or along the coasts. George Pepper writes, for instance, "The smile of heaven has fallen nowhere more softly and sweetly than it has fallen upon Kentucky" (12). Like other commentators, Pepper makes only positive comments about the environment, but he also argues that southern society has ruined what nature made so beautiful. According to Pepper, "Kentucky is a State for which nature has done everything and men nothing. Her fertile soil and genial climate, her immense forests of timber and boundless pastures—are some of the advantages which might make it the bode of a numerous, prosperous and happy people" (12). Despite failing to take full advantage of their land, however, the people of Kentucky have benefited, for "[t]he healthiness of the climate is seen in the vigor, robust manhood and physical beauty of its sons," writes Pepper (12). Likewise, George Stephens finds the land beautiful but the people at fault: "The country bordering on the river is beautiful; nature has done everything for it, but a cursed institution has blighted it. There is not a country in the world where nature has been more lavish with its blessing, and yet it is forsaken, worn out, almost a wilderness" (25). Most Union soldiers, however, simply gaze bewildered at the beauty of the mountain scenery. According to Edward Ripley, one valley he views "is perfectly magnificent, rich and well cultivated, splendidly watered and well wooded" (11). At times, the landscape seems almost too beautiful to be real. According to Rhodes, the scenery near Harper's Ferry "was delightful and reminded me of stories of fairy land as we looked off into the valleys. Little villages with white church spires were seen in all directions" (73). In fact, according to George Pepper, the southern mountains are so magnificent that they rival the Alps and would make an ideal tourist destination. According to Pepper, one portion of Tennessee is "denominated *par excellence* the Switzerland of America" (27). Because of the landscape of the southern mountains, Pepper argues, "No citizen of America can be justified in traveling to Italy and Switzerland in search of beauty and rugged mountain grandeur, until he has visited this northern region of Georgia" (27). "From the summit of Lookout," Pepper boasts, "a glorious view is presented; here the tourist may observe at one glance, the mountains of four States" (28).[12]

Pepper's desire to remake Lookout Mountain, the scene of several bloody Civil War battles, into a national tourist destination is appropriate given his belief in the link between the North and the South provided by the mountains. "The vast chain of the Appalachian Mountains, which commences in the State of New York," Pepper explains, "terminates in Georgia, sixty miles South of its northern boundary" (33). Thus, the mountains serve as a testament that the Union should be preserved. Rather than simply providing beautiful landscape through which to march or producing annoying insects with which soldiers must contend, Pepper claims, nature proves that the North and the South are in essence one. According to Pepper,

> Nature, in her sublime economy, foreseeing the grand destiny of the Republic, piled up mountains high and interminable, but left a narrow valley between, when

time was in its infancy, to be another link in the golden chain that binds the States of the Union. Man in his madness may attempt to deface the beauties of nature, but here the great Architect of the Universe has stamped in living letters the word Union, on every created object, bid these august mountains to be friendly, the rivulets to lave their alternate sides, and the birds to woo their mates across the narrow valley, and forever to sing the song of peace and union. (36)

The South becomes almost a park for northern visitors in Pepper's description, as he recreates himself and his fellow soldiers as the first wave of sightseeing tourists. While the environment may be slightly unfamiliar to Pepper, its unique characteristics do not differentiate South from North but come to prove that the South must exist in a friendly, yet subservient, relationship to the North.

Even more than the mountains, Alonzo Quint argues, both American nature and the constructed features of the American landscape illustrate the union between the two regions. "Our country's coasts, its rivers, its mines, its roads, its telegraphs, demand that it be one" (47), Quint writes. Not only the natural environment links the two regions but also those features of the landscape constructed by the members of the republic; not only mountains and rivers but also roads and telegraphs join North and South. In constructing the communication and transportation networks that link the various parts of the nation, Quint suggests, Americans have only respected that law that the entire natural environment illustrates: North and South are one. This desire to join the two regions is common in many of these Union narratives, and writers frequently focus much of their narratives on those connections between the two regions and the qualities that North and South share.

A common ancestry, racial, cultural, and historical, was one of the primary links posited by these writers, as they attempted to show that southerners were essentially the same peoples as inhabited the northern states. For instance, George Pepper remarks of Tennessee, "The original inhabitants of this State were chiefly emigrants from Pennsylvania. The ancestors of these people were generally of the Scotch nation, some of whom emigrated to Ireland, thence to America. A few German and English were intermixed" (25). George Stephens, traveling through Virginia, visits a church graveyard where he sees the graves of "the forefathers of the village," with some tablets "dating back as far as 1706" (27). Stephens attempts to suggest both a common racial ancestry and a historical heritage, reminding his readers of the colonial period the two regions share. Newton Curtis points to a similar heritage, arguing that he has been able in the South to visit scenes from the nation's colonial past: "We passed over territory which recalled many interesting incidents connected with the Colonial and

Revolutionary periods." He explains, "At Mechanicsville, we came to the scene of a most important event in the history of the Jamestown colony. . . . It was here, or near this place, on the 16th day of December, 1607, that Captain John Smith was captured, while in search of corn for the colonists of Jamestown" (106). Curtis proceeds to remind his readers of Smith's story, recounting how the Native American maiden Pocahontas had shielded the Englishman Smith from death by interceding on his behalf. This story is important to the history of both North and South, Curtis suggests, because the essential incidents of their pasts are the same.[13] He also describes important national figures who had settled in the area. According to Curtis, "One of the most interesting characters in that part of Virginia, was George Mason; he was a typical representative of an old and distinguished family which, from the early colonial days, had furnished in every generation one or more occupants of important official positions in the State or Federal governments" (61). As with John Smith, George Mason becomes in Curtis's text a figure who is central to Virginia's, and thus the South's, history but also is represented as having contributed greatly to the Revolutionary government and to the colonies' fight for independence. Both Smith and Mason testify to the common ancestry the two regions share and suggest that the nation's identity may have grown out of southern roots.

The use of Revolutionary historical sites is perhaps the most notable strategy in a number of these Civil War accounts for linking the North and the South. According to Curtis, for instance, the house presently inhabited by the wife of Robert E. Lee has more historical than contemporary significance. "It attracted much attention on account of the Colonial and Revolutionary memories which surrounded it," Curtis explains; "here Washington had courted and married Mrs. Martha Custis" (105). Elisha Rhodes, too, finds significance in the house, explaining, "This is historic ground for in yonder house George Washington was married" (58). Many other soldiers are reminded of the founder of the American nation while they travel through Virginia, but it is frequently Washington's home, Mount Vernon, that draws the most comment. According to George Stephens, "We passed Mount Vernon—the bells of the fleet tolling. The tomb lies in the midst of a clump of firs just south and a little below the house; the mansion and the grounds are nearly as they were left by Washington, and the whole looks down upon the river, calling upon the passer-by for a thought upon the great man whose dust lies beneath the fir trees" (25). Mount Vernon, argues Stephens, is of national importance for a number of reasons. For one, it was the home of the nation's founder, as Stephens does not need to remind his readers, and it has been preserved as Washington had kept it in order to give later generations a glimpse into the life of this famous American. Even more important, however, Mount Vernon is now the resting place of Washington's remains. This Virginia soil, Stephens tells his readers, has become sacred because it serves as the burial ground of the republic's first president. Thus, the site calls forth not only the bells of the fleet but also private meditations on the "great man" by innumerable individual members of the Union Army.

Of course, not only those sites in the South associated with George Washington are found to be historically significant by these Union travelers. For Curtis, the entire city of Williamsburg speaks of the nation's glorious past and its promising, united future. Encamped near the city, Curtis exclaims,

> Williamsburg, Virginia! What memories were awakened by its sight! This ancient city, incorporated in 1632, with a population which has never exceeded that of many of our modern villages, had been the scene of more important events in Colonial and Revolutionary times than any other town or city in the colonies. Here was founded, in 1692, by royal charter, the second college in America: the College of William and Mary. On its rolls were to be placed the names of Washington, Jefferson, Madison, Monroe, John Marshall,—in fact, all of the leading men of the South, who rendered conspicuous service in winning our National Independence and in establishing a government which has proved the most permanent and the best yet devised for the welfare and happiness of its citizens. (152)

As Washington's tomb and home are worthy of preservation and reverence, so, too, should Williamsburg be celebrated and honored for the central role it played in securing the freedom of the American colonies. Williamsburg's citizens, Curtis argues, the "leading men of the South," were essential members of the emerging national government who designed and served the American republic from its very founding.

Elisha Rhodes views Richmond in a similar light, but he seems to urge the American people to rescue the city from its appropriation by the Confederacy. As he is stationed near Richmond after the end of the war, Rhodes writes, "We then took a look at the Capitol which sheltered the Rebel Congress and whose walls heard much treasonable talk. The Capitol stands in a fine park in which is a famous statue of Washington. Jefferson, Mason, Clay, and Patrick Henry stand guard over it. Here under the eye of Washington treason was plotted and traitors made their plans" (232). Again, this site has more historical than contemporary significance, although Rhodes argues that the Capitol had to be saved from the grasp of a traitorous mob. The treason of the Confederate leaders seems even more treacherous to Rhodes having been planned and discussed under the gaze of the nation's founders. The area is doubly significant now that the rebellion has ended, Rhodes suggests, for it has importance both to the Revolutionary and Civil Wars. "The road to Richmond will take us through the country that is now historic," Rhodes states, "and we shall get an idea of the inside of the late southern confederacy" (232). Now, in addition to the Capitol, the entire city and its surroundings are a part of the nation's past, speaking even more loudly of its destiny as a united republic.

According to many soldier-travelers, however, the two regions are not only tied by a common past, since many current inhabitants of the South share concerns with their northern brethren about the destiny of the nation and the possibility of a united future. That is, many people in the South sympathize with the Union and fervently desire a peaceful reconciliation between the northern and Confederate states. Of course, many writers note, the slaves and former slaves of the South hope for a future in which they will be free citizens of the united nation. As a result, Union troops frequently receive assistance from these southerners. As Solomon Northup had anticipated years earlier, few slaves do anything to protect the southern way of life, according to accounts. In *Twelve Years a Slave*, Northup claims, "[T]here are not fifty slaves on the shores of Bayou Boeuf, but would hail with unmeasured delight the approach of an invading army" (190). One of Northup's readers would in fact later help liberate the area and indeed receive the welcome Northup had promised. William Root was a second lieutenant under General N. P. Banks when his regiment moved in to occupy the area described in Northup's narrative.[14] De Forrest apparently agrees with Northup, explaining, "As to the Negroes, they are all on our side, although thus far they are mainly a burden" (qtd. in Masur 83). Of course, many former slaves were anything but a burden, especially once the Union Army began to accept them as recruits. Both Robert Shaw and Thomas Higginson commanded highly decorated units of troops made up of free black northerners and former slaves. Like many other Union soldiers, Elisha Rhodes became convinced of the excellence of African American soldiers after seeing them in action, stating, "I have not been much in favor of colored soldiers, but yesterday's work convinced me that they will fight. So Hurrah for the colored troops!" (155). George Stephens recognized the slave not as a burden but as a fellow fighter striving for justice. He writes, "When the Union soldier meets the negro in the enemy's country he knows him as a friend and asks him to strive for freedom in spite of fugitive-slave laws, proclamations and orders" (204). Susie King Taylor, whose husband, a former slave, was in a Union regiment, argues forcefully that Union soldiers in the South benefited greatly from the assistance of the slave population. Years after the end of the war, Taylor hoped to remind her readers of the contribution women had made during the war, writing, "There are many people who do not know what some of the colored women did during the war. There were hundreds of them who assisted the Union soldiers by hiding them and helping them to escape. Many were punished for taking food to the prison stockades for the prisoners. . . . Others assisted in various ways the Union army" (67). Both men and women were fighting for the eradication of slavery, Taylor explains, and southerners both slave and free contributed to the Union victory. All were soldiers and members of southern society, regardless of race or gender, she argues.

There were also many white citizens in the South who felt sympathy with the Union Army, these narratives suggest. Of course, the Quaker inhabitants of the South did not participate in the fighting, a few explain, but they did contribute positively to the Union's war effort. According to William Burson, "All the Quakers with whom I conversed, claimed to be neutral, in reference to the war, but on a lengthy conversation with them, it was easy to discern that their sympathies were with the Federal Government" (66). Newton Curtis writes, "We found the members of the Quaker Meeting, who had settled in Virginia . . . an industrious, Union-loving people who abhorred war, but were ever ready to care for our sick, supply us with fruits and vegetables, and do all that was possible to promote our well-being" (64). These Quakers are southern citizens, Burson and Curtis remind their readers, but they are not aiding the rebellion.

Some entire cities, even regions, within the South were largely Union, according to many accounts. Arriving in Nashville, Tennessee, for instance, George Pepper exclaims, "What a visible change in the sentiments of the people. Three years ago, when our soldiers entered this haughty and fashionable city, they were greeted with imprecations and defiant looks. Now, peals of bells and salvos of cannon salute the brave veterans with a hundred thousand welcomes. The Union sentiment, pure and unconditional, has been growing wonderfully of late, in Nashville" (22).[15] In Raleigh, North Carolina, too, Pepper notes, "There are a large number of Unionists" (389). Not surprisingly, some soldiers find Union sentiment further north, in parts of Virginia. According to Alonzo Quint, "Our regiment was sent on the next day to occupy Harper's Ferry. We did so, and received a flag which the women had privately prepared to present to the first regiment of Union troops which should enter the town" (16).[16] But even in the Deep South, in Georgia, for instance, Union travelers encountered white people who were on their side. The widow of an eminent Georgian, Pepper explains, was "a splendid patriot" who "did everything in her power to prevent the secession of Georgia" (278). According to Pepper, "Herself and two accomplished daughters did everything in their power to make our weary boys as comfortable as possible" (278). And Burson speaks with a woman

who "would rather die in prison than see her brothers go into the army to fight
for Jeff. Davis and against the Union" (71). These women, too, were southerners,
the soldiers explain, as well as patriotic Americans.

According to a number of writers, however, not only the female portion of
the southern citizenry was sympathetic with the Union, and not only slaves and
women desired peace. Even many of the men fighting in the Confederate Army
believed in the Union cause and fought only because they had been forced into
service, several writers suggest. According to Taylor, for instance, when she was
a slave her landlord's son gave her reading lessons, until, in 1861, "the Savannah volunteer Guards, to which he and his brother belonged, were ordered to
the front under General Barton" (6). Although his brother was killed, Taylor
explains, her tutor "deserted over to the Union side, and at the close of the
war went to Washington, D.C., where he has since resided" (6). According to
Taylor, then, at least some Confederate soldiers were ready to desert at the first
opportunity.

Burson, captured and led to Andersonville prison, discovers that a number
of his captors are Union sympathizers: "As we marched along I had several opportunities of conversing with the guards, and I found a pretty strong Union
feeling existing among them. They had lost so many of their men by desertions
that neither regiment numbered more than three or four hundred; and for fear
they would all desert, they were sent to the rear to do provost duty" (28). Later,
Burson even speaks with some members of the Confederate Army who do fight
but claim not to aim at Union soldiers. "They declared that they could not fight
against their principles," he explains. "Though forced into several hard battles
in the vicinity of Richmond," he adds, these southern soldiers "said they always
shot so high that no one was ever hurt by their bullets, as they expected to be
killed themselves, and wanted to die with a clear conscience" (80). Burson also
discovers a secret organization with members throughout the South who all
work to dismantle the Confederacy. After his escape from Andersonville prison,
Burson attempts to flee to Knoxville, Tennessee, because he knows it is a Union
stronghold. Along the way he accepts assistance from a group of slaves, who
direct him to a "Union man." After providing the group of escapees directions
to the Union lines, Burson explains, the southern man "gave me to understand
that there was a secret organization in the South, whereby Union men were en-
abled to recognize each other, and said if we could get initiated into the order,
that we would have no trouble getting through to Tennessee" (64). In fact, this
man tells Burson, if he were to become a member of this "Union League," then
he would be safe even among the infamous "Home Guard," for, Burson writes,
"we would find many friends among them, who would assist us in making our

escape" (64). "This man," Burson concludes, "though dressed in rebel garb, was Union at heart, and I found that the Jeff. Davis government was losing more by such soldiers than it was gaining" (64). So, while there were many members of southern society who openly and actively supported the United States government, there were perhaps even more who worked behind the scenes to overthrow the Confederacy and reestablish the union of North and South, according to many of these Union writers. For many in the South, even those who appeared to be supporters of the Confederate government, union was far more important than secession.[17]

Because the Union soldiers who write these travel accounts so often find members of southern society professing Union sentiment, they frequently describe the enemy not in regional but in ideological terms. That is, many writers refer to the enemy not as "southerners" but as "secessionists" or "rebels." For instance, George Stephens writes, "The people were evidently strongly 'secesh,' although some of them professed to be glad to see us" (20). Robert Shaw describes a talk his quartermaster had with General Banks "about making use of the negroes against the Secessionists" (125). After his capture, Burson laments, "I was now a prisoner and in the hands of rebels who had no respect for the flag of their country—and but little regard for its defenders" (25). Even though "the conduct of the citizens toward us as we marched along was in almost every instance becoming," Burson writes of the group of Georgia militiamen who guard them, he says, "a meaner, more uncouth looking set of 'scalawags,' styling themselves soldiers, it had never been my privilege to look upon" (33). These men are the enemy, Burson suggests, not the regular citizens of Georgia. In fact, the enemy is not necessarily southern at all, argues George Pepper. "It is a well known fact, to most of the traveling public," he explains, "that there is a large number of English secessionists, who constantly denounce the administration and the present war for the destruction of the rebellion, and at the same time lauding up Jeff. Davis and his cohorts" (14). Pepper agrees with Burson and others, that the real enemy of the Union Army and the American people is not the South but various groups of radical secessionists.

According to Pepper, the slaveholders and those who support their aristocratic society are the true enemy of the American republic. "In accounting for this horrible condition of affairs," Pepper argues, "it is just and fair to ascribe it all to the mercenary slave-holders. They were haughty, improvident, intemperate and full of hate to the poor whites and blacks" (270). The war, according to these writers, does not pit one region against another but rather a superior culture against a decadent one. As Pepper suggests, the war is between democracy and aristocracy.[18] Southerners dislike democracy "and prefer the aristocracy of the South," according to Alonzo Quint (47). Most Confederates, suggests George Whitman, are wealthy, and the poor have not benefited from either the institution of slavery or the Civil War. Suggesting that east Tennessee had probably been beautiful prior to the war but was now quite desolate, Whitman writes, "The most of the large farmers and rich men seems to have gone off with the rebs, and the poor folks have about all they can do, to get bacon and corn meal enough to keep them alive" (116). This rhetoric also continues after the war, as Shelby Foote explains in his description of a speech given by the Reverend Beecher in April 1865 at the ruins of Fort Sumter. According to Foote, although Beecher "predicted that the common people North and South would soon unite to rule the country, he entertained no notion of forgiveness for those 'guiltiest and most remorseless traitors,' the secessionist aristocrats" (972). The guilty, Beecher believed, were the wealthy of the region, not the poor folk who rarely benefited from the institution of slavery but were forced to fight many of the battles.

Because they defined the enemy so narrowly, as "secessionists" or "rebels," many of these Union soldiers were able to establish close relationships with other members of southern society. Burson, of course, frequently receives assistance from southerners; once he is initiated into the Union League, he feels himself closely attached to a group of southerners and shares with them a set of values and goals. Friendly relations are even seen to arise between soldiers of the two armies. For instance, during a brief truce called in order to retrieve wounded soldiers, George Stephens finds, "They were all in good humor and lively, and the hours passed pleasantly, as the men from the two opposing armies chatted in the shade of some oak trees" (213). Alonzo Quint, too, describes friendly relations between the soldiers, at least occasionally: "On the opposite bank are rebel troops in plenty, with whom ours exchange various kinds of courtesies, sometimes with good-natured greetings, sometimes with crashing shot and bursting shell" (20). Susie Taylor explains that Confederate soldiers would not only talk with members of the Union Army but would even desert given the opportunity. "Some mornings I would go along the picket line," she writes, "and I could see the rebels on the opposite side of the river. Sometimes as they were changing pickets they would call over to our men and ask for something to eat, or for tobacco, and our men would tell them to come over. Sometimes one or two would desert to us" (25). For Taylor, Quint, Stephens, and others, these southerners are more like themselves than different. While they might temporarily be serving different governments, these current differences do not hide the fact of their common qualities and goals.[19]

Often the connections drawn are based on what are seen as similar class backgrounds. The poor of the two regions are seen to share a particular understanding, and both are often represented as fighting for democracy against the wealthy slaveholders. The deserters Taylor describes, for instance, join the Union cause because they "had no negroes to fight for" (25). Union officers, too, frequently establish relationships with members of the opposing army. For example, when his staff is traveling with five hundred Confederate prisoners, Edward Ripley welcomes to his staff a southern surgeon. Ripley writes of this man, "The Texan is a fine fellow. We have taken a decided liking for each other, and as there is no need of stirring up this troublesome apple of discord, politics, he is established in our family as one of us" (88). While he and this Texan may have their disagreements, Ripley suggests, they share enough to become close friends. Likewise, when he is an officer, Elisha Rhodes establishes fairly close relations with southerners, although he generally comes to know southern civilians rather than Confederate soldiers. Rhodes frequently dines in the homes of the southerners among whom he is encamped, especially after the end of the war, when he seems particularly eager to encourage these relationships. He seems to have become, because of his rank as a lieutenant colonel, equal to those southerners who have fairly high social status. As with poorer soldiers, these class-based links seem almost as strong as those uniting members of the same army. For instance, although Dr. Shore, a Virginian, had been a slave owner prior to the war, Rhodes manages to become quite friendly with him while camped near the doctor's home after the surrender of Lee. After riding with part of his staff to Dr. Shore's house to accept a dinner invitation, Rhodes writes, "We found him a true southern gentleman and very hospitable, while the ladies were very kind and pleasant. The dinner was enjoyed by we soldier people and was well served. After dinner a servant passed pipes with long reed stems to each of us. The people are really kind to us and try to make our life here pleasant. They send me flowers from their gardens, and I in turn furnish them with little luxuries which they have been deprived of for many a long month" (229). As with the other Union soldiers, Rhodes seeks to establish friendly relations with this group of southerners and in one way or another to become a part of their group and ensure that they become part of his. He focuses on his host's hospitality and the kindness of the ladies he meets. Both Rhodes and these southerners work to make the relationship mutually beneficial and cordial, ignoring or downplaying the bitterness or anger each might have felt.

In establishing connections with various groups of southerners, northern soldiers are seeking to define these people as part of the same population as themselves. These southerners, the soldiers seem to argue, are not "other" but are part of "us." Only radical "secessionists," "rebels," or "slave owners" are not truly American, they argue, for most people of the South hold values or possess characteristics essentially identical to those northerners hold or possess. Of course, the South and southerners are different, these narratives acknowledge. While speech patterns, social conventions, natural surroundings, or household environments may differ, however, the similarities between North and South are far more significant. Most southerners, for instance, believe in democracy and are opposed to the aristocratic slaveholders, according to many writers. On the other hand, officers often suggest that the manners and habits of the wealthy, even some who had owned slaves, are similar enough to those of the northern elite as to allow for mutual consideration and friendly relations. In addition, many northern soldiers suggest that former slaves have been friends with Union soldiers and should be considered fellow citizens of the American republic. These former slaves, soldiers frequently argue, are ready to become Americans. "The end of the war will be the end of slavery," writes Rhodes, "and then our land will be the 'Land of the free'" (215). By the end of the war, then, many northern commentators have come to believe that the United States could (and did) contain a greater variety of peoples, races, cultures, and environments than they had previously believed. Travel had convinced them of this fact. Moving through the North and the South with the Union Army, these soldiers had seen sights, encountered diversity, and traversed landscapes they scarcely could have imagined before leaving their homes. All of these—sights, sites, peoples, and places—constituted America, they concluded, and were part of their nation, recently defended and newly reunified.

These broadened imaginations and conceptions are illustrated by the wonder, amazement, and interest with which northern writers encountered new experiences. For instance, as Ambrose Bierce explains, for the numerous soldiers who had never traveled outside of the flatlands of the Midwest, the sight of mountains opened up entirely new beliefs about their world: "It was a strange country. Nine in ten of us had never seen a mountain, nor a hill as high as a church spire, until we had crossed the Ohio River. In power upon the emotions nothing, I think, is comparable to a first sight of mountains. To a member of a plains-tribe, born and reared on the flats of Ohio or Indiana, a mountain region was a perpetual miracle. Space seemed to have taken on a new dimension; areas to have not only length and breadth, but thickness" (4). Likewise, Rhodes begins to recognize the variety and diversity that form the United States when he arrives in the nation's capital for the first time, as Washington, D.C., comes for Rhodes to represent synecdochically the entire country. "Hurrah we are in

Washington and what a city!" he exclaims. "Mud, pigs, geese, Negroes, palaces, shanties everywhere" (12). Once accustomed to the city, Rhodes and his regiment move on to new ground. He writes, "We moved through Washington with crowds of people looking at us from the sidewalks and houses, and at last we reached Long Bridge and crossed into Virginia. It is my first visit to the Old Dominion and every object is of interest" (16). Over a month later, Rhodes is still finding himself in new territory. In one city in Virginia, Rhodes is reminded of the common colonial heritage of North and South but is also intrigued by the differences he finds: "I was much surprised at the appearance of Yorktown. We entered town through a gate in a fort built upon a bluff. There are not more than twenty houses in the village and some of these must have been built before the Revolutionary War for they are of the gamble roof style and all tumbling down. Passing through the main street we saw the old forts built by the British Army when it was besieged by Washington in 1781" (70). Although this Virginia city appears so different than those in his native Rhode Island, he is still within his own nation, he suggests, for this is land that George Washington won for his country. America, Rhodes realizes, is bigger, broader, and more varied than he had realized.

In addition to encouraging him to revise his beliefs about his country and to broaden the scope of his national vision, Rhodes's travels also allow him growth of a more personal nature. Rhodes is constantly confronted by novel experiences because of his movement across unfamiliar terrain and, in his particular case, because of his rapid promotion through the ranks. However, while Rhodes's set of personal experiences was broadened by the Civil War, he was not unique in the impact the travel had on his personal identity. Thomas Wentworth Higginson had already been a military leader before he took charge of the troops in his South Carolina regiment, but he had never before been among so many African Americans. As he explains, "Already I am growing used to the experience, at first so novel, of living among five hundred men, and scarce a white face to be seen,—of seeing them go through all their daily processes, eating, frolicking, talking, just as if they were white. . . . [N]or is it till the line of white officers moves forward, as parade is dismissed, that I am reminded that my own face is not the color of coal" (9). This experience is so unique for Higginson, in fact, that he almost loses his own identity and becomes someone other than who he is. Ambrose Bierce captures some of the wonder with which so many soldiers greeted their novel experiences with the war in his story "A Son of the Gods," where he writes, "How curiously we had regarded everything! how odd it all had seemed! Nothing had appeared quite familiar" (109). This novelty grows out of a number of factors, as these soldiers encounter new

environments, landscapes, cultures, and experiences, and are thus further transformed as American travelers.[20]

It is not only the Union soldiers themselves who encounter a variety of new
scenes and people during the war, however, for many people who accompanied these northern men also came across previously unknown aspects of their
country. "One of the darkey servants," Rhodes writes, "has never seen a river
before and called it a 'Right smart brook.' While watching a steamboat sail by
he said, 'Does dat dar wheel turn on de ground?' He also asked 'How they got
dot boat out of the water nights' " (154). Even though, according to Rhodes, "We
have had much fun with him" (154), this man's amazement at these new sights
was not a reaction with which Rhodes and his comrades were unaccustomed.
They, too, had been astounded and surprised by many of the characteristics of
the land as they traveled. Susie Taylor even experiences her own hometown in a
whole new way while traveling with the Union Army. "I remember, when going
into Savannah in 1865," she writes, Colonel Trowbridge "said that he had been
there before the war, and told me many things I did not know about the river.
Although this was my home, I had never been on it before" (46). Because of his
previous travels, Trowbridge, it seems, can offer Taylor new insight into her own
city. Like so many of the soldiers in her husband's regiment and in the entire
army, Taylor is offered a new perspective from which to view her world through
travel with the troops.

Thus, while the movement in which these writers participated during the
four years of war gave them an expanded vision of their nation, their travel also
served to make them more fully American, as they participated in one of the
freedoms on which the United States was founded. Thus, like William Bartram
and Hector St. John de Crèvecoeur, these soldiers proved their status as Americans in the exercise of their rights. Travel served as both symbol and proof of
that freedom and of their full membership in the American nation. Despite the
contrast drawn by Elisha Rhodes between soldiers and citizens, these Union
soldiers became fully functioning members of their society even as they traveled in order to define that country. By exercising their freedom to travel, they
also served as exemplary American citizens for those throughout the South who
were just coming to understand what membership in the republic might mean.
As much as they have enjoyed this freedom to travel, many suggest, so should
all citizens of the American republic feel free to travel throughout their newly
unified nation. Many of these soldiers would have applauded the sentiment expressed in the farewell speech by Colonel Trowbridge, the leader of the regiment
in which Susie Taylor's husband served: "The flag of our fathers, restored to its
rightful significance," he stated, "now floats over every foot of our territory,

from Maine to California, and beholds only free men!" (qtd. in Taylor 48).[21] Because the flag floats over the entire nation, Trowbridge suggests, Americans of all races now have the right to travel freely throughout that same space, for the flag serves as a sign of freedom of movement.

The travel of these countless individual soldiers and others was not the only movement deeply significant for the reunification of the American nation, however. Perhaps even more important was the overall movement of the troops of the opposing armies. After all, war is all about the occupation of territory by one army instead of another. Thus, the movement of the Union Army literally reconfigured the land over which it passed as American instead of Confederate. The landscape had threatened to become something other than American until Union troops occupied it and marked it as once again a segment of the United States. Susie Taylor illustrates this process clearly when she describes an island near their camp that is disputed territory. According to Taylor, "Between Barnwell and the mainland was Hall Island. I went over there several times with Sergeant King and other comrades. One night there was a stir in camp when it was found that the rebels were trying to cross, and next morning Lieutenant Parker told me he thought they were on Hall Island; so after that I did not go over again" (26). The island, it seems, is essentially American territory when the Union Army controls it. When it is, Taylor has the freedom to travel there, and she does not fear imprisonment or the loss of her rights. However, once the Union Army does not fully control the island, it is essentially no longer American territory. Were she to travel there once Confederate soldiers had made inroads, then she would be open to capture, imprisonment, enslavement, and the complete loss of those rights that she holds dear as a member of the Union and the American nation.

According to Abraham Lincoln, once the Confederate Army has surrendered, the issue of whether the southern states were in fact a separate country during the war is immaterial, as long as the nation as a whole has become fully unified again and the rights of all are respected. During his "Speech on Reconstruction," given within days of the end of the war, Lincoln states,

> We all agree that the seceded States, so called, are out of their proper practical relation with the Union; and that the sole object of the government, civil and military, in regard to those states is to again get them into that proper practical relation. I believe it is not only possible, but in fact, easier, to do this, without deciding, or even considering, whether these states have even been out of the Union, than with it. Finding themselves safely at home, it would be utterly immaterial whether they had ever been abroad. Let us all join in doing the acts necessary to restoring the

proper practical relations between these states and the Union; and each forever
after, innocently indulge his own opinions whether, in doing the acts, he brought
the states from without, into the Union, or only gave them proper assistance, they
never having been out of it. (699)

The South is now home, Lincoln argues, and the question of whether it or its
inhabitants have traveled abroad is of no consequence. Whether or not southern
territory was something other than the United States, Lincoln argues, is immaterial now that the Union Army has conquered the Confederates and overtaken
the land, as long as the people of the northern states now do all in their power to
ensure "proper relations" with their former enemies and present fellow citizens.

In the end, travel narratives by Union soldiers seem to have developed naturally
out of the long history of accounts by northern writers describing their experiences in the American South. For all of these writers, the travel experienced
and described not only served to expand their own subjectivity but also worked
to enlarge and redefine the nation in its entirety. If the American South, the internal "other" in the accounts of so many northern writers, has gradually come
to be identified, and to identify itself, with the United States, these accounts
certainly played a part in that transformation. While some accounts may have
played a larger or more fruitful part than others, the full mass of these narratives
perhaps became a force not to be withheld or denied. Accordingly, the narratives by Union soldiers can be seen to recapitulate the history of American travel
writing about the South as a whole.

   In addition, if tourists constitute an expeditionary force without guns, as
Dean MacCannell suggests, then perhaps these Union soldiers also illustrate
vividly the ideological work performed by all travelers (and tourists), especially
those with pens. Like soldiers, travelers reconfigure the land over which they
travel and about which they write as they seek to establish or confirm some type
of relationship with the cultural, social, geographical, or racial "other." Like an
expeditionary force, northern travelers in the American South cleared the ideological ground and prepared the region for the broader encounter with the
North that has been occurring ever since. While individual travelers and travel
accounts may have contributed in varying degrees to the South's gradual incorporation into the American nation, their true significance lies in the cultural
work the entire body of these accounts performed during the years between the
Revolutionary and Civil Wars.

Conclusion

[I]t is difficult to stay in one place when meditating on the issue of travel.

GEORGES VAN DEN ABBEELE

As I have argued throughout this work, travel literature played an integral role in the struggle to create a national identity. Between the Revolutionary and Civil Wars, numerous northern travelers headed south to investigate the region that was widely seen to constitute the primary barrier to a clearly unified national culture. While previous studies have investigated the function of travel narratives in the evolving understanding of the characteristics of this American nation, most of these works have defined "travel literature" very narrowly and thus included only those texts describing, for instance, leisure travel across national borders. But travel literature shouldn't be defined so restrictively, as individuals travel for myriad reasons and produce numerous types of text. Even when many of their movements are restricted by factors larger than themselves—slavery, the military, gender ideology—individual travelers have often been able to determine *how* or *why* they journey, if not *where* they are moved. As a result of these considerations, I have sought to broaden the parameters of "travel literature" and to analyze texts not frequently viewed within this generic category.

Of course, as much recent work with travel texts has argued, previous attempts to define "travel literature" have frequently depended on unstable or theoretically unsophisticated distinctions, but if the category is expanded too widely, "travel literature" is in danger of disappearing as a useful critical term. In fact, according to Glenn Hooper and Tim Youngs in the introduction to their recent *Perspectives on Travel Writing*, "The point to determine, therefore, is whether *travel writing* is really a genre at all" (13). It is not a distinct genre, they conclude; rather, "travel writing" should be thought of as "a collective term for a variety of texts both predominantly fictional and non-fictional whose main theme is travel" (13). That is, Hooper and Youngs believe the borders of "travel literature" territory should be enlarged even further than I have defined it in my own work, to include additional types of works, including obviously fictional texts.

While I am not ready to dispense entirely with "travel literature" as a distinct category, I do appreciate the benefits in using the travel paradigm to analyze a variety of texts, both nonfictional and fictional. For example, during the decades following the Civil War, the cultural work that had been performed by the texts of Bartram, Northup, Kemble, Jacobs, Olmsted, or the others I have discussed was perhaps continued most obviously by the vast amount of regional writing published, for the nation's most important literary magazines regularly featured regional fiction along with other travel pieces.[1] During the years between the Revolutionary and Civil Wars, northerners had turned to travel literature for information about the South, but their desire to understand more fully this "internal Other" was satisfied after the Civil War to an increasing degree not solely by the literature of travel but also by the writings of the nation's regional authors.

One of the most popular at the time was Mary Noailles Murfree, who, between 1884 and her death in 1921, published stories in a number of the nation's leading literary and cultural journals, including *Lippincott's* and *Atlantic Monthly*, and authored eighteen novels and six collections of short stories. Writing under the pseudonym Charles Egbert Craddock, Murfree introduced a host of colorful "backwoods" Tennessee mountain folk to the nation's urban readers, who eagerly consumed Murfree's literary offerings; *In the Tennessee Mountains*, published in 1884, "went through seventeen editions in its first two years" (Brodhead 118). Many of Murfree's tales, while not literally true, certain resemble travel literature and can be read productively in these terms.

Murfree's famous story "The Dancin' Party at Harrison's Cove," originally published by *Atlantic Monthly* in 1878 and later included in *In the Tennessee Mountains*, is exemplary of her early tales. The story is set in the southern mountains at a fashionable watering hole, in the log cabins of neighboring families, and along the mountain paths connecting these locales. Two groups are clearly delineated: the "mountain people" who live permanently in the area and the "summer sojourners" visiting "New Helvetia Springs" for a break from their city lives (Craddock 216). The narrator, who is never named, is obviously educated and purports to provide special information about both the area and the "native" inhabitants.[2] Of course, the speech patterns of these two groups differ dramatically. While the urban tourists and the narrator speak in formal, standard English, the rural characters' voices are represented in a barely comprehensible dialect.[3]

The central role of the tourist in this tale is not incidental. Although the numbers of both intranational and international tourists had been steadily increasing throughout the nineteenth century, tourism became especially popular in the decades following the Civil War, so this story reflected contemporary realities about Americans and travel.[4] The South was previously "other" for northern culture and society, but in Murfree's tale the postwar South has apparently become little more than a tourist destination, a playground or natural reserve to which the inhabitants of the North can retire when they require rest, relaxation, and diversion. Far from constituting a dangerous region to be understood and controlled, the South has become a safe space that nourishes and rejuvenates.[5]

This tourist figure is additionally significant, however, because local color stories replicate many features and themes of "standard" travel narratives: an outsider journeys through a geography and society not his or her own and then writes an account, published and consumed in a social and cultural arena not inhabited by those described within.[6] The similarities are not complete, of course; unlike in most travel narratives, which tend to place the narrator/author at the center of the text, the narrators of local color tales are often hidden from the reader's view, and these stories are generally read as fictional, unlike traditional travel narratives, which are primarily received as factually true.[7] Still, the tales do resemble traditional travel narratives, for the fictional elements in these stories have been seen to refer less to the information included about the setting or the people than to the details of the specific plot narrated. As critics of regional texts have pointed out, these stories not only entertained but also provided knowledge for a largely urban audience about those regions outside the nation's cities. Local color stories, then, are perhaps even more slippery than more obvious travel narratives in their blending of the fictional and nonfictional. Of course, distinctions can be drawn between regionalist fiction and travel writing, even if such distinctions are somewhat difficult to maintain, but interpreting the former in terms of the latter yields provocative results.

Like travel narratives, these stories perform cultural work; while the particular plots related might not be taken as true, they still provided readers with purportedly "true" information about spaces outside of their knowledge and also reflected the tensions, contradictions, and ideologies of the cultures that produced them. As Murfree's story illustrates, much local color writing addressed the continuing struggle for northern hegemony, rewritten as a search for national harmony. According to Brodhead, "This genre's great public flowering began with the Northern victory in the Civil War, in other words with the forcible repression of sectional autonomy in favor of national union and the legal supplanting of the locally variant by national norms of citizenly rights" (119). For Brodhead, these tales reflect the impact of economic forces rapidly unifying the nation. While these economic factors are undoubtedly important, regionalist fiction serves, too, to carry on the cultural work of antebellum travel literature. As with the travel literature throughout the nation's history, postwar regional writing shifts the contradictions of the national culture into one of regional and geographical difference; according to Amy Kaplan, "By rendering social difference in terms of region, anchored and bound by separate spaces, more explosive social conflicts of class, race, and gender made contiguous by urban life could be effaced" (251). Once again, problems central to the nation as a whole were shifted onto the South. And, once again, northerners headed south, to understand the nation's internal "other" and to exercise a fundamental American right: travel.

The interpretive result of re-viewing Murfree's story as a travel text suggests that one frustration of travel literature might, in fact, constitute its utility as a critical tool, for the problems, difficulties, and frustrations of travel literature as a genre represent, ironically, some of its primary strengths as a lens through which to view early American literary and cultural texts. Travel literature might be impossible to pin down in terms of particular conventions, characteristics, or subjects, but this very fluidity makes it a particularly useful critical tool, for looking at a wide variety of texts *as* travel narratives frequently provides insight into the cultures that produced these texts and those described within the texts. Thus, not just regionalist works but many texts not generally connected to travel writing should be read in terms of their connections to travel writing.

For example, numerous works generally read as nature writing need to be reread through the lens of travel writing, for although these texts focus on nature, travel is generally an essential element. The journals of John James Audubon or the works of John Muir certainly warrant investigation as travel pieces, even though neither was published during the lifetime of the author. John Muir's *A Thousand-Mile Walk to the Gulf* incorporates a number of the issues, themes, and metaphors of earlier travel narratives, and Audubon's journals clearly link his travels to those of William Bartram, for instance. But not only those texts describing the South need to be studied; for instance, *Walden* can productively be read as a travel narrative, despite the relative stasis of the narrator, particularly given that Thoreau's other important works, such as *A Week on the Concord and Merrimack Rivers*, *Cape Cod*, and *The Maine Woods*, revolve around the travels of the narrator. All of these texts are frequently read by ecocritics but only very rarely studied as narratives of travel.

In addition, much antebellum American fiction needs to be reexamined in light of recent critical and theoretical work in travel writing. Certainly, most critics would agree that *Typee* is a travel narrative, and many might grudgingly agree with analyzing *Moby-Dick* in these terms, but *The Scarlet Letter* or *The Blithedale Romance* should also be studied as travel texts. After all, both of these texts, too, involve the travels of at least one figure into the social and cultural worlds of a new group, and both texts were undoubtedly influenced by the travels and experiences of the author. The freedom to travel and the pleasures and insights afforded by such travel seem integral to many early American texts, so perhaps it is time to read far more major texts of American literature in the light of critical and theoretical work on travel and travel writing. That is, critics, too, should travel—theoretically, generically, critically, and methodologically.[8]

However, using the insights of those who study "travel literature" to analyze a variety of texts does not eradicate all generic distinctions, for travel texts are produced and received differently than other types of writing. If nothing else, travel writing's production and reception differentiate the texts I have included and discussed; all of the writers in this study made truth claims about their individual travels and the accounts they produced. Of course, later research might have pointed to inaccuracies (particularly in Bartram's account), and many were greeted with intense skepticism even when published. Still, travel these individuals did, across boundaries of many types—geographical, social, racial, ideological, rhetorical, and, of course, regional. As a result, their texts, too, have traveled—across the regions within the United States, across the national borders to other countries and continents, and across the years since their initial publication to eager readers in the present.

Notes

INTRODUCTION

1. Ironically, this increase in travel and apparent freedom came at a cost, according to James Buzard, who argues, "The greater freedom to travel, offered to a greater number, was real, but it was gained only by reconstructing 'freedom' within an infrastructural and cultural network that limited the actual field of choices" (47).

2. For information on southerners traveling north, see John Hope Franklin's *A Southern Odyssey: Travelers in the Antebellum North.*

3. For Susan-Mary Grant, this voice has been ignored in studies of American nationalism because of its predominance: "The northern ideology survived—albeit in a changed form—and because it survived, it has been ignored. It is too obvious, it is all-pervasive, it is America" (18).

4. Still, the critical work of postcolonial critics has been useful for understanding this relationship; two useful collections of essays have been Ashcroft et al.'s *The Post-Colonial Studies Reader* and Williams and Chrisman's *Colonial Discourse and Post-Colonial Theory: A Reader.*

5. Marlon B. Ross points to a similar disruption in the growth of nationalist sentiment: "Whereas growth, both temporal and spatial, implies natural continuity and preformation, like the predestined movement from birth to maturity or the form of the body predetermined by the enlargement of the cell, change and expansion are inherently discontinuous and disruptive. . . . [C]hange and expansion are distressing phenomena, disrupting the relation between past and present, between internal and external, between native and exotic" (56).

6. Studies of the culture of travel and tourism have also increased dramatically in recent years. See, for instance, John Urry's *The Tourist Gaze* or *Touring Cultures: Transformations of Travel and Theory,* edited by Chris Rojek and Urry.

7. Two signs of the critical attention travel writing currently enjoys are worth mentioning. One is the creation of the International Society for Travel Writing, which hosts a biannual conference devoted exclusively to travel writing. The second is the sheer volume of essay collections on and studies of travel and travel writing. Many of these collections focus on modern or contemporary travel literature; two of the more noteworthy include *Travellers' Tales,* edited by George Robertson et al., and *Temperamental Journey,* edited by Michael Kowaleski. On the other hand, *Travel Writing and Empire,* edited by Steve Clark, covers a vast time span, including essays on travelers from Hakluyt to Bill Bryson. Other useful recent studies not described elsewhere in this introduction include Dennis Porter's *Haunted Journeys: Desire and Transgression in European Travel Writing;*

Tourists with Typewriters, by Patrick Holland and Graham Huggan; Lynne Withey's readable *Grand Tours and Cook's Tours*; and Casey Blanton's *Travel Writing: The Self and the World*. Two texts that address travel itself more than travel writing but that nonetheless are useful guides are *Hosts and Guests*, edited by Valene Smith, and *Travel Culture: Essays on What Makes Us Go*, edited by Carol Traynor Williams. And Eric J. Leed, in *The Mind of the Traveler: From Gilgamesh to Global Tourism*, provides a useful overview of the figure of the traveler in his or her various journeys and manifestations throughout Western societies.

8. Certainly, other texts that looked at travel literature had been published prior to these. For instance, Foster Rhea Dulles published *Americans Abroad: Two Centuries of European Travel* in 1964. Like Dulles's book, however, these earlier texts are generally more historical studies than sustained critical investigations.

9. For more information on the impact that travel literature, especially the literature of exploration, has had on American literature, see William Spengemann's *The Adventurous Muse*; according to Spengemann, his book analyzes the "complex interrelations among New World travel-writing, European literature, and Romantic aesthetics on the development of American fiction" (3).

10. In contrast, James Buzard argues in *The Beaten Track*, "It should be clear that for the rhetorical purposes involved in distinguishing tourists and travellers, negative value did not attach so much to any particular form of transport, but rather to whichever form seemed at that moment to threaten the older ways, which then retroactively assumed positive value" (37). Buzard's work provides an especially informative analysis of these terms.

11. For additional analysis on travel literature's role in imperialism, see David Spurr's excellent and thorough *The Rhetoric of Empire: Colonial Discourse in Journalism, Travel Writing, and Imperial Administration*.

12. Several scholars have also written important studies on "travel theory" and on the connections among travel, writing, and theory. See especially Edward Said's "Traveling Theory," Michel Butor's "Travel and Writing," Georges Van Den Abbeele's *Travel as Metaphor: From Montaigne to Rousseau*, and Caren Kaplan's *Questions of Travel: Postmodern Discourses of Displacement*.

13. For Greenblatt, the writings of European travelers to the New World are significant more for what they tell us about European culture than for what they reveal about American landscape; "the early modern discourse of discovery," Greenblatt argues, "is a superbly powerful register of the characteristic claims and limits of European representational practice" (23).

14. In addition to the works discussed below, see also Christopher Mulvey's books *Anglo-American Landscapes: A Study of Nineteenth-Century Anglo-American Travel Literature* and *Transatlantic Manners: Social Patterns in Nineteenth-Century Anglo-American Travel Literature*.

15. According to Stowe, "A growing class of privileged, influential Americans in the nineteenth century exploited all of the features of their favorite pastimes to claim social

and professional positions for themselves, to gratify their desire for pleasure and especially for prestige, and to justify their privileges by demonstrating their superior taste
and sensitivity" (15).

16. Buzard's text was clearly influenced by Dean MacCannell's now classic work *The
Tourist: A New Theory of the Leisure Class*, first published in 1976, which argues, "the em-
pirical and ideological expansion of modern society [is] . . . intimately linked in diverse
ways to modern mass leisure, especially to international tourism and sightseeing" (3). For
MacCannell, tourism is, ultimately, "a kind of collective striving for a transcendence of
the modern totality, a way of attempting to overcome the discontinuity of modernity, of
incorporating its fragments into unified experience" (13). For further discussions of the
significance of travel to modern societies, see James Clifford's excellent and wide-ranging
Routes: Travel and Translation in the Late Twentieth Century, which focuses especially on
those border areas where cultures and societies interact, what Pratt calls "contact zones,"
and see Jonathan Culler's fascinating essay "The Semiotics of Tourism" in his *Framing
the Sign*, which explains that tourists are exemplary semioticians, for "all over the world
they are engaged in reading cities, landscapes and cultures as sign systems" (155).

17. In *Exotic Journeys: Exploring the Erotics of U.S. Travel Literature, 1840–1930*, Justin
Edwards argues that travel writing includes descriptions of contact zones that are "presented in erotic terms" (3). According to Edwards, "While American travel to foreign
regions is usually presented as a commodious signifier, providing everything from civilization to primitivism, freedom to danger, and fulfillment to corruption, the images of
eroticism remain a constant trope" (14).

18. A number of the differences described by Mills will be discussed in more detail
in chapter 3.

19. For instance, in her list of travel books published between 1830 and 1900, Mary
Suzanne Schriber includes only those that describe *foreign* travel.

20. While this definition would certainly encompass both books and, for instance,
magazine or newspaper articles, I have generally limited my study to book-length man-
uscripts, even in the case of Frederick Law Olmsted, whose newspaper reports were later
republished in book form.

21. This aspect of travel literature has frequently been described in terms of a double
movement, in which a travel narrative describes both an outward and an inward journey;
unfortunately, this simple dichotomy simplifies the complexity of many travel texts into
a neat public/private pair of journeys.

CHAPTER ONE. Representing America

1. Historians and critics have long recognized that Crèvecoeur's *Letters* exemplifies the argument that what America promised during the seventeenth and eighteenth
centuries was the opportunity to put the ideals of the European Enlightenment to a
practical test. Elayne Rapping explains that Crèvecoeur, influenced as he was by the
philosophes and other Enlightenment thinkers, "saw the significance of the fact that the

Age of Enlightenment, in which men began to suspect they could discover rationally the laws of nature which governed an intelligible universe, was also the age in which a new nation was being established on a newly settled land, offering an opportunity to test these theories" (707). According to this view, the freedoms enjoyed by this "new man" in America rested on two related bases: the government and the land. Ultimately these are the same phenomenon for Crèvecoeur since, he argues, the government of America, like its inhabitants, has grown out of the natural environment.

2. As Christine Holbo has pointed out, most critics base their arguments on "an assumed narrative decline involving a change of heart, a gap between author and narrator, or both" (59). This "narrative decline" toward the end of the book is most often seen as a response to one of two things: slavery or the American Revolution. Doreen Saar, for instance, argues, "After James's experience in Charles Town, the tone of the last three letters becomes progressively darker" (192). Other critics, such as Albert Stone, argue that after James's experiences with southern slavery, his view of humanity is so altered that his entire belief system is affected and he becomes completely disillusioned with America's prospects and with human nature. Stone further argues, as do many critics, that Crèvecoeur's personal experiences during the early stages of the American Revolution—he was imprisoned in New York, fled to England, and returned from France several years later to find his wife had been killed and his children dispersed—infect the later chapters of the text and cast a shadow over the author's earlier optimism. Stone writes, "The anxieties of this troubled time suffuse the later letters—some of which may have been written in New York—and are vividly dramatized in the later sketches" (12). This reading weakens the text, however, by reducing the criticisms to simple individual responses to personal injustice, rather than recognizing the larger skepticism toward American society that the text represents. In his biography of Crèvecoeur, Thomas Philbrick argues, "*Letters* follows a downward arc of the dream gone sour, of a promised land which is discovered to be no haven from history and change, of a chosen people who are found to have no exemption from the follies and sins of mankind at large" (88). Regardless of their views on the importance of similarities between James and Crèvecoeur or of the details they use to support their arguments, however, all of these critics agree that *Letters from an American Farmer* charts a progression from the ideal to the real, from a world largely of Crèvecoeur's making to the unpleasant realities of southern slavery and the American Revolution.

3. Even many contemporary critics who question the simple progression (or regression) sketched out by earlier generations of critics argue that reality invades the text only in the final chapters. These recent critics generally recognize the split between Crèvecoeur and his narrator described by Christine Holbo but not always emphasized by earlier critics. Nonetheless, while these arguments often complicate the idea of a neat progression from the ideal to the real, most continue to subscribe to the general outline of that movement. Some critics, such as David Robinson, argue that the utopian model described by James in the early chapters becomes the basis for Crèvecoeur's critique of American society; Robinson suggests that most critics believe there to be "a conscious

utopian design and serious social criticism implied by the chosen structure of the work" (19). James Machor concurs, stating, "most critics now agree that Crèvecoeur uses the farmer's plight to undermine Enlightenment assumptions and assert the failing of the American ideal" (75). Despite the repeated attempts to construct an American ideal, these critics suggest, James's efforts are confounded by the intrusion of contemporary history. For Machor, by the end of the work, "The great world of power, complexity, alliances, political contentions—in a word, the city—has intruded upon the farmer's domain" (74). Stephen Arch argues, "James is made to confront realities gilded by the rhetoric of his and the minister's romantic notions" (150). What James learns to do late in the book, Arch continues, is to "defictionalize his world" and begin to see the reality behind the rhetoric of colonial America (154). Similarly, Grantland Rice claims that Crèvecoeur's attempts to represent this New World are undermined by the realities of the historical situation. *Letters*, Rice writes, is a work of fiction about a naive writer "who attempts to write an originary epic for an emerging nation only to discover this epic collapsing under the onslaught of the historical contingencies predicted by Abbé Raynal and accentuated by the aesthetic imperatives of his own pen" ("Crèvecoeur" 94). While Rice makes a novel argument about Crèvecoeur's creation and use of a new genre, his argument again charts the general progression from the ideal to the real, suggesting, as the vast majority of critics do, that the agrarian ideal that James establishes is undermined only very late in the book. While many critics, including Rice, point to the attempt by James in the final chapter to reassert the power of his earlier ideal, all argue that his attempt is a *re*-assertion, suggesting that the utopia of which James dreams at the end is identical to that of the initial three chapters. This early ideal, however, is so consistently undermined from the very beginning of the text as to be completely discredited by the final chapters of the book. In response, James attempts in the final episode to create a markedly different ideal in which travel plays a more significant role.

4. Ironically, as the narrator recreates himself as a traveling farmer, the gap between James and Crèvecoeur narrows, so the narrative and authorial personae may be closest at the end of the book, the point at which most critics have suggested the two are most distinct.

5. Two critics who have recognized Crèvecoeur's work as primarily a travel narrative are Seelye and Barbeito. Seelye, however, focuses his criticism on those letters not included in *Letters* during the author's lifetime but published since as *Sketches of Eighteenth-Century America*. Barbeito, in her recent dissertation, focuses more narrowly on the importance of the captivity narrative genre to Crèvecoeur's *Letters*.

6. When James might have seen this soil is unclear, for, as usual, he does not describe an actual journey to North Carolina.

7. Obviously, Nantucket has its own problems, despite the view of many critics. The women of Nantucket, for instance, are all opium addicts, according to James, not a habit generally practiced by those who are completely satisfied with their situation. See, also, Anna Carew-Miller's "The Language of Domesticity in Crèvecoeur's *Letters from an American Farmer*," in which she argues, "Clearly, for Crèvecoeur, there is something

wrong with the model community [on Nantucket]. When the natural order of domestic relations is disturbed—the father-husband no longer the authority—anything can
happen: chaos, men become passive; women take drugs" (248).

8. See also Kolodny's discussion of the feminization of the American landscape in
The Lay of the Land; especially useful were chapters 2 and 3, "Surveying the Virgin Land"
and "Laying Waste Her Fields of Plenty."

9. There has been a curious critical lacunae concerning James's wife and her remarks
about Mr. F. B. and writing. Rice and a few others have something to say about her
view of writing as a political activity, but no critics have anything to say concerning her
biting comments about James's correspondent. For instance, as James, his wife, and their
minister discuss the sincerity of Mr. F. B.'s request, James's wife asks, "Would'st not thee
be ashamed to write unto a man who has never in his life done a single day's work, no,
not even felled a tree; who hath expended the Lord knows how many years in studying
stars, geometry, stones, and flies and in reading folio books?" (40). Comments such as
this can surely be read as more ironic than critics have recognized.

10. James also notes, "Good and evil, I see, are to be found in all societies, and it is in
vain to seek for any spot where those ingredients are not mixed" (51), a notable comment
in a letter generally said by critics to be one of the two most optimistic of the book.

11. Interestingly, when describing the law, James uses rhetoric similar to that used to
discuss slavery. James states the law should serve as a bridle, a device used to harness and
guide horses. The problems in the South seem to result from the wrong application of restraint. Rather than helping to curb the excess greed and power of the entire population,
the law assists some as it enslaves others. Slaves are controlled too tightly and are thus
unable to act freely within the bo(u)nds of the mild restraint the law should provide.

12. Christine Holbo argues that "the language of sensibility and imaginative association" were used by writers during this period as they "theorized the links between
natural order, social order, and individual psychology" (21).

13. In letter 2, James recounts the pleasures he has received and the lessons learned
from watching birds: "The astonishing art which all birds display in the construction
of their nests, ill-provided as we may suppose them with proper tools, their neatness,
their convenience, always make me ashamed of the slovenliness of our houses; their love
to their dame, their incessant careful attention, and the peculiar songs they address to
her while she tediously incubates their eggs, remind me of my duty could I ever forget
it" (61). But James is unable to maintain this positive picture of nature and instinct,
for while watching a swallow and a wren, he observes a very different scene. James has
provided the wren with a small but adequate box for nesting, and he has built a larger
box for the swallow, a larger bird. For some reason unknown to James, the wren dislikes
its own box and drives the larger bird from its more sizable nest. "This exploit was no
sooner performed" than the wren "removed every material to its own box with the most
admirable dexterity; the signs of triumph appeared very visible . . . [and] an universal
joy was perceivable in all its movements" (63). "Where did this little bird learn that spirit
of injustice?" James wonders (63). From nature, of course, is the answer, as he realizes

once he has traveled to Charles Town and confronted directly a different aspect of nature. In these early chapters, however, a positive view predominates, while darker visions only periodically intrude, a ratio that is inverted later in the text.

14. Note once again the common device of describing not the travels of the narrator but those of a generic "European."

15. "In another century," James worries, "the law will possess in the north what now the church possesses in Peru and Mexico," two New World countries that have failed to rid their societies of the problems of the Old.

16. The rhetoric of slavery might also refer to the relationship between the colonies and England, as several critics have noted. Doreen Saar, for instance, argues, "For Whigs, slavery symbolized the relationship between Britain and the American colonies" (195). While not actively a Whig himself, Crèvecoeur has nonetheless incorporated Whig discourse into his text; it would perhaps have been impossible not to do so given his subject matter. If one takes the rhetoric of slavery to refer also to the relationship of the colonies to England, then to argue for emancipation is implicitly to argue for national independence. Part of the interest of this work arises from the author's ambivalence on both of these issues—an ambivalence that produces fertile ambiguities in the language of the text.

17. Many critics argue that this chapter represents the complete failure of James's ideal, as his farm is destroyed due to his refusal to participate in the American Revolution. These critics point to passages in which James bemoans his inability to maintain a middle position between two extremes. For instance, James wonders, "What can an insignificant man do in the midst of these jarring contradictory parties, equally hostile to persons situated as I am?" (205). Stephen Arch claims that by the final chapter, "James no longer has faith in his culture and his culture's fictions" (156). Similarly, Elayne Rapping argues that James "has carefully built a world for himself on the basis of certain principles which have all proved false" (713). Other critics, however, emphasize James's attempt in the final chapter to reassert his earlier agrarian ideal. A. W. Plumstead writes, Crèvecoeur, the "responsible family man[,] must retreat with his loved ones from this chaos and attempt to recapture the peace and joy of former days in an Indian village" (216). Robert Winston argues that James heads west in order to "reassert the power of the idyll" (261), and David Robinson believes that James goes west as a statement of his beliefs in agrarian self-determination, beliefs elucidated in the early chapters of the book. All of these critics are partially correct, for the final chapter does describe the intrusion of the American Revolution into James's idyll, and his move west is certainly an attempt to create an ideal. These critics fail to realize, however, that this new ideal differs in important ways from James's earlier utopian creation, most notably in its attempt to forge a new ideal by combining farming with travel.

18. Annette Kolodny argues that what James is trying to maintain in the final chapter "is the integrity of the human social community—nurtured by the landscape, but not, like the backwoodsmen or the indolent southerners, so totally dependent upon it as to become regressively 'mongrel' or infantile, engulfed by its plentitude" (62).

19. Because of his new understanding of the importance of freedom of movement, James will also free his slaves, he claims. As he explains, he will tell them, "In the name of God, be free, my honest lads; I thank you or your past services; go, from henceforth, and work for yourselves; be sober, frugal, and industrious, and you need not fear earning a comfortable subsistence" (219).

20. Significantly, much of the last chapter refers to a time in the future, supposedly after the writing of the letter but before James's correspondent receives it, a sort of ideal time in the very near future.

21. Crèvecoeur's work shows John becoming interested in botany after spotting a daisy one day while plowing. Bertram then exclaims, "What a shame . . . that thee shouldest have employed so many years in tilling the earth and destroying so many flowers and plants without being acquainted with their structures and their uses!" (194). Thus, Crèvecoeur does recognize the botanist's obsession with the productive capabilities of nature.

22. See, for instance, Michael Branch's "Indexing American Possibilities."

23. See especially N. Bryllion Fagin's *William Bartram: Interpreter of the American Landscape.*

24. John Seelye argues in "Beauty Bare," for instance, "Like his father (and like George Washington), William Bartram is an instrument of empire as well as of the Enlightenment as he explores the rich Floridian savannas" (53). Likewise, Philip Terrie states, "His travels, research, and obvious joy in nature consistently reflect his conviction that nature exists to be used and that his own mission in discovering and describing nature was to hasten the process of exploitation" (22).

25. Mary Mattfield seems to know Bartram especially well, claiming that he emerges from the text as "a man of great personal charm" (344).

26. Of course, the Bartrams' projects not only reflect the development of the South as a region but also help produce this sense of southern distinctiveness.

27. Pratt describes her use of the term "anti-conquest" as follows: "Natural history asserted an urban, lettered, male authority over the whole of the planet; it elaborated a rationalizing, extractive, dissociative understanding which overlaid functional, experiential relations among people, plants, and animals. In these respects, it figures a certain kind of global hegemony, notably one based on possession of land and resources rather than control over routes. At the same time, in and of itself, the system of nature as a descriptive paradigm was an utterly benign and abstract appropriation of the planet. Claiming no transformative potential whatsoever, it differed sharply from overtly imperial articulations of conquest, conversion, territorial appropriation, and enslavement. The system created . . . a utopian, innocent vision of European global authority, which I refer to as an anti-conquest" (38).

28. I disagree with the rather narrow view of imperial travel implicit in John Seelye's characterization of William Bartram as a man "in the hire of a single individual, on a particular errand, serving as the vicarious agent of another man's curiosity, his purpose tied to neither colonial nor commercial considerations" (*Beautiful Machine* 141).

29. Thomas Slaughter argues that even this map illustrates Bartram's doubts concerning development of the Alachua Savanna, for Bartram rotates the savanna ninety degrees, thus rendering the map, in Slaughter's view, practically useless (*Natures* 187).

30. David Spurr argues that "naturalization" is one of the fundamental tropes of travel writing and colonial discourse (156).

31. Bryllion Fagin suggests, "His objects come to him merged with the landscape as unbroken impressions, before he proceeds to dismember them for scientific classification. Thus his trees, shrubs, and flowers often come to him in forests and groves and fields and meadows, and he describes them from the outside, as it were, before he approaches them and the forest is lost in the trees that stand out" (84).

32. Patricia Medeiros states that in *Travels*, "Scientific precision and poetic extravagance are joined, sometimes with absurd results" (203). Charles Adams points to the "dizzying succession of discourses" that Bartram employs in describing the Altamaha River (17), and Robert Arner argues that Bartram's complex experiences are paralleled by a disparity of styles.

33. Interestingly, Bartram fails to mention slavery in his discussion of Charleston; in fact, the institution of slavery is conspicuously absent from his entire book.

34. Londa Schiebinger observes, "Linnaeus's term *Mammalia* helped legitimize the sexual division of labor in European society by emphasizing how natural it was for females—both human and nonhuman—to suckle and rear their own offspring. Linnaean systematics had sought to render nature universally comprehensible, yet the categories he devised infused nature with middle-class European notions of gender" (qtd. in Slaughter, *Natures* 28).

35. The placement of the Linnaean term in a footnote is an ambiguous gesture on Bartram's part, for it might suggest an inferior status for the Latin designation in Bartram's discursive hierarchy, but it could also suggest a more objective, extratextual status for the term.

36. As Charles Adams argues, "Theological, didactic, metaphorical, affective, scientific: each of these discourses might characterize nature absolutely, but Bartram balances each against the other, so that the truth of one is dependent on the truth of all" (119).

37. In some passages, Bartram represents the Native American as "other" through a process of romanticization. This process is particularly notable when Bartram is describing native women. For example, as Bartram and a companion are making their way through the mountains back to town, they come upon some "exuberant sweet pastures" and encounter a group of Cherokee maidens: "[we] enjoyed a most enchanting view; a vast expanse of green meadows and strawberry fields; a meandering river gliding through, saluting in its various turnings the swelling, green, turfy knolls, embellished with parterres of flowers and fruitful strawberry beds; flocks of turkies strolling about them; herds of deer prancing in the meads or bounding over the hills; companies of young, innocent Cherokee virgins, some busy gathering the rich fragrant fruit, others having already filled their baskets, lay reclined under the shade of floriferous and fragrant native bowers of Magnolia, Azalea, Philadelphus, perfumed Calycanthus, sweet

Yellow Jessamine and cerulean Glycine frutescens, disclosing their beauties to the flutter-
ing breeze, and bathing their limbs in the cool fleeting streams; whilst other parties more
gay and libertine, were yet collecting strawberries, or wantonly chasing their companions, tantalising them, staining their lips and cheeks with the rich fruit" (291). Although
Bartram seems to classify these "innocent Cherokee virgins" with the "turkies," deer, and
other wildlife, he is clearly interested in more than classification. These Native Americans
are not entirely "other," for, as Bartram notes, he and his friend attempt to join the scene,
which is simply "too enticing for hearty young men to continue idle spectators" (291). It
seems in this scene as if, as Slaughter has argued, Bartram sees gender before race, so that
any "otherness" these figures possess arises not from their identity as Native Americans
but from their identity as women (Interview).

   38. Without directly stating such, Bartram suggests through this description that he
is not only on foot but is also alone, neither of which was actually true, according to
Thomas Slaughter (*Natures* 208). This change obviously alters the situation that Bartram
here describes.

   39. In a rather bizarre passage, Bartram even claims to be able to read this warrior's
thoughts (44).

   40. Bruce Silver, for instance, describes William as "the apolitical son of the Quaker
botanist John Bartram" (597).

   41. "Whether as Puc Puggy or frontier tale-spinner," Adams continues, "Bartram is
cast as a man happily adrift in the South, chanting Latin through the swamps and Indians
camps, or quaintly letting his imagination run away with him" (113).

   42. Douglas Anderson agrees, arguing, "The Wilderness enables Bartram to place his
own eventful times in a context wide enough to provide a basis for measured skepticism
as a corrective for patriotic fervor" (5), and Charles Adams writes, "The Linnaean system here stands synecdochically for a structure of knowledge about natural and human
history that is permanent, orderly, and comprehensible" (115).

   43. Philip Terrie is not specific enough to the contemporary American political scene
when he argues that Bartram's "view of nature as alternating between the blissful and
the fearsome develops in the context of Bartram's profound skepticism concerning the
character of human affairs, and . . . reflects a projection of Bartram's anxieties about
human nature and human history onto the natural world he is exploring" (20).

   44. Given the obvious contradictions in Bartram's representations of Indians, it is
clear that Bartram maintained his culture's fear of Native Americans in general despite
the numerous positive individual interactions he enjoyed throughout *Travels*.

   45. Bartram is at pains to gain the belief of the reader in these passages. He writes,
"How shall I express myself so as to convey an adequate idea of it to the reader, and at the
same time avoid raising suspicions of my veracity" (117). As Thomas Slaughter argues,
pointing out that in reality the bear episode did not occur at the same time that William
Bartram was in danger of alligator attack, Bartram is more concerned with emotional
than factual truth (*Natures* 201). Berta Grattan Lee seems to concur, stating, "Bartram's

usual method of literary intensification is to combine a series of observations into one striking scene" (128).

46. This passage again brings up Bartram's complex relationship with and reaction to Native American history, culture, and society. Although Native Americans frequently seem to be part of the danger that Bartram fears, he also seems to view himself as somehow heir to the history and culture of these tribes. Furthermore, he clearly admires many whom he encounters, and he is provided with a name, Puc-Puggy, which means "Flower-Hunter," by the Seminoles.

47. Of the historical (as opposed to the textual) William Bartram, Thomas Slaughter states that, in Charleston when war broke out in 1775, William Bartram headed inland to avoid the fighting. However, although he was a Quaker and thus generally opposed to warfare, Bartram did serve "as a spy for Patriot forces in 1776 during his travels" (*Natures* 196).

48. Bartram's statement that the face of nature was not present during the storm suggests that he depends upon nature to at least appear benign, but it also exemplifies Philip Terrie's point that Bartram's "primary organizing device" is the "violent moment followed by the anxiously desired peaceful resolution" (30).

49. One can't help but wonder if Bartram didn't add this sentence during his revisions and thus have in mind both his southern travels and his journey through life, as well as the course of the nation as a whole. The use of the present tense is telling.

CHAPTER TWO. Moving Slaves

1. Are black residents "constituent members of this sovereignty?" Taney wondered. "We think they are not, and that they are not included, and were not intended to be included, under the word 'citizens' in the Constitution" (*Historic* 128).

2. Eric Foner argues that this decision marks a shift in the definition of American citizenship from one based on class to one based on race (75).

3. In his dissenting opinion, Justice McLean wrote:

There are several important principles involved in this case, which have been argued, and which may be considered under the following heads:

1. The locality of slavery, as settled by this court and the courts of the States.

2. The relation which the Federal Government bears to slavery in the States.

3. The power of Congress to establish Territorial Governments, and to prohibit the introduction of slavery there.

4. The effect of taking slaves into a new State or Territory, and so holding them, where slavery is prohibited.

5. Whether the return of a slave under the control of his master, after being entitled to his freedom, reduces him to his former condition.

6. Are the decisions of the Supreme Court of Missouri, on the questions before us, binding on this court, within the rule adopted. (Howard 533)

4. Elsewhere Baker has written, "For once literacy has been achieved, the black self, even as represented in the *Narrative* [by Frederick Douglass], begins to distance itself from the domain of experience constituted by the oral-aural community of the slave quarters" ("Autobiographical" 104).

5. Ironically, many critics use the language of travel in their analyses. In *Long Black Song*, for instance, Houston Baker writes of David Wilson and Frederick Douglass, "Both writers labored along freedom's road, under the dim light of the north star, and though they chose different modes of travel, both achieved their goals, contributing to humanity on the way" (83).

6. See, also, Robert Stepto's "Narration, Authentication, and Authorial Control in Frederick Douglass' *Narrative* of 1845" and Robert O'Meally's essay about the connections between Douglass's work and the sermon tradition.

7. The reference to Baker is useful here, for the development of Baker's thought in relation to Douglass's *Narrative* is indicative of much criticism of the author and his work. Like other critics writing at the time, Baker argued in his 1972 work *Long Black Song* that the *Narrative* is a bildungsroman and that it should be placed "in the realm of sophisticated literary autobiography" and viewed as "a spiritual autobiography akin to the writings of such noted white American authors as Cotton Mather, Benjamin Franklin, and Henry Adams" (78). In his later work, however, Baker's focus shifted to confront more directly the complicated relationship between Douglass and literacy and language. In *The Journey Back: Issues in Black Literature and Criticism*, Baker argued that in order to establish and define his personal identity, Douglass had to work within a representational system that sought to define him in particular ways. "Unlike white Americans who could assume literacy and familiarity with existing literary models as norms," Baker argues, "the slave found himself without a system of written language—'uneducated,' in the denotative sense of the word. His task was not simply one of moving toward the requisite largeness of soul and faith in the value of his experiences. He first had to seize the word. His being had to erupt from nothingness. Only by grasping the word could he engage in the speech acts that would ultimately define his selfhood" (31). Douglass grasped the word, according to Baker, by redefining linguistic terms that had served to keep him enslaved. For instance, Douglass "ultimately controls the competition among the various markers of *nigger*," argues Baker, "because he has employed meanings (e.g., agent having the power of literacy) drawn from his own field of experience to represent the competition in a way that invalidates «subhuman agency of labor»" (34). According to Baker in *The Journey Back*, however, "In Douglass's case, a conception of the preeminent form of being is conditioned by white, Christian standards" (36); ultimately Douglass "is comforted, but also restricted, by the system he adopts" (39).

8. "What begins as an indictment of mainstream practice," Valerie Smith writes of Douglass's *Narrative*, "actually authenticates one of its fundamental assumptions" (26).

9. Sam Worley agrees, remarking, "Criticism of Douglass' first autobiography has repeatedly shown the extent to which it is complicit with the individualist bourgeois thought both through its elevation of Douglass as a self-made man as well as its down-playing of the crucial role of the slave community" (244). Likewise, Teresa Goddu and Craig Smith argue that Douglass is unable to free himself from the "white ideological framework," in part because his work is so frequently appropriated by others, particularly those in the abolitionist movement. "Even though he attains his freedom, it remains precarious, subject always to subtle appropriation," these two critics argue (840).

10. Zafar views Douglass as Franklin's alter ego rather than his cultural or literary progeny, "for Douglass's repeated inversions of the myth first articulated by Franklin represent more than imitation and simple reversal" (99).

11. According to Carolyn Porter, "In addressing a white audience, the slave incorporated its ideology; but he often did so in ways that exposed its limits" (359), and Zafar argues, "Ambivalence and strain may only prove that Douglass's struggles with the limitations of self-presentation are, after all, those of a genuinely representative man" (115).

12. Not only Douglass's written works illustrate this tension, Sundquist argues, for in his July 4 speech, Douglass "placed himself *outside* the American dream but *within* the circle of the post-Revolutionary generation's principal rhetoric" (Introduction 14).

13. John Carlos Rowe concurs: "Douglass does not unequivocally appeal to his 'inner resources' as his means to freedom; by invoking the power of language in the quest for freedom, Douglass appeals to a common and culturally maintained resource potentially available to all" (270).

14. Once he realizes the power of language, Douglass explains, he understood the white man's power to enslave the black man. Douglass writes, "From that moment, I understood the pathway from slavery to freedom" (58).

15. Rowe argues that ships were a particularly rich symbol for Douglass, suggesting as they do both merchant ships and slave ships. Rowe argues, "If at first the young Douglass merely copies the letters of the ships' carpenters, the author of the 1845 *Narrative* writes *on* those ships another message, which runs counter to the commercial purposes of trade in the North and the South in Douglass' lifetime. The romantic vision of freedom is a consequence of Douglass' rhetorical deconstruction of the 'white' metaphor of the ship as freedom only for some" (110).

16. For an interesting interpretation of the individual's appropriation of the city landscape, see "Walking in the City" in *The Practice of Everyday Life*, in which Michel de Certeau argues that walking can be compared with speech: "The act of walking is to the urban system what the speech act is to language or to the statements uttered. At the most elementary level, it has a triple 'enunciative' function: it is a process of *appropriation* of the topographical system on the part of the pedestrian (just as the speaker appropriates and takes on the language); it is a spatial acting-out of the place (just as the speech act is an acoustic acting-out of language); and it implies *relations* among differentiated positions, that is among pragmatic 'contracts' in the form of movements (just as verbal enunciation is an 'allocution,' 'posits another opposite' the speaker and puts contracts

between interlocutors into action)" (98). In a similar way to the relationship between individual speech acts and a system of language, de Certeau argues, "Walking affirms, suspects, tries out, transgresses, respects, etc., the trajectories it 'speaks,' " (99). Douglass, likewise, in his perambulations through the city, appropriates individual aspects of larger ideological structures and puts them to his own, subversive use. The fact that this use involves his learning a language makes the connections to de Certeau's essay all the more intriguing.

17. He is saddened to realize, however, that his mistress simultaneously undergoes a transformation that inversely parallels his own. As he is becoming less of a slave, her life is becoming more determined by slavery. Slavery, Douglass repeatedly points out, is detrimental to both the slaves and the slaveholders. Sophia Auld manifests this argument more clearly than any other figure in the book, for she changes from a loving, kind mistress to one who continually attempts to catch the young Douglass disobeying his master's commands. Douglass writes of his mistress, "Slavery proved as injurious to her as it did to me. When I went there, she was a pious, warm, and tender-hearted woman. . . . Slavery soon proved its ability to divest her of these heavenly qualities. Under its influence, the tender heart became stone, and the lamblike disposition gave way to one of tiger-like fierceness. The first step in her downward course was in her ceasing to instruct me" (59–60). To the extent that Douglass becomes free, it seems, Mrs. Auld is enslaved.

18. As if to prove that this journey marks the emergence of a new traveler-figure, Douglass undergoes a ritualized cleansing process prior to his departure from the plantation. "I spent the most part of all these three days in the creek, washing off the plantation scurf, and preparing myself for my departure," he writes (54).

19. Douglass explains also that slaves were pleased to be asked to run errands for their owners. He writes, "A representative could not be prouder of his election to a seat in the American Congress, than a slave on one of the out-farms would be of his election to do errands at the Great House Farm" (45).

20. Unruly slaves, like untamed horses, had to be "broken," taught to move only in accordance with their masters' orders.

21. Douglass hopes his movements will be validated by his owner, but Auld simply sends him back to Covey.

22. Of course, the very existence of these patrols necessarily demonstrates the existence of slave subjectivity, for if slaves had been unable to move themselves, as slave ideology suggested, then, obviously, there would have been no use for the patrols.

23. In fact, Douglass criticizes those who do describe the routes used by escaping slaves, especially those participating in the Underground Railroad. As Douglass argues, "I have never approved of the very public manner in which some of our western friends have conducted what they call the *underground railroad,* but which, I think, by the open declarations, has been made most emphatically the *upper-ground railroad*" (95).

24. The historical Frederick Douglass's later break with William Lloyd Garrison illustrates further his ability to determine his own movements, for he left Garrison's

organization after coming to the conclusion that he was being paraded around the lecture circuit as physical proof of the brutalities of slavery, rather than acting as an intelligent, capable traveling lecturer in his own right. Douglass did not allow Garrison and his followers to decide how he should best be put to use but left the organization in order to control more fully his own travels, both around the country and on the stage. He again determined when and how to approach the podium rather than allow his fellow abolitionists to do so.

25. It is significant, I think, that two of the three examples Baker provides here—the Underground Railroad and the North Star—are concerned primarily with issues of travel.

26. In "'As to Nation I Belong to None': Ambivalence, Diaspora, and Frederick Douglass," Russ Castronovo argues that critics' focus on Douglass's patriotism are misguided. Douglass, Castronovo argues, expresses particularly ambivalent thoughts concerning his membership in the nation, for while Douglass "desires to experience national belonging" (248), he also understands that African Americans are not offered full participation in American society. As Castronovo explains, "The conflicted aspects of Douglass's own thinking correspond to his attempts to contest the nation, to alienate its traditions and unsettle its hallowed doctrines so that descendants of the African diaspora can call—however uncertainly or uneasily—America home" (247). While I do find compelling Castronovo's assessment of Douglass's later thoughts on his role in the American nation, I do not agree that these beliefs surface in his earlier texts, particularly Douglass's 1845 *Narrative*. The narrator of this early autobiography seems particularly eager to struggle for citizenship in the United States, despite its problems at that time.

27. The general preference of Douglass's 1845 autobiography over his later ones, which actually include more details about his years as a slave and about his escape, might suggest the critical and popular dependence on this model.

28. In fact, the large sales of Northup's narrative encouraged his publishers, Derby and Miller, to publish other first-hand accounts of slavery, "including an expanded edition of Frederick Douglass' 1845 autobiography" (Eakin and Logsdon xv).

29. See, for instance, Eugene Genovese's *Roll, Jordan, Roll* or Elizabeth Fox-Genovese's *Within the Plantation Household*.

30. There are, of course, political considerations that can help explain the trust Phillips afforded Northup's text and withheld from others. Because Northup's situation was so unique, even southerners could support the veracity of his book without agreeing that all slave narratives should be considered worthy historical sources.

31. Rare but not unique, by any means. The editors of *Twelve Years a Slave* include brief descriptions of two similar cases (Eakin and Logsdon x).

32. David Wilson's contribution to the narrative is impossible to calculate, especially since Northup was himself literate even before he was sold into slavery and would not have had to depend on Wilson for the writing had he desired to produce a narrative by himself. The few critics who have discussed Wilson's influence generally agree that the more literary flourishes of the narrative are Wilson's contribution, while Northup's are

seen to be the bare facts of the horrifying narrative itself, particularly the astounding amount of detail incorporated into the text.

33. Particularly during the 1960s, when slave narratives came to the fore as important historical and political documents, perhaps Northup's lack of outspoken condemnation of the institution was not as politically attractive as was that openly expressed in the writings of figures such as Douglass or Delany.

34. Of course, the one time Douglass does depend on others, when he and a group of friends try to escape, his attempt is unsuccessful because they have included too many people.

35. Of course, even large numbers cannot make travel safe for slaves. Northup describes a tragic attempt on the part of a large group of slaves to fight their way to freedom in Mexico. When the group's plans are exposed by one of the initial instigators, the group is slaughtered as an example for others. In contrast, Lew Cheney, the treacherous slave traitor who had exposed the others, was granted his freedom by the state of Louisiana and even provided with a five hundred dollar reward.

36. Northup also includes several descriptions of the Native Americans of the region. For instance, of a group of Chickasaws, he writes, "They were a rude but harmless people, and enjoyed their wild mode of life. They had little fancy for the open country, the cleared lands on the shores of the bayous, but preferred to hide themselves within the shadows of the forest. They worshipped the Great Spirit, loved whiskey, and were happy" (72). Interestingly, Northup adopts several standard ethnographic attitudes toward his subject here. The people are "harmless" and "happy," he explains, and their understandable avoidance of open spaces is chalked up to an inexplicable preference "to hide themselves within the shadows of the forest."

37. Their plans fail when one of the three, Robert, dies of smallpox.

38. One important difference was that he was almost thrown overboard by proslavery southern passengers.

CHAPTER THREE. Domestic Travel

1. According to Hayden in *The Grand Domestic Revolution*, "Because domestic space was as much an economic and social product as public, urban space, the farmhouse, with its capacious storage and work spaces, gave way to urban and suburban dwellings with less space and more areas devoted to the consumption and display of manufactured goods" (12).

2. Furthermore, according to Egan, "Because it balanced individual desires against a drive for social control, the home necessarily produced conflict among its members" (20), as well as between competing models of the household.

3. The development of these two ideals is particularly important to Fox-Genovese, who argues, "The history of southern women does not constitute another regional variation of the main story; it constitutes another story" (42). Of course, even for Fox-Genovese the story of antebellum southern women, both slave and free, is integrally

tied to the story of women in the antebellum North, for both regions did, after all, form one nation. So while these two domestic ideals were distinct from each other, they were not entirely unrelated.

4. While Pratt is analyzing travel texts by European writers about "undeveloped" regions, specifically Africa and South America, much of her discussion is applicable to texts written about late-eighteenth- and early-nineteenth-century American society.

5. Of course, not only women have produced this type of travel narrative; in fact, Pratt's only examples in this article are narratives by men, such as those by Mungo Park and John Stedman.

6. The editor of the 1984 edition doesn't seem to share Fanny Kemble's concern for the individuality of the slaves, for John A. Scott's appendix C, "A List of Persons Referred to in the *Journal*, with Biographical Notes," is a list only of those *white* persons to whom Kemble refers. There are no slaves included, although Kemble's Irish servant, Margery O'Brien, is.

7. According to Diane Roberts: "These slave women now occupy another category for Kemble: they are *mothers* and within the web of pieties which Victorian culture created for motherhood. By *naming* them . . . and telling their stories, Kemble releases them from their designated location at the bottom of the white/black binary: she makes common cause with them as *women* and so puts at risk her own placement above them as the mistress" (112). Roberts is careful to point out that Kemble does not push herself into complete solidarity with these slaves, for Kemble maintains a number of the prejudices of her class and race. But, says Roberts, she does begin to bring slave women "up" to her standards of health as well as to "lower" herself in order to deal with the filth of slavery.

8. Sara Mills writes that women narrators are "more aware of the way the narrator appears to others, of themselves as object," because of their socialization as sexualized objects of the male gaze (98).

9. Describing Psyche, a slave who believes she will soon be forced to abandon her husband in order to accompany her owner to another state, Kemble writes, "With this deadly dread at her heart she was living day after day, waiting upon me and seeing me, with my husband beside me, and my children in my arms in blessed security, safe from all separation but the one reserved in God's great providence for all His creatures" (135).

10. Romines, describing the work of fiction writers around the time of the Civil War, writes, "For when a writer turned to domestic life and its recurring rhythm as a primary subject, placing her central characters inside, not outside, this world, she found herself in a literary and psychic realm with few precedents and little terminology, a domestic realm that traditionally privileged privacy and unwritten texts" (8).

11. Kemble had learned of these issues when she had previously published a travel book on her experiences during her first year of travel in the United States. This book had caused quite a stir in New York, for the young Kemble had mistakenly believed that the absence of names would shield her subjects from her criticisms.

12. However, unlike many women travelers in North America or Europe, according to Pratt, Graham and Tristan find that "the indoor private world does not mean family

or domestic life, but in fact their absence: it is the site above all of solitude, the private place in which the lone subjectivity collects itself, creates itself in order to sally forth into the world" (159).

13. It is ironic, given her history as an internationally famous stage actress, that Kemble should focus on the domestic sphere as a place in which to fashion an identity, but she seems to have fallen into the domestic role with some readiness if not, perhaps, with much enthusiasm or competence. According to Margaret Armstrong, "Fanny did honestly believe that the husband was the head of the house in all temporal matters, such as the source of the family income. On the other hand, in spiritual matters the husband had no jurisdiction, and slavery was sinful; therefore the question became spiritual" (204).

14. According to Mills, "Denied the outlet of waged work, middle-class women were encouraged to care for others and consider the maintenance of relationships as their domain" (96).

15. When Kemble uses a "discourse of philanthropy," she may have been inserting herself into the social environment in the only way available for one of her position, for, according to Pratt, "social reformism might be said to constitute a form of female imperial intervention in the contact zone" (*Imperial Eyes* 160).

16. Ironically, travel literature by men is often valued most highly when it is unique or is the product of a singular personality.

17. For example, women's writing has long been criticized for being overly emotional or too involved in the popular issues of the day, unlike "classic" male literature that is supposedly more self-referential and rhetorically complex. But in works such as *Sensational Designs: The Cultural Work of American Fiction, 1790–1860,* her groundbreaking study of nineteenth-century popular fiction, Jane Tompkins argues that much of the popular literature of the period, particularly women's fiction, did not attempt to free itself from the pressing social concerns of the day but was explicitly propagandistic. The sentimental novel, most notably *The Wide, Wide World* or *Uncle Tom's Cabin,* should be read as "a political enterprise, halfway between sermon and social theory, that both codifies and attempts to mold the values of its time" ("Sentimental Power" 270). Because American women lacked the resources for direct confrontation of the social norms, they were forced to appropriate the system of values for their own ends, argues Tompkins (*Sensational* 161). This appropriation was accomplished in and through the home, for what domestic space offered these novelists, as it offered women writers of travel texts, was a site purportedly removed from the patriarchal worlds of politics and economics from which women could interrogate these traditionally masculine arenas. Women did not simply remain within the home, even though, according to Tompkins, "[t]hey had to stay put and submit," for women used the safety of their home environments in order to move outside of those realms and examine the nation's political and economic institutions (*Sensational* 161).

18. According to Dolores Hayden, "[Stowe's] ultimate objective was to give women control over the domestic space of the household to match male involvement in agricultural or industrial production. . . . Her suburban house was designed to put the Ameri-

can woman, newly described as a 'minister of home' and a 'true professional,' in charge of a well-organized private domestic workplace in a democratic society where public life was run by men" (*Redesigning* 22). Jane Tompkins argues that Beecher and Stowe had even grander plans, arguing that their book "is a blueprint for colonizing the world in the name of the 'family state' . . . under the leadership of Christian women" ("Sentimental Power" 286).

19. This interruption is most obvious in the differences in the numerous kitchens described in the novel, particularly those of Dinah, the slave cook in the St. Clare house in New Orleans, and the Quaker Rachel Halliday. The St. Clare kitchen is the epitome of disorder. Dinah has no system of organization whatsoever, and the household as a whole suffers from the lack of a strong central female figure. As a result, the household falls apart after the untimely death of Augustine St. Clare, the kind but ineffectual patriarch of the family. In fact, the only character able to carry out Augustine's wishes is his aunt Ophelia, a strong New England woman whose housekeeping skills are second to none but are out of place in the slaveholding household that her nephew heads. Rachel Halliday, in contrast, is firmly in charge of the Halliday home. Halliday combines organization and Christian morality, which encourages the use of the house as a haven for the runaway slave Eliza; in fact, the home even serves to reunite Eliza's family, as this is where she and her child meet her husband after having escaped separately from slavery. Rachel Halliday represents the perfect homemaker, for she maintains the smooth functioning of her sphere and is able, as a result, to offer her assistance to all of those who enter her domain. Her home is thus the foundation of a new political order based on Christian principles and community rather than competition and the values of the marketplace.

20. Helen Fiddyment Levy makes a similar point about the later nineteenth- and twentieth-century women novelists she analyzes in *Fiction of the Home Place*: "The spiritual emphasis of these women's writing also asserts the morality of the home place by offering a vision of a purer American democracy, one which admits cooperative communal relationships and undertakings as an alternative both to the competitive individualism of their contemporary dominant discourse and the repressive hierarchy of the earlier paternalistic family. The home place throughout serves the ideal of moderation" (10).

21. In her "Appeal to the Women of the Free States," Stowe argues, "However ambition and the love of political power may blind the stronger sex, God has given to woman a deeper and more immovable knowledge, in those holier feelings, which are peculiar to womanhood, and which guard the sacredness of the family state" (427).

22. As Diane Roberts explains, "Controlling the representation means controlling the culture: if blacks are the ignorant, over-sexed savages of pro-slavery literature, then laws must be made to keep them separate from the white women they might harm—or seduce. If they are Christlike, living, innocent souls, they must be educated and brought along to citizenship; and if they are intelligent, resourceful, mature beings, then they must be granted the full rights of citizenship. Representation is intimately involved with power" (7).

23. This letter and another are included in most modern editions of the book.

24. According to Gillian Brown, "The distinction between work and family is eradicated in the slave, for whom there is no separation between economic and private status" (15).

25. Ironically, living in a slave household thus seems to have a democratizing effect on Kemble, who waits on herself rather than rely on servants, perhaps prompting or further encouraging her charity toward the slaves.

26. While the slaves do attempt to clean their houses and the hospital, as well as themselves and their children, it is unclear whether they are attempting to please Kemble because they understand the importance of cleanliness, because they believe she is ordering them to do so, or because they hope to receive some favor by pleasing her. Kemble herself seems to think that her disavowal of power over them proves that the first is the case.

27. Earlier she has wondered, "How is it that the fable ever originated of God's having cursed man with the doom of toil? . . . How invariably have the inhabitants of the southern countries, whose teeming soil produced, unurged, the means of life, been cursed with indolence, with recklessness, with the sleepy slothfulness which, while basking in the sunshine, and gathering the earth's spontaneous fruits, satisfied itself with this animal existence, forgetting all the nobler purposes in the mere ease of living?" (26).

28. The acting paradigm is extremely important to Kemble's text. As Allmendinger argues, "We see Kemble filtering her experience of the South through the medium of her experience on the stage and we see that for her acting became a metaphor for slavery. She characterized the degradation of the black slave by focusing upon slaves as practitioners of the arts of imitation and of performance: singing and dancing, using theatrical gestures" (508). Allmendinger focuses on the importance of imitation, but the acting metaphor is even more significant than he recognizes. Because of the erasure of the public and the private in their lives, slaves are always on stage and always performing. Thus, Kemble suggests, slaves are unable to live their own lives because of the ceaseless production in which they are forced to perform and participate, and the lives they lead are reduced to complex imitations of life.

29. Of course, another difficulty that Kemble frequently mentions is that the institution of marriage is made a mockery under slavery, for slave families are broken up when one member is sold, women are often forced to have sex with an overseer or master, and many masters break up a marriage if they think there are problems, simply assigning each partner a new spouse. Compared to other families, then, engineer Ned and his unnamed wife are fortunate, as their marriage has apparently been accepted by Mr. Butler and allowed to continue. The numerous children produced by the marriage undoubtedly have something to do with this.

30. The ease with which crops are grown in the South is frequently cited by travelers as a cause for the supposed lack of a work ethic among southerners, both black and white. For instance, see letter 9 in Crèvecoeur's *Letters from an American Farmer*.

31. Under the cult of domesticity, writes Eric Foner, "For both sexes, freedom meant fulfilling their respective inborn qualities" (71).

32. Alison Booth argues, "The system depends on her ineffectuality; the mistress not only may but must be useless to sharpen the definition of slave labor" (238).

33. As if to illustrate the social and ideological threat apparently posed by movement and travel, Kemble describes "the separation of men and women so rigidly observed by all traveling Americans" (21).

34. Another time, "I pursued my voyage of discovery by peeping into the kitchen garden," she writes, but "dared do no more; the aspect of the place would have rejoined the very soul of Solomon's sluggard of old" (82).

35. As Fox-Genovese argues, "The persistence in the South of the household as the dominant unit of production and reproduction guaranteed the power of men in society, even as measured by nineteenth-century bourgeois standards" (38).

36. Interestingly, many critics of Kemble's book believed she had, like her popular character Lady Macbeth, "unsexed herself." See Roberts 103.

37. Arguing that Kemble's work sought to solidify cultural codes and traditions while simultaneously crossing those lines, Alison Booth argues, "As she strives to set the limit that others may not cross, Kemble also seems attracted to freedom of movement" (235).

38. Like most critics who write about this text, I use "Linda Brent" when referring to the character in the work but "Harriet Jacobs" when discussing the creator of this narrative voice and the author of the text.

39. For instance, when a slave in the colonel's home says of her master, "Indeed, he is a father to us all," Kemble remarks, "Whether she spoke figuratively, or literally, we could not determine" (31).

40. Lydia Maria Child, the editor of Jacobs's *Incidents in the Life of a Slave Girl*, was obviously aware of the shocking nature of the story being presented. In her introduction, Child writes, "I am well aware that many will accuse me of indecorum for presenting these pages to the public; for the experiences of this intelligent and much-injured woman belong to a class which some call delicate subjects, and others indelicate. This peculiar phase of Slavery has generally been kept veiled; but the public ought to be made acquainted with its monstrous features, and I willingly take the responsibility of presenting them with the veil withdrawn" (3–4). Apparently, an introduction by an authorizing voice such as Child's made such indecorum more acceptable.

41. Even though, according to Diane Roberts, Fanny Kemble's "Georgia *Journal* is the most explicit white text on slavery as institutionalized rape" (105), Kemble's text cannot equal the force, immediacy, or honesty of the narrative by Jacobs, a black slave.

42. According to Donald Gibson in "Harriet Jacobs, Frederick Douglass, and the Slavery Debate: Bondage, Family, and the Discourse of Domesticity," Douglass, in his 1855 text *My Bondage and My Freedom,* and Jacobs in her autobiography "to a much greater extent than most other narrators, insist that whatever slavery might be, there is little of the character of benevolent domesticity associated with family life about it. Both narrators make it abundantly clear that slavery and family life, as conceived in the antebellum South, are much at odds, the property relationship between slave and slaveowner precluding any such analogy" (158).

43. Jacobs does describe, however, several white women who help her as she makes her escape to the North and avoids recapture. In her introduction to the Harvard University Press edition, Jean Fagan Yellin writes, "A central pattern in *Incidents* shows white women betraying allegiances of race and class to assert their stronger allegiance to this sisterhood of all women" (xxxiii). Southern racial ideology is apparently not without its local ruptures, particularly when it conflicts with individual beliefs about domestic womanhood.

44. Debra Humphreys argues that because Brent's grandmother operates a business in her home, her house is actually both a public and a private space (149). While the operation of a business in her grandmother's home is clearly significant, however, Jacobs suggests that it is the institution of slavery that destroys the boundaries between public and private and opens the house, for instance, to the constant threat of search by unruly slave catchers.

45. Of her aunt Nancy, Jacobs writes, "This aunt had been married at twenty years of age; that is, as far as slaves *can* marry. She had the consent of her master and mistress, and a clergyman performed the ceremony. But it was a mere form, without any legal value" (143).

46. As I've suggested in the previous chapter, Solomon Northup is a notable exception.

47. "Her focus on the family," argues Gibson, "lends her a vision that does away completely with the distinction between freedom and the establishment of a home. The two motives become wholly one" ("Harriet Jacobs" 172).

48. According to Elizabeth C. Becker, "Instead of assuming a passive role as her grandmother suggests, Brent emulates her father, brother, and uncle" (414), all of whom have actively resisted their enslavement.

49. Anne Goodwyn Jones and Susan Donaldson, in their introduction to *Haunted Bodies*, argue that Jacobs's rebellion against Dr. Flint "threatens his very sense of manhood," which could explain his apparent obsession with retrieving her. Jones and Donaldson suggest, "Apparently, the smallest assertion of freedom and defiance on the part of a slave woman had the power to shrivel a white slave-owning man's confidence in the power of his gender—because he believed his society's prescriptions requiring white male control" (2).

50. Elizabeth Becker argues further that, "in rejecting Dr. Flint's definition of her, Linda rebelliously denies the definitions of true womanhood—passivity and purity" (417).

51. This may suggest that Brent's freedom actually depends on, and begins at, the borders of her body, for she is able to create a domestic space for her children even though the physical space in which she survives hardly exceeds the bounds of her person. Control of her own body is thus identical to control of her domestic space, and vice versa.

52. This might, in fact, suggest that travel, too, begins with the ability to control even one's most basic movements, as Northup experienced when he could not do so.

53. Skinfill writes, "Racial identity is less resolved as a question in the North than it is

subsumed into a problem of class position. Jacobs begins to work within the literal and not simply literary constraints of domesticity" (74).

CHAPTER FOUR. Yeomen All

1. After making his decision to become a farmer, Olmsted wrote to a friend, "I suppose it's no very great stretch of ambition to anticipate my being a Country Squire in Old Connecticut in the course of fifteen years. I should like to help then as far as I could—in the popular mind—generosity, charity, taste &c.—independence of thought, of voting and of acting. The education of the ignoble vulgus ought to be much improved and extended" (qtd. in Beveridge 7–8).

2. His friend and traveling companion Charles Loring Brace had introduced him to Henry J. Raymond, editor of the newspaper, who had hired Olmsted after speaking with him for five minutes.

3. The first trip produced fifty letters, which appeared under the heading "The South" in the *New-York Daily Times* from February 16, 1853, until February 13, 1854. A second series, which was based on Olmsted's trip in 1853 and 1854, appeared in the *Times* under the heading "A Tour of the Southwest," contained only fifteen letters, and ran from March 6 until June 7, 1854, when the series ended abruptly. A final ten articles from this second trip, entitled "The Southerners at Home," appeared several years later in the *New York Daily Tribune*, from June to August 1857.

4. Hereafter, those quotations taken from *The Papers of Frederick Law Olmsted*, vol. 2, entitled *Slavery and the South: 1852–1857*, will be designated *SS* in the parenthetical citation. Olmsted quotations marked with only a page number are from *The Cotton Kingdom*.

5. During his tenure at the publishing house, Olmsted completed "work with Henry David Thoreau on his *Cape Cod* manuscript and was influential in publishing Herman Melville's *Benito Cereno*" (Lee Hall 48). He also worked with a number of *Putnam's* writers, such as Ralph Waldo Emerson, Henry Wadsworth Longfellow, and Harriet Beecher Stowe, and met other important literary figures, including Edgar Allan Poe, Horace Greeley, and Margaret Fuller (Lee Hall 48).

6. Describing the beginnings of nationalism in Europe after the Reformation, Anderson argues, for instance, "What, in a positive sense, made the new communities imaginable was a half-fortuitous, but explosive, interaction between a system of production and productive relations (capitalism), a technology of communications (print), and the fatality of human linguistic diversity" (42–43).

7. In fact, once his publishing house failed, Olmsted quickly abandoned the "republic of letters" to begin his next career, for which he is most widely known, as the designer (with Calvert Vaux) and superintendent of the Central Park project.

8. In a review of vol. 2 of Olmsted's collected papers, edited by Beveridge and McLaughlin, Thomas Bender argues that Olmsted assumed the "role of 'the representative man'—representative of his class, that is" (qtd. in Kalfus 166).

9. *The Cotton Kingdom*, then, is a text created by several hands, particularly those of Olmsted, his newspaper editors, and Goodloe, the editor of a Washington antislavery newspaper. Also very influential on Olmsted were his friend Charles Loring Brace and his brother, John. In fact, John had accompanied Frederick on his second journey through the South and had assembled *A Journey through Texas* from Frederick's notes, essays, and letters. Despite the influence of these others, however, Olmsted is clearly the central figure in the text, for *The Cotton Kingdom* describes his travels through the South; thus, the book ought to be viewed as primarily his creation. Although Goodloe may have cut some passages and ensured that the condensation was Olmsted's most ardently abolitionist text, Olmsted's beliefs about slavery and the complex relationship between the North and the South remain the central characteristic of the book. Furthermore, Olmsted's new introduction, written specifically for the publication of *The Cotton Kingdom*, reveals the evolution of his thoughts regarding slavery and suggests that Goodloe's revisions were in line with Olmsted's thinking at the time of the outbreak of the Civil War.

10. None of Olmsted's books sold particularly well. According to Dana White, all three of Olmsted's books on the South sold, probably, fewer than twenty-five thousand copies from 1856 until the outbreak of the Civil War (27). However, *The Cotton Kingdom* did sell better than the three from which it was constructed.

11. Not surprisingly, Olmsted's books were neither favorably received nor reviewed in the South; in fact, *The Cotton Kingdom* itself contains an unfavorable review of *A Journey through Texas* from *De Bow's Review*. The review begins, "Mr. Frederick Law Olmsted, after signalizing himself by two very wordy volumes, abounding in bitterness and prejudice of every sort, and misrepresentations upon the 'Seaboard Slave States,' finding how profitable such literature is in a pecuniary point of view, and what a run is being made upon it throughout the entire limits of abolitiondom, vouchsafes us now another volume, entitled a 'Journey Through Texas, or a Saddle-trip on the South-western Frontier.' Here, again, the opportunity is too tempting to be resisted to revile and abuse the men and the society whose open hospitality he undoubtedly enjoyed, and whom we have no doubt, like every other of his tribe travelling at the South, he found it convenient at the time to flatter and approve" (543).

12. Even very recent studies of Olmsted, such as Rybczynski's, have accepted Olmsted's argument that he was simply presenting the facts. Rybczynski argues that Olmsted "never stoops to punditry. He does not lecture but generally steers the reader to the conclusion that the facts demand" (123).

13. Describing nineteenth-century travel writing in general, Porter writes, "Whatever pattern travel writing took, reviewers insisted that it be objective. In practice, however, a travel writer's credibility derived not from his objectivity but from the degree to which he maintained the distinction between 'us' and 'them.' In *Typee*, Melville blurred the boundaries between civilization and savagery, lost credibility, and became the 'man who had lived among cannibals.' In *The Cotton Kingdom*, however, Olmsted reinforced the boundary between North and South and was praised for his dispassionate objectivity" (362).

14. In his study of the American novel, Philip Fisher argues, "Culture, as we commonly say, articulates, in the sense of giving shape to and sorting out, some part of the past as it can be of use to a particular present" (3). But, continues Fisher, culture also "does work that, once done, becomes obvious and unrecoverable because it has become part of the habit structure of everyday perception" (3).

15. Olmsted hoped to avoid the moral arguments used by northern abolitionists, for he believed their rhetoric served to distance southern slaveholders from the North and accomplished little in the way of reforming the South and its institutions and economy. Rather than argue his thesis directly, however, Olmsted claims he will simply describe what he has encountered and let the facts speak for themselves. As Laura Roper explains, "His method of reporting was the same that he had used in *Walks and Talks*: he presented a profusion of concrete, specific details from which the reader could draw conclusions, and he offered his own" (86). Accordingly, much of Olmsted's writing consists of descriptions of the landscape, accounts of his interactions with people met along the way, and statistics or figures on agricultural production, all of which, he claims, should serve to convince the South to abolish slavery. Of course, these anecdotes are frequently punctuated by brief commentary, and Olmsted's opinions quickly surface. Almost upon entering Virginia, for instance, Olmsted notes that the countryside is noticeably undeveloped. Even though Virginia, "this old country," was "settled before any part of Massachusetts," Olmsted sees little evidence of industry. There is hardly any manufacturing to speak of, and the people seem particular lazy and unmotivated. "Altogether," he claims, "the country seen from the railroad, bore less signs of an active and prospering people than any I ever travelled through before, for an equal distance" (33). This conclusion is reached after viewing from the train only seventy-five miles of Virginia countryside.

16. According to Edmund Wilson, Olmsted's "interest is primarily economic, but to explain the economic aspects of life in the South involved also a detailed account of the habits of Southern society" (222).

17. Olmsted believes nature can, even needs to be, improved upon, as his equation here of "nature" with "decay" suggests. The "natural" scenes that he finds most beautiful are those that combine the "natural" with the "manmade," such as a park in Natchez overlooking the Mississippi River. Of course, this attitude finds its most significant outlet several years later in Olmsted's work as a landscape architect.

18. By arguing that the North produces the only efficient travel equipment he finds in the South, Olmsted suggests that the northern locomotives and stagecoaches he praises are not only signs of the excellence of northern systems of transportation and manufacturing but also symbols of the superiority of a free-market economy in which products, ideas, and people can move freely throughout the nation.

19. Part of Olmsted's distress at this work crew in particular is undoubtedly the presence of women who "were engaged at exactly the same labour as the men" (161). As I discuss at more length below, Olmsted is frequently shocked by the lack of appropriate gender boundaries in southern society.

20. It is important to note that, despite his belief that slaves could and should be taught the responsibilities of free and full participation in American society, Olmsted could be extremely racist at times. Describing a group of slaves in Washington, D.C., who are particularly "inferior in the expression of their face," for instance, Olmsted remarks, "all the negro characteristics were more clearly marked in each than they often are in any at the North" (28). And his racism extended to groups other than those of African descent. In Richmond, Olmsted notes disapprovingly, "very dirty German Jews, especially, abound, and their characteristic shops (with their characteristic smells, quite as bad as in Cologne) are thickly set in the narrowest and meanest streets, which seem to be otherwise inhabited mainly by negroes" (38).

21. Of course, Olmsted could just as easily be describing here his view of the southern planter class, too, for he finds them almost as lazy, indifferent, indolent, and immoral as their slaves.

22. Like his description of southern society as "aristocratic," Olmsted's equation of poor southerners with a "peasantry"—which would not move as freely as would a "citizenry"—suggests that the South is more similar to the European past than to an American future. As his title states, the South is a *kingdom*, not truly part of a *nation*.

23. It may be that in Olmsted's view, moral and cultural considerations are essentially indistinguishable.

24. Olmsted's use of the word "home" only in reference to the nonslaveholding household is indicative, I think, of many of the issues raised in my previous chapter on the works of Fanny Kemble and Harriet Jacobs.

25. Of course, Olmsted is particularly impressed by the German immigrants of Texas, because, like northern immigrants to the South, they have exhibited purposeful travel with the aim of rejuvenating a declining society.

26. Olmsted was frustrated in his attempt to get inside as many southern homes, especially plantation homes, as he had hoped prior to his journeys, despite the numerous letters of introduction he carried with him. The most common way for him to gain entrance to a home in the South is to ask someone he meets on the road where they think he might be able to find lodging for the night. Much to his disgust, when seeking shelter he is often turned away, even late at night or when he is ill, and he argues vehemently against the characterization of southerners as "hospitable." See, for instance, pages 517–20 or 545–53 in *The Cotton Kingdom*.

27. In response to the difficulties of determining an individual southerner's class, Olmsted constructs a rather elaborate system of comparison for people of various classes in the North and the South. For instance, Olmsted explains, "The great difference in character between the third class of the South and that of the North, as indicated by their respective manners, is found in the much less curiosity and ready intelligent interest in matters which have not an immediate personal bearing in that of the South" (559).

28. Slavery is, thus, once again characterized primarily by the restrictions it places on action and movement.

29. Olmsted's beliefs concerning "free" labor are perhaps best illustrated by his actions as the superintendent of the Central Park project. According to Kalfus, "That Olmsted was an effective administrator of labor and a fair and decent employer are not to be doubted. But it is equally clear that he regarded the free laborer (free, but not free to strike) in much the same authoritarian, paternalistic manner that he had the 'childlike' slave laborer" (165). Olmsted did have concerns about the justice of the northern economy, however, and occasionally noted the difficult conditions many poor laborers in the North faced. In *The Cotton Kingdom*, Olmsted writes, for instance, "I am not [at] all disposed to neglect the allegation that there is sometimes great suffering among our free labourers. Our system is by no means perfect; no one thinks it so: no one objects to its imperfections being pointed out" (489). As a reformer rather than a revolutionary, Olmsted's solution to these problems generally involved moral and cultural uplift instead of serious alterations to the economic system.

30. Ironically, Olmsted fails to mention that southerners frequently hired Irishmen or other immigrants to perform such work for extremely low wages rather than risk the loss of as large an investment as a group of slaves would constitute. After all, the death of an immigrant worker was not nearly as costly for the southerner as the death of a slave.

31. Of course, "overlooking the aged and diseased" is exactly what opponents of free-labor capitalism have long argued capitalist societies do. In contrast, southern opponents frequently argued, slave society took care of its aged or diseased slave members, an argument not generally supported by the experiences or accounts of most slaves. In his *Narrative*, for instance, Frederick Douglass specifically charges his owner with failing to take care of Douglass's elderly grandmother once she could no longer work.

32. It is significant, too, that the group Olmsted most admires are travelers who have, essentially, carried the city into the country, as they have brought literature, music, painting, and other high cultural productions and institutions into the "wilderness" of the Texas frontier. These immigrants serve, in a sense, as "carriages" of northern values and culture, carting a free-market ideology into a slave-based society.

CHAPTER FIVE. Tourists with Guns (and Pens)

1. According to Foote, "Men who never before had been fifty miles from their places of birth now knew, from having slept and fought in its fields and woods and cane brakes, gawked at its cities, such as they were, and trudged homeward through its desolation, that they too had had a country. Not secession but the war itself, and above all the memories recurrent through the peace that followed—such as it was—created a Solid South, more firmly united in defeat than it had been during the brief span when it claimed independence" (1042).

2. Of course, Olmsted's most popular book, *The Cotton Kingdom*, was published just as the war was starting, in 1861.

3. In his nonfictional essay "The Crime at Pickett's Mill," Ambrose Bierce nicely captures the ignorance many soldiers felt of their location, their destination, or their enemy. Bierce explains, "The civilian reader must not suppose when he reads accounts of military operations, in which relative position of the forces are defined, as in the foregoing passages, that these were matters of general knowledge to those engaged. . . . It is seldom, indeed, that a subordinate officer knows anything about the disposition of the enemy's forces—except that it is unamiable—or precisely whom he is fighting. As to the rank and file, they can know nothing more of the matter than the arms they carry. They hardly know what troops are upon their own right or left the length of a regiment away. If it is a cloudy day they are ignorant even of the points of the compass. It may be said, generally, that a soldier's knowledge of what is going on about him is coterminous with his official relation to it and his personal connection with it; what is going on in front of him he does not know at all until he learns it afterward" (39).

4. Movement up through the ranks should follow a logical progression, most soldiers believed, so political appointments of the leadership positions apparently frustrated many soldiers who had been passed over for promotion. Rhodes requested the governor of Rhode Island not to make political appointments but to allow the current officers to choose from the ranks of enlisted men. Rhodes himself was promoted rapidly through the ranks; as he explains, "I have been a Private, a Corporal, Sergeant Major, Second Lieutenant, and Adjutant, and if everything works well I shall climb higher" (150), which he did, leaving the army as a lieutenant colonel. Despite his ambition, however, he turned down an appointment when he believed that there were men above him who had been passed over for promotion. Colonel Robert Shaw complains about the practice of appointing officers rather than moving enlisted up from the ranks in a letter home in which he responds to a piece of writing by Frederick Law Olmsted, who, as always, apparently had much to say concerning the issues of his day. Shaw writes, "I saw a letter in the Tribune of 27 inst. from Mr. Olmsted speaking of the duties of captains and how seldom they were properly attended to. Like everyone else who writes about it he pitched into the Captains but never said a word about the government having appointed 3000 officers without requiring them to pass any examination, and everyone of whom may be, for all the govt knows, as unfit for his place as the most ignorant private in the ranks" (132). Because Olmsted was not a member of the army but was in charge of the Sanitary Commission during the war, Shaw believed Olmsted was perhaps not as aware of the complexities of issue as he might have been.

5. Rhodes's contrast of citizens and soldiers suggests a level of servitude almost comparable to southern slavery. Of course, Union soldiers retained their citizenship, however, even if their actions were largely determined by their superiors, so this distinction is perhaps misleading. Nonetheless, it seems particularly ironic that northern soldiers willingly (or unwillingly) gave up some of their freedom to travel in order to secure that right for southern slaves. Surprisingly, none of the writers included draw explicit connections between soldiers and slaves, and they do not seem particularly aware of the parallels between their situations and the situations of the slaves.

6. Some soldiers may prove an ability to travel, rather than simply move, by sur-passing their assigned duties. For instance, Thomas Wentworth Higginson writes of one member of his regiment, "Our most untiring scout during this period was the chaplain of my regiment,—the most restless and daring spirit we had, and now exulting in full liberty of action" (115). This man exercises his freedom, then, by choosing even during his free time to assist the Union Army and help bring about the abolition of slavery.

7. Later, however, Rhodes learns to appreciate a pleasant situation when he experi-ences one. "I hope we shall be allowed to spend the winter in Winchester," he writes, "for it is great fun" (179).

8. It could be argued, in fact, that the Union Army accomplished much of what Olm-sted had had in mind but had been unable to bring about through the publication of his texts, particularly the start of the shift from a slave-based to a free-labor economy that Olmsted thought so essential. Certainly there was much focus on the economy during and after the war. Edward Ripley wrote, for instance, "There was never so splendid a chance for individual enterprise as right now. Everyone is getting rich" (170), and, in a letter to his soldier brother, John Sherman wrote, "The truth is, the close of the war with our resources unimpaired gives an elevation, a scope to the ideas of leading capitalists, far higher than anything ever undertaken before. They talk of millions as confidently as formerly of thousands" (qtd. in Shelby Foote 1042).

9. Coulter might argue that Higginson was allowing his hatred of slavery to influence his response to southern nature. According to Coulter, "It hardly need be stated that many Northerners wrote with a feeling of hostility to almost everything Southern except natural scenery, and some of these even permitted their hatred of slavery to deny beauty in landscapes or to allow that a Southern sunset could be alluring" (xi).

10. Given that huge numbers of Union soldiers did indeed die of illness, De Forrest has some right to be concerned.

11. Higginson seems aware of his participation in a tradition of travel writing, for he locates his experiences by explaining, "This was not the plantation which Mrs. Kemble has since made historic, although that was on the same island" (67).

12. Apparently, Lookout Mountain has since grown, as roadside advertisements for Rock City, located on Lookout Mountain, now claim that a visitor can "See Seven States" from the summit.

13. The story may also be significant because it illustrates the possibility of "union" between two distinct groups, here Europeans and Native Americans rather than North and South.

14. For more information, see the footnote by Eakin and Logsdon in Northup 190.

15. Of course, as illustrated above, some of the changes were attributed to an increase in northern immigration.

16. Not all parts of Virginia were pro-Union, however, and Quint is quick to point out his disappointment when he does not find the sympathy he expects. "I see much in the Northern papers about freeing the Union sentiment, awaking loyalty, and the like," he writes. "But I did not see such sentiment in Central Virginia, where it ought, above

all places on rebel soil, to have been exhibited" (41). Elisha Rhodes is surprised by the greeting his troops receive in one Virginia town: "Greatly to our surprise we were welcomed by the ladies of this village with waving Union flags and handkerchiefs" (164). "Such loyal demonstrations in a Virginia town were never seen by the 6th Corps before," he adds.

17. Of course, some soldiers are suspicious of the speed with which the population professes Union sympathy. According to Higginson, for instance, "Every white man, woman, and child is flattering, seductive, and professes Union sentiment; every black ditto believes that every white ditto is a scoundrel, and ought to be shot" (110). After crossing into Virginia, Rhodes, who seems to spend much of his time in the homes of southerners, remarks with suspicion, "I found a house where there were two pretty girls who claimed to be Unionist" (78). In another part of Virginia, when Rhodes's regiment is plagued by troubles from local Confederate sympathizers, he exclaims, "The people are honest farmers during the day, but at night they arm themselves and mounting their horses are guerrillas" (181). No doubt these "honest farmers" also pledge allegiance to the Union cause when Federal soldiers are near.

18. Of course, not only Union soldiers viewed the war in these terms. Ralph Waldo Emerson, for instance, argued, "We have attempted to hold together two states of civilization: a higher state, where labor and the tenure of land and the right of suffrage are democratical; and a lower state, in which the old military tenure of prisoners or slaves, and of power and land in a few hands, makes an oligarchy: we have attempted to hold these two states of society under one law. But the rude and early state of society does not work well with the later, nay, works badly, and has poisoned politics, public morals, and social intercourse in the Republic, now for many years" (qtd. in Masur 127). In fact, Emerson found war itself as a threat to democratic institutions. According to Emerson, "The misfortune of war is that it makes the country too dependent on the action of a few individuals, as the generals, cabinet officer &c. who direct the important military movement & action of the great masses of citizens" (125).

19. Ambrose Bierce would probably have disagreed, however, for he argues, "The soldier never becomes wholly familiar with the conception of his foes as men like himself; he cannot divest himself of the feeling that they are another order of beings, differently conditioned, in an environment not altogether of the earth. The smallest vestiges of them rivet his attention and engage his interest. He thinks of them as inaccessible; and, catching an unexpected glimpse of them, they appear farther away, and therefore larger, than they really are—like objects in a fog. He is somewhat in awe of them" (109).

20. This search for the novel was apparently felt even by those far removed from the fighting. For example, Louisa May Alcott, who traveled from her home in Massachusetts to Washington, D.C., to become a nurse, writes in her journal, "I want new experiences, and am sure to get 'em if I go. So I've sent in my name, and bide my time writing tales" (qtd. in Masur 21). Although she did not stay in the nation's capital for very long, Alcott apparently found what she was looking for, describing in her journal a "most interesting

journey into a new world full of stirring sights and sounds, new adventures, and an
evergrowing sense of the great task I had undertaken" (22).

21. Of course, plenty of Union soldiers argued that the war was not about slavery or
the extension of citizenship rights to freed slaves. "Our men are fighting for the flag, not
for the abolition of slavery," wrote Alonzo Quint (48). Still, Quint argues, these men did
believe the South was (or should be) part of their nation, even if they did not believe
African Americans were (or should be) included in the reconstituted republic.

CONCLUSION

1. As Richard Brodhead argues, a staple of the major literary magazines during this
period was "the short piece of touristic or vacationistic prose, the piece that undertakes
to locate some little-known place far away and make it visible in print" (124–25).

2. For instance, Mrs. Johns, who sells fruit to the tourists, has "such a face as one
never sees except in these mountains" (Craddock 217).

3. These two discourses are frequently juxtaposed, highlighting their contrast; for
instance, according to the narrator, "Mrs. Johns, sitting on the extreme edge of a chair
and fanning herself with a pink calico sun-bonnet, talked about her husband, and a
misery in his side and in his back, and how he felt it 'a-comin' on nigh on ter a week
ago'" (217).

4. As Amy Kaplan argues, "Regionalism performs a kind of literary tourism in a period that saw the tourist abroad and at home as a growing middle-class phenomenon;
tourism was no longer limited to the grand tours of the upper class" (252).

5. The figure of the urban tourist in a rural backwater also incorporates the nostalgia many critics have recognized in regionalist writing. According to Stephanie Foote,
"Although regional texts focused almost exclusively on rural concerns, their nostalgic
tone shows them to have been profoundly shaped by an awareness of the globalizing
and standardizing tendencies of urbanization and industrialization" (3). Furthermore,
nostalgia points to the desire to erase difference or to fashion national reunification—
to reimagine the past as unified rather than divisive. As Christopher Wilson argues, the
regional fiction published by postwar genteel magazines exhibited "a nostalgia that often
subtly underwrote a growing political reconciliation of North and South (with disastrous
consequences for African Americans)" (158).

6. According to Brodhead, regional fiction has an "easily identified set of formal
properties. It requires a setting outside the world of modern development, a zone of
backwardness where locally variant folkways still prevail. Its characters are ethnologi-
cally colorful, personifications of the different humanity produced in such non-modern
cultural settings. Above all, this fiction features an extensive written simulation of regional vernacular, a conspicuous effort to catch the nuances of local speech" (115).

7. The tendency to downplay the narrator's presence in favor of the details of story
and setting point to the journalistic background of many regional authors; for example,

Mark Twain's professional experience included journalism and travel writing, both of which certainly influenced his later fiction.

8. Of course, a number of recent critics have looked specifically at the confluence of travel and theory. See, for instance, Caren Kaplan's *Questions of Travel: Postmodern Discourses of Displacement* and Georges Van Den Abbeele's *Travel as Metaphor: From Montaigne to Rousseau.*

Works Cited

Adams, Charles H. "William Bartram's *Travels*: A Natural History of the South." *Rewriting the South: History and Fiction.* Ed. Lothar Hönnighausen. Tübingen: A. Francke, 1993. 112–20.

Adams, Percy G. *Travelers and Travel Liars, 1660–1800.* University of California Press, 1962.

———. *Travel Literature and the Evolution of the Novel.* Lexington: University Press of Kentucky, 1983.

Addeman, J. M. *Reminiscences of Two Years with the Colored Troops.* Providence: N. Bangs Williams, 1880.

Adorno, Theodor W. *Aesthetic Theory.* Ed. Gretel Adorno and Rolf Tiedemann. Trans. C. Lenhardt. New York: Routledge and Kegan Paul, 1984.

Allmendinger, Blake. "Acting and Slavery: Representations of Work in the Writings of Fanny Kemble." *Mississippi Quarterly* 41 (1988): 507–13.

Anderson, Benedict. *Imagined Communities: Reflections on the Origin and Spread of Nationalism.* Revised edition. New York: Verso, 1991.

Anderson, Douglas. "Bartram's *Travels* and the Politics of Nature." *Early American Literature* 3.2 (1990): 3–17.

Andrews, William L., ed. *Critical Essays on Frederick Douglass.* Boston: G. K. Hall, 1991.

Arac, Jonathan. "Narrative Forms." Bercovitch 605–778.

Arch, Stephen Carl. "The 'Progressive Steps' of the Narrator in Crèvecoeur's *Letters from an American Farmer*." *Studies in American Fiction* 18 (1990): 145–58.

Armstrong, Margaret. *Fanny Kemble: A Passionate Victorian.* New York: Macmillan, 1938.

Arner, Robert D. "Pastoral Patterns in William Bartram's *Travels*." *Tennessee Studies in Literature* 18 (1973): 133–45.

Ashcroft, Bill, Gareth Griffiths, and Helen Tiffin, eds. *The Post-Colonial Studies Reader.* New York: Routledge, 1995.

Baker, Houston. "Autobiographical Acts and the Voice of the Southern Slave." Andrews 94–107.

———. *Blues, Ideology, and Afro-American Literature: A Vernacular Theory.* Chicago: University of Chicago Press, 1984.

———. *The Journey Back: Issues in Black Literature and Criticism.* Chicago: University of Chicago Press, 1980.

———. *Long Black Song: Essays in Black American Literature and Culture.* Charlottesville: University Press of Virginia, 1972.

Barbeito, Patricia Felisa. "Captivity as Consciousness: The Literary and Cultural Imagination of the American Self." Diss. Harvard University, 1998.

Bartram, John. *Travels in Pensilvania and Canada.* 1751. Ann Arbor: University Microfilms, 1966.

Bartram, William. *Travels and Other Writings.* Ed. Thomas P. Slaughter. New York: Library of America, 1996.

Becker, Elizabeth C. "Harriet Jacobs's Search for Home." *CLA Journal* 35 (1992): 411–21.

Beecher, Catharine E. *A Treatise on Domestic Economy.* 1841. New York: Source Book, 1970.

Beecher, Catharine E., and Harriet Beecher Stowe. *The American Woman's Home: or, Principles of Domestic Science.* 1869. New York: Arno Press, 1971.

Beidler, Philip D. "Franklin's and Crèvecoeur's 'Literary' Americans." *Early American Literature* 13 (1978): 50–63.

Bercovitch, Sacvan, ed. *The Cambridge History of American Literature: Volume 2, 1820–1865.* Cambridge: Cambridge University Press, 1995.

Beveridge, Charles E. Introduction. Olmsted, *Slavery and the South* 1–39.

Bhabha, Homi. *The Location of Culture.* New York: Routledge, 1994.

Bierce, Ambrose. *Ambrose Bierce's Civil War.* Ed. William McCann. Washington, D.C.: Regnery Gateway, 1956.

Blanton, Casey. *Travel Writing: The Self and the World.* New York: Twayne, 1997.

Boorstin, Daniel. *The Americans: The National Experience.* New York: Random House, 1965.

Booth, Alison. "From Miranda to Prospero: The Works of Fanny Kemble." *Victorian Studies* 38 (1995): 227–54.

Branch, Michael. "Indexing American Possibilities: The Natural History Writing of Bartram, Wilson, and Audubon." *The Ecocriticism Reader.* Ed. Cheryll Glotfelty and Harold Fromm. Athens: University of Georgia Press, 1996. 282–302.

Brodhead, Richard. *Cultures of Letters: Scenes of Reading and Writing in Nineteenth-Century America.* Chicago: University of Chicago Press, 1993.

Brown, Gillian. *Domestic Individualism: Imagining Self in Nineteenth-Century America.* Berkeley: University of California Press, 1990.

Burson, William. *A Race for Liberty; or, My Capture, Imprisonment, and Escape.* Wellsville, Ohio: W. G. Foster, 1867.

Bush, Clive. *The Dream of Reason: American Consciousness and Cultural Achievement from Independence to the Civil War.* New York: St. Martin's Press, 1977.

Butor, Michel. "Travel and Writing." Kowalewski 53–70.

Buzard, James. *The Beaten Track: European Tourism, Literature, and the Ways to Culture, 1800–1918.* New York: Oxford University Press, 1993.

Caesar, Terry. *Forgiving the Boundaries: Home as Abroad in American Travel Writing.* Athens: University of Georgia Press, 1995.

Carew-Miller, Anna. "The Language of Domesticity in Crèvecoeur's *Letters from an American Farmer.*" *Early American Literature* 28 (1993): 242–54.

Carson, Barbara G. "Early American Tourists and the Commercialization of Leisure." *Of Consuming Interest: The Style of Life in the Eighteenth Century.* Eds. Cary Carson, Ronald Hoffman, and Peter J. Albert. Charlottesville: University Press of Virginia, 1994: 373–405.

Castronovo, Russ. " 'As to Nation I Belong to None': Ambivalence, Diaspora, and Frederick Douglass." *American Transcendental Quarterly* ns 9.3 (September 1995): 245–60.

Certeau, Michel de. *The Practice of Everyday Life.* Trans. Steven Rendall. Berkeley: University of California Press, 1984.

Chandler, Marilyn R. *Dwelling in the Text: Houses in American Fiction.* Berkeley: University of California Press, 1991.

Clark, Steve, ed. *Travel Writing and Empire: Postcolonial Theory in Transit.* New York: Zed Books, 1999.

Clark, Thomas. Editor's foreword. Coulter vii–ix.

Clifford, James. *Routes: Travel and Translation in the Late Twentieth Century.* Cambridge, Mass.: Harvard University Press, 1997.

Coffin, Charles Carleton. *Four Years of Fighting: A Volume of Personal Observation with the Army and Navy.* Boston: Ticknor and Fields, 1866.

Corbett, Mary Jean. *Representing Femininity: Middle-Class Subjectivity in Victorian and Edwardian Women's Autobiographies.* New York: Oxford University Press, 1992.

Coulter, E. Merton. *Travels in the Confederate States: A Bibliography.* 1948. Baton Rouge: Louisiana State University Press, 1994.

Craddock, Charles Egbert [Mary Noailles Murfree]. *In the Tennessee Mountains.* 1884. Ridgewood, N.J.: Gregg Press, 1968.

Crèvecoeur, J. Hector St. John de. *Letters from an American Farmer* and *Sketches of Eighteenth-Century America.* New York: Penguin, 1986.

Culler, Jonathan. *Framing the Sign: Criticism and Its Institutions.* Norman: University of Oklahoma Press, 1998.

Curtis, Newton Martin. *From Bull Run to Chancellorsville: The Story of the Sixteenth New York Infantry together with Personal Reminiscences.* New York: G. P. Putnam's Sons, 1906.

Douglass, Frederick. *My Bondage and My Freedom.* 1855. *Autobiographies.* New York: The Library of America, 1994.

———. *Narrative of the Life of Frederick Douglass, an American Slave.* 1845. Ed. David W. Blight. Boston: Bedford Books, 1993.

Dulles, Foster Rhea. *Americans Abroad: Two Centuries of European Travel.* Ann Arbor: University of Michigan Press, 1964.

Eakin, Sue, and Joseph Logsdon. Introduction. *Twelve Years a Slave.* By Solomon Northup. Baton Rouge: Louisiana State University Press, 1968.

Earnest, Ernest. *John and William Bartram.* Philadelphia: University of Pennsylvania Press, 1940.

Edwards, Justin D. *Exotic Journeys: Exploring the Erotics of U.S. Travel Literature, 1840–1930.* Hanover, N.H.: University Press of New England, 2001.

Egan, Ken, Jr. *The Riven Home: Narrative Rivalry in the American Renaissance.* Selins-
grove: Susquehanna University Press, 1997.

Elliott, Emory, et al., eds. *The Columbia History of the American Novel.* New York: Columbia University Press, 1991.

Fagin, N. Bryllion. *William Bartram: Interpreter of the American Landscape.* Baltimore:
Johns Hopkins University Press, 1933.

Fein, Albert, ed. *Landscape into Cityscape: Frederick Law Olmsted's Plans for a Greater
New York City.* New York: Van Nostrand Reinhold, 1967.

Fish, Cheryl J. *Black and White Women's Travel Narratives: Antebellum Explorations.*
Gainesville: University Press of Florida, 2004.

Fisher, Dexter, and Robert B. Stepto, eds. *Afro-American Literature: The Reconstruction
of Instruction.* New York: Modern Language Association, 1979.

Fisher, Philip. *Hard Facts: Setting and Form in the American Novel.* New York: Oxford
University Press, 1987.

Foner, Eric. *The Story of American Freedom.* New York: Norton, 1998.

Foote, Shelby. *The Civil War, a Narrative: Red River to Appomattox.* New York: Random
House, 1974.

Foote, Stephanie. *Regional Fictions: Culture and Identity in Nineteenth-Century American
Literature.* Madison: University of Wisconsin Press, 2001.

Fox-Genovese, Elizabeth. *Within the Plantation Household: Black and White Women of
the Old South.* Chapel Hill: University of North Carolina Press, 1988.

Franklin, John Hope. *A Southern Odyssey: Travelers in the Antebellum North.* Baton
Rouge: Louisiana State University Press, 1976.

Franklin, Wayne. *Discoverers, Explorers, Settlers: The Diligent Writers of Early America.*
Chicago: University of Chicago Press, 1979.

Fryer, Judith. *Felicitous Space: The Imaginative Structures of Edith Wharton and Willa
Cather.* Chapel Hill: University of North Carolina Press, 1986.

Fussell, Paul. *Abroad: British Literary Traveling between the Wars.* New York: Oxford University Press, 1980.

Gates, Henry Louis, Jr. "Binary Oppositions in Chapter One of *Narrative of the Life of
Frederick Douglass an American Slave Written by Himself.*" Fisher and Stepto 212–31.

————. *Figures in Black: Words, Signs, and the "Racial" Self.* New York: Oxford University Press, 1987.

Gellner, Ernest. *Nations and Nationalism.* Ithaca: Cornell University Press, 1983.

Genovese, Eugene D. *Roll, Jordan, Roll: The World the Slaves Made.* New York: Random
House, 1974.

Gibson, Donald B. "Harriet Jacobs, Frederick Douglass, and the Slavery Debate: Bondage, Family, and the Discourse of Domesticity." *Harriet Jacobs and Incidents in the Life
of a Slave Girl: New Critical Essays.* Ed. Deborah M. Garfield and Rafia Zafar. New
York: Cambridge University Press, 1996. 156–78.

————. "Reconciling Public and Private in Frederick Douglass' *Narrative.*" *American
Literature* 57 (December 1985): 549–69.

Gilroy, Paul. *The Black Atlantic: Modernity and Double Consciousness.* Cambridge, Mass.: Harvard University Press, 1993.

Goddu, Teresa A., and Craig V. Smith. "Scenes of Writing in Frederick Douglass's *Narrative*: Autobiography and the Creation of Self." *The Southern Review* 25.4 (1989): 822–40.

Grabo, Norman S. "Crèvecoeur's American: Beginning the World Anew." *William and Mary Quarterly* 3rd ser. 48 (1991): 159–72.

Grant, Susan-Mary. *North over South: Northern Nationalism and American Identity in the Antebellum Era.* Lawrence: University Press of Kansas, 2000.

Greenblatt, Stephen. *Marvelous Possessions: The Wonder of the New World.* Chicago: University of Chicago Press, 1991.

Hall, Catherine. "Missionary Stories: Gender and Ethnicity in England in the 1830s and 1840s." *Cultural Studies.* Ed. Cary Nelson, Paula A. Treichler, and Lawrence Grossberg. New York: Routledge, 1992.

Hall, Lee. *Olmsted's America: An "Unpractical" Man and His Vision of Civilization.* New York: Little, Brown, 1995.

Hayden, Dolores. *The Grand Domestic Revolution: A History of Feminist Designs for American Homes, Neighborhoods, and Cities.* Cambridge, Mass.: MIT Press, 1981.

———. *Redesigning the American Dream: The Future of Housing, Work, and Family Life.* New York: Norton, 1984.

Herbst, Josephine. *New Green World.* New York: Hastings House, 1954.

Higginson, Thomas Wentworth. *Army Life in a Black Regiment.* 1870. Williamstown, Mass.: Corner House, 1984.

Historic Opinions of the United States Supreme Court. New York: Vanguard, 1935.

Holbo, Christine. "Imagination, Commerce, and the Politics of Associationism in Crèvecoeur's *Letters from an American Farmer.*" *Early American Literature* 32 (1997): 20–65.

Holland, Patrick, and Graham Huggan. *Tourists with Typewriters: Critical Reflections on Contemporary Travel Literature.* Ann Arbor: University of Michigan Press, 1998.

Hooper, Glenn, and Tim Youngs, eds. *Perspectives on Travel Writing.* Studies in European Cultural Transition 19. Burlington, Vt.: Ashgate, 2004.

Howard, Benjamin C. *A Report of the Decision of the Supreme Court of the United States, and the Opinions of the Judges Therof, in the Case of Dred Scott versus John F. A. Sandford.* New York: Appleton, 1857.

Humphreys, Debra. "Power and Resistance in Harriet Jacobs' *Incidents in the Life of a Slave Girl.*" *Anxious Power: Reading, Writing, and Ambivalence in Narrative by Women.* Ed. Carol J. Singley and Susan Elizabeth Sweeney. Albany: State University of New York Press, 1993. 143–56.

Jacobs, Harriet A. *Incidents in the Life of a Slave Girl, Written by Herself.* 1861. Ed. Jean Fagan Yellin. Cambridge, Mass.: Harvard University Press, 1987.

Jefferson, Thomas. "Autobiography." *Writings.* New York: Library of America, 1984. 1–102.

Jehlen, Myra. "J. Hector St. John Crèvecoeur: A Monarcho-Anarchist in Revolutionary America." *American Quarterly* 31 (1979): 204–22.

Johnson, Richard. "What Is Cultural Studies Anyway?" *What Is Cultural Studies? A Reader.* Ed. John Story. London: Arnold, 1996. 75–114.

Jones, Anne Goodwyn, and Susan V. Donaldson, eds. *Haunted Bodies: Gender and Southern Texts.* Charlottesville: University Press of Virginia, 1997.

Kalfus, Melvin. *Frederick Law Olmsted: The Passion of a Public Artist.* New York: New York University Press, 1990.

Kaplan, Amy. "Nation, Region, and Empire." Elliott 240–66.

Kaplan, Caren. *Questions of Travel: Postmodern Discourses of Displacement.* Durham, N.C.: Duke University Press, 1996.

Kemble, Frances Anne. *Journal of a Residence on a Georgian Plantation in 1838–1839.* 1863. Ed. John A. Scott. Athens: University of Georgia Press, 1984.

Kibbey, Ann, and Michele Stepto. "The Antilanguage of Slavery: Frederick Douglass's 1845 *Narrative.*" Andrews 166–91.

Kolodny, Annette. *The Lay of the Land: Metaphor as Experience and History in American Life and Letters.* Chapel Hill: University of North Carolina Press, 1975.

Kowalewski, Michael, ed. *Temperamental Journeys: Essays on the Modern Literature of Travel.* Athens: University of Georgia Press, 1992.

Lawrence, D. H. *Studies in Classic American Literature.* 1923. New York: Penguin, 1961.

Lawson-Peebles, Robert. *Landscape and Written Expression in Revolutionary America.* Cambridge: Cambridge University Press, 1988.

Lee, Berta Grattan. "William Bartram: Naturalist or 'Poet'?" *Early American Literature* 7 (1972): 124–29.

Leed, Eric J. *The Mind of the Traveler: From Gilgamesh to Global Tourism.* New York: Basic Books, 1991.

Levy, Helen Fiddyment. *Fiction of the Home Place: Jewett, Cather, Glasgow, Porter, Welty, and Naylor.* Jackson: University Press of Mississippi, 1992.

Lewis, Robert. "Frontier and Civilization in the Thought of Frederick Law Olmsted." *American Quarterly* 29 (1977): 385–403.

Lincoln, Abraham. *Speeches and Writings, 1859–1865.* New York: Library of America, 1989.

Looby, Christopher. "The Constitution of Nature: Taxonomy as Politics in Jefferson, Peale, and Bartram." *Early American Literature* 22 (1987): 252–73.

MacCannell, Dean. *The Tourist: A New Theory of the Leisure Class.* 1976. Berkeley: University of California Press, 1999.

Machor, James L. "The Garden City in America: Crèvecoeur's *Letters* and the Urban-Pastoral Context." *American Studies* 23 (1982): 69–83.

Masur, Louis P., ed. *"The Real War Will Never Get in the Books": Selections from Writers during the Civil War.* New York: Oxford University Press, 1993.

Mattfield, Mary S. "Journey to the Wilderness: Two Travellers in Florida, 1696–1774." *Florida Historical Quarterly* 45 (1967): 327–51.

McCurry, Stephanie. *Masters of Small Worlds: Yeoman Households, Gender Relations, and the Political Culture of the Antebellum South Carolina Low Country.* New York: Oxford University Press, 1995.

Medeiros, Patricia M. "Three Travelers: Carver, Bartram, and Woolman." *American Literature, 1764–1789: The Revolutionary Years.* Ed. Everett Emerson. Madison: University of Wisconsin Press, 1977. 195–211.

Mills, Sara. *Discourses of Difference: An Analysis of Women's Travel Writing and Colonialism.* New York: Routledge, 1991.

Mitchell, Broadus. *Frederick Law Olmsted: A Critic of the Old South.* Baltimore: Johns Hopkins University Press, 1924.

Moore, L. Hugh. "The Aesthetic Theory of William Bartram." *Essays in Arts and Sciences* 12 (1983): 17–35.

Morgan, Winifred. "Gender-Related Difference in the Slave Narratives of Harriet Jacobs and Frederick Douglass." *American Studies* 35.2 (1994): 73–94.

Mudimbe, V. Y. *The Invention of Africa: Gnosis, Philosophy, and the Order of Knowledge.* Bloomington: Indiana University Press, 1988.

Mulvey, Christopher. *Anglo-American Landscapes: A Study of Nineteenth-Century Anglo-American Travel Literature.* Cambridge: Cambridge University Press, 1983.

———. *Transatlantic Manners: Social Patterns in Nineteenth-Century Anglo-American Travel Literature.* Cambridge: Cambridge University Press, 1990.

Northup, Solomon. *Twelve Years a Slave.* 1853. Ed. Sue Eakin and Joseph Logsdon. Baton Rouge: Louisiana State University Press, 1968.

Norton, Oliver Willcox. *Army Letters, 1861–1865.* Chicago: O. L. Deming, 1903.

Olmsted, Frederick Law. *The Cotton Kingdom.* 1861. Ed. Arthur M. Schlesinger Sr. New York: Modern Library, 1984.

———. *Slavery and the South: 1852–1857.* Vol. 2 of *The Papers of Frederick Law Olmsted.* Ed. Charles E. Beveridge and Charles Capen McLaughlin. Baltimore: Johns Hopkins University Press, 1981.

O'Meally, Robert G. "Frederick Douglass' 1845 *Narrative*: The Text Was Meant to Be Preached." Fisher and Stepto 192–211.

Pepper, George W. *Personal Recollections of Sherman's Campaigns in Georgia and the Carolinas.* Zanesville, Ohio: Hugh Dunne, 1866.

Philbrick, Thomas. *St. John de Crèvecoeur.* New York: Twayne, 1970.

Phillips, Ulrich B. *American Negro Slavery.* 1918. Baton Rouge: Louisiana State University Press, 1966.

Plumstead, A. W. "Hector St. John de Crèvecoeur." *American Literature, 1764–1789: The Revolutionary Years.* Ed. Everett Emerson. Madison: University of Wisconsin Press, 1977. 213–32.

Porter, Carolyn. "Social Discourse and Nonfiction Prose." *Columbia Literary History of the United States.* Ed. Elliott Emory. New York: Columbia University Press, 1988. 345–63.

Porter, Dennis. *Haunted Journeys: Desire and Transgression in European Travel Writing.* Princeton: Princeton University Press, 1991.

Powell, Lawrence N. Introduction. Olmsted, *The Cotton Kingdom* ix–xl.

Pratt, Mary Louise. *Imperial Eyes: Travel Writing and Transculturation.* New York: Routledge, 1992.

———. "Scratches on the Face of the Country; or, What Mr. Barrow Saw in the Land of the Bushmen." *Critical Inquiry* 12 (1985): 119–43.

———. "Travel Narrative and Imperialist Vision." *Understanding Narrative.* Ed. James Phelan and Peter J. Rabinowitz. Columbus: Ohio State University Press, 1994. 199–221.

Quint, Alonzo H. *The Potomac and the Rapidan: Army Notes.* Boston: Crosby and Nichols, 1864.

Rapping, Elayne Antler. "Theory and Experience in Crèvecoeur's America." *American Quarterly* 19 (1967): 707–18.

Reising, Russell J. *The Unusable Past: Theory and the Study of American Literature.* New York: Methuen, 1986.

Rhodes, Elisha Hunt. *All for the Union: The Civil War Diary and Letters of Elisha Hunt Rhodes.* Ed. Robert Hunt Rhodes. New York: Vintage, 1985.

Rice, Grantland S. "Crèvecoeur and the Politics of Authorship in Republican America." *Early American Literature* 28 (1993): 91–119.

———. *The Transformation of Authorship in America.* Chicago: University of Chicago Press, 1997.

Ripley, Edward Hastings. *Vermont General: The Unusual War Experiences of Edward Hastings Ripley, 1862–1865.* Ed. Otto Eisenschiml. New York: Davin-Adair, 1960.

Roberts, Diane. *The Myth of Aunt Jemima: Representations of Race and Region.* New York: Routledge, 1994.

Robertson, George, et al., eds. *Travellers' Tales: Narratives of Home and Displacement.* New York: Routledge, 1994.

Robinson, David M. "Community and Utopia in Crèvecoeur's *Sketches.*" *American Literature* 62 (1990): 17–31.

Rojek, Chris, and John Urry, eds. *Touring Cultures: Transformations of Travel and Theory.* New York: Routledge, 1997.

Romero, Lora. *Home Fronts: Domesticity and Its Critics in the Antebellum United States.* Durham, N.C.: Duke University Press, 1997.

Romines, Ann. *The Home Plot: Women, Writing, and Domestic Ritual.* Amherst: University of Massachusetts Press, 1992.

Roper, Laura Wood. *FLO: A Biography of Frederick Law Olmsted.* Baltimore: Johns Hopkins University Press, 1973.

Ross, Marlon B. "Romancing the Nation-State: The Poetics of Romantic Nationalism." *Macropolitics of Nineteenth-Century Literature: Nationalism, Exoticism, Imperialism.* Ed. Jonathan Arac and Harriet Ritvo. Durham, N.C.: Duke University Press, 1995: 56–85.

Rowe, John Carlos. *At Emerson's Tomb: The Politics of Classic American Literature.* New York: Columbia University Press, 1997.

Rybczynski, Witold. *A Clearing in the Distance: Frederick Law Olmsted and America in the Nineteenth Century.* New York: Scribner, 1999.

Saar, Doreen Alvarez. "Crèvecoeur's 'Thoughts on Slavery': *Letters from an American Farmer* and Whig Rhetoric." *Early American Literature* 22 (1987): 192–203.

Said, Edward. "Traveling Theory." *The World, the Text, the Critic.* Cambridge, Mass.: Harvard University Press, 1983.

Scheper, George L. "The Reformist Vision of Frederick Law Olmsted and the Poetics of Park Design." *New England Quarterly* 62 (1989): 369–402.

Schriber, Mary Suzanne. *Writing Home: American Women Abroad, 1830–1920.* Charlottesville: University Press of Virginia, 1997.

Seelye, John. *Beautiful Machine.* New York: Oxford University Press, 1991.

———. "Beauty Bare: William Bartram and His Triangulated Wilderness." *Prospects: The Annual of American Cultural Studies.* Vol. 6. Ed. Jack Salzman. New York: Burt Franklin, 1981. 37–54.

Shaw, Robert Gould. *Blue-Eyed Child of Fortune: The Civil War Letters of Colonel Robert Gould Shaw.* Ed. Russell Duncan. Athens: University of Georgia Press, 1992.

Silver, Bruce. "William Bartram's and Other Eighteenth-Century Accounts of Nature." *Journal of the History of Ideas* 39 (1978): 597–614.

Skinfill, Mauri. "Nation and Miscegenation: *Incidents in the Life of a Slave Girl.*" *Arizona Quarterly* 52.2 (1995): 63–79.

Slaughter, Thomas P. *The Natures of John and William Bartram.* New York: Knopf, 1996.

———. Personal interview. Oxford, Mississippi. May 1998.

Slotkin, Richard. *Regeneration through Violence: The Mythology of the American Frontier, 1600–1860.* Hanover, N.H.: Wesleyan University Press, 1973.

Smith, Valene, ed. *Hosts and Guests: The Anthropology of Tourism.* 2nd ed. Philadelphia: University of Pennsylvania Press, 1989.

Smith, Valerie. *Self-Discovery and Authority in Afro-American Narrative.* Cambridge, Mass.: Harvard University Press, 1987.

Spengemann, William C. *The Adventurous Muse: The Poetics of American Fiction, 1789–1900.* New Haven: Yale University Press, 1977.

Spurr, David. *The Rhetoric of Empire: Colonial Discourse in Journalism, Travel Writing, and Imperial Administration.* Durham, N.C.: Duke University Press, 1993.

Stephens, George E. *A Voice of Thunder: The Civil War Letters of George E. Stephens.* Ed. Donald Yacovone. Urbana: University of Illinois Press, 1997.

Stepto, Robert B. "Narration, Authentication, and Authorial Control in Frederick Douglass' *Narrative* of 1845." Fisher and Stepto 178–91.

Stevens, Charles Carleton. *Three Years in the Sixth Corps.* New York: D. Van Nostrand, 1867.

Stone, Albert E. "Identity and Art in Frederick Douglass's *Narrative.*" Andrews 62–78.

———. Introduction. *Letters from an American Farmer* and *Sketches of Eighteenth-Century America.* 1916. By J. Hector St. John de Crèvecoeur. New York: Penguin, 1986.

Stowe, Harriet Beecher. "Appeal to the Women of the Free States." *Uncle Tom's Cabin.* New York: Norton, 1994. 427–29.

———. *The Key to Uncle Tom's Cabin.* 1853. New York: Arno and the New York Times, 1969.

———. *Uncle Tom's Cabin.* 1852. Ed. Elizabeth Ammons. New York: Norton, 1994.

Stowe, William W. *Going Abroad: European Travel in Nineteenth-Century American Culture.* Princeton: Princeton University Press, 1994.

Sundquist, Eric J., ed. *Frederick Douglass: New Literary and Historical Essays.* Cambridge: Cambridge University Press, 1990.

———. Introduction. Sundquist, ed., *Frederick Douglass* 1–22.

———. "The Literature of Expansion and Race." Bercovitch 125–328.

Tate, Claudia. *Domestic Allegories of Political Desire: The Black Heroine's Text at the Turn of the Century.* New York: Oxford University Press, 1997.

Taylor, Susie King. *Reminiscences of My Life in Camp.* 1902. New York: Arno Press, 1968.

Terrie, Philip G. "Tempests and Alligators: The Ambiguous Wilderness of William Bartram." *North Dakota Review* 59 (1991): 17–32.

Tompkins, Jane. *Sensational Designs: The Cultural Work of American Fiction, 1790–1860.* New York: Oxford University Press, 1985.

———. "Sentimental Power: *Uncle Tom's Cabin* and the Politics of Literary History." *Ideology and Classic American Literature.* Ed. Sacvan Bercovitch and Myra Jehlen. New York: Cambridge University Press, 1986. 267–92.

Travers, Len. *Celebrating the Fourth: Independence Day and the Rites of Nationalism in the Early Republic.* Amherst: University of Massachusetts Press, 1997.

Urry, John. *The Tourist Gaze.* 2nd ed. London: Sage Publications, 2002.

Van Den Abbeele, Georges. *Travel as Metaphor: From Montaigne to Rousseau.* Minneapolis: University of Minnesota Press, 1992.

Washington, George. "Eighth Annual Message to Congress." *Writings.* New York: Library of America, 1997. 978–85.

Weber, Max. *The Protestant Ethic and the Spirit of Capitalism.* 1904. Translated by Talcott Parsons. London: HarperCollins, 1930.

Welter, Barbara. *Dimity Convictions: The American Woman in the Nineteenth Century.* Athens: Ohio University Press, 1976.

Wesley, Marilyn C. *Secret Journeys: The Trope of Women's Travel in American Literature.* Albany: State University of New York Press, 1999.

White, Dana. "A Connecticut Yankee in Cotton's Kingdom." White and Kramer 11–51.

White, Dana, and Victor A. Kramer. *Olmsted South: Old South Critic/New South Planner.* Westport, Conn.: Greenwood Press, 1979.

Whitman, George Washington. *Civil War Letters of George Washington Whitman.* Ed. Jerome M. Loving. Durham, N.C.: Duke University Press, 1975.

Williams, Carol Traynor, ed. *Travel Culture: Essays on What Makes Us Go.* Wesport, Conn.: Praegor, 1998.

Williams, Patrick, and Laura Chrisman, eds. *Colonial Discourse and Post-Colonial Theory: A Reader.* New York: Columbia University Press, 1994.

Wilson, Christopher P. "Introduction[: The Late Nineteenth Century]." Elliott 157–59.

Wilson, Edmund. *Patriotic Gore: Studies in the Literature of the American Civil War.* New York: Oxford University Press, 1962.

Winston, Robert P. " 'Strange Order of Things!': The Journey to Chaos in *Letters from an American Farmer.*" *Early American Literature* 19 (1984–85): 249–66.

Withey, Lynne. *Grand Tours and Cook's Tours: A History of Leisure Travel, 1750–1915.* New York: W. Morrow, 1997.

Worley, Sam. "Solomon Northup and the Sly Philosophy of the Slave Pen." *Callaloo* 20.1 (1997): 243–59.

Yellin, Jean Fagan, ed. Introduction. Jacobs xiii–xxxiv.

Zafar, Rafia. "Franklinian Douglass: The Afro-American as Representative Man." Sundquist, ed., *Frederick Douglass* 99–117.

Ziff, Larzer. *Return Passages: Great American Travel Writing, 1780–1910.* New Haven: Yale University Press, 2000.

———. *Writing in the New Nation: Prose, Print, and Politics in the Early United States.* New Haven: Yale University Press, 1991.

Index

Abroad (Fussell), 10

Adams, Charles, 55, 207 (nn. 32, 36)

Adams, Percy, 10

Age of Nationalism, 2

Allmendinger, Blake, 119

American identity: construction of, 7; as founded on movement, 1; and immigration, 1; and international travel, 1; struggle to define, 1

American Negro Slavery (Phillips), 83

Americans, The (Boorstin), 147

Anderson, Benedict: "imagined community" concept of, 2; on modern-nation characteristics, 6, 22, 143; on print culture, 22, 143; on U.S. founding documents, 7

Andrews, William, 70

Arac, Jonathan, 79

Articles of Confederation, 2–3, 6

Audubon, John James, 196

Baker, Houston, 65, 69, 70, 79, 81, 83, 210 (n. 5)

Barbeito, Patricia, 24, 203 (n. 5)

Bartram, John, 45; botanical garden of, 42; Florida trip of, 42; Linneaus's view of, 41; portrait of, in Crèvecoeur's *Letters*, 41–42; as Royal Botanist, 42; *Travels in Pensilvania and Canada*, 42

Bartram, William: and Alachua Savanna, 48–52; on alligators, 56–58; and American Revolution, 59; as businessman, 43; critical views of, 44; as disciple of Linneaus, 43; drawings of, for Fothergill, 42, 47, 48–51; as Enlightenment figure, 21, 42–43, 44; and epistemology, 15–16, 21; and father, 42; as forerunner of Emerson and Thoreau, 44; and Fothergill, John, 42–43, 47–48, 52; hurricane description of, 58–59; on Little Saint Johns River, 47–48; and narrative persona, 20; and Native Americans, 49, 53–55, 57, 58; and natural history, 46, 52; as nature writer, 196; as Puc-Puggy, 43; and report to Fothergill, 41–43, 45; as representative American, 15–16, 19, 44, 54, 56, 61; revisions of *Travels* by, 44, 209 (n. 49); and Romanticism, 21, 44; and Saint Johns River, 55–61; and slave narratives, 83, 84; and slavery, 43; soldiers compared with, 166, 190; and travel, 20; as traveler, 61–62; traveling companions of, 26. See also *Travels* (W. Bartram)

Becker, Elizabeth C., 134, 220 (nn. 48, 50)

Beecher, Catharine, 111

Beecher, Henry Ward, 186

Beidler, Philip, 41

Beveridge, Charles E., 143, 154, 221 (nn. 1, 8)

Bhabha, Homi, 9

Bierce, Ambrose, 188, 189–90, 226 (n. 3), 228 (n. 19)

Black and White Women's Travel Narratives (Fish), 13

Boorstin, Daniel, 147

Brace, Charles Loring, 141, 142, 222 (n. 9)

Bremer, Fredrika, 105

Brent, Linda. See *Incidents in the Life of a Slave Girl* (Jacobs); Jacobs, Harriet

Brodhead, Richard, 195–96, 229 (n. 1)

Brown, Gillian, 125, 218 (n. 24)

Burson, William: and Andersonville Prison, 184; and Quakers, 183; and slavery's effect on southern society, 175; and "Union League," 184–85, 186; and Union sentiment in the South, 183–85

Butler, Pierce, 16, 114, 118, 121, 124. *See also* Kemble, Fanny

Buzard, James, 12, 199 (n. 1), 200 (n. 10)

Caesar, Terry, 11–12, 13

Carson, Barbara, 4

Chandler, Marilyn, 104

Citizenship: of black Americans, 64; and slavery, 66; travel as component of, 71

Civil War: movement of army during, 166, 168–70; number of travelers during, 165–66; and relationship of North and South, 191–92. *See also* Travelers, Civil War soldiers as

Clark, Thomas, 171

Constitution, U.S., 3–4, 7

Corbett, Mary Jean, 108

Cotton Kingdom, The (F. L. Olmsted): as abolitionist text, 145, 222 (n. 9); argument of, 148–49; British attitudes toward, 146; creation of, 142, 145; influence of, on North, 146; method of, 148, 223 (n. 15); North/South division in, 143, 145; objectivity of, 146–48; as paradigmatic, 145; poor white view of, 154–55; publication of, 146; reception of, critical, 146–48; relation of, to Olmsted's landscape architecture, 147–48; reviews of, 146; sales of, 222 (n. 10); tone of, 145–46

Coulter, E. Merton, 165, 227 (n. 9)

Craddock, Charles Egbert (Mary Noailles Murfree), 194–96

Crèvecoeur, J. Hector St. John de: authorial voice of, 25; and Bartram, William, 61; and Charles Town (Charleston), 25; and definition of American, 6, 15; and Enlightenment, 35; and farmer ideal, 15; and middle colony, 24; and Olmsted, Frederick Law, 143; and ontology, 21; as representative American, 15, 20; and slave narratives, 67, 71; and slavery, 30–32; soldiers compared with, 190; and travel, 20, 25; as traveling farmer, 21; use of nature by, 35. *See also* James (narrator of *Letters from an American Farmer*); *Letters from an American Farmer* (Crèvecoeur)

"Cult of True Womanhood," 112–13

Curtis, Newton, 179–81, 183

"Dancin' Party at Harrison's Cove, The" (Murfree), 194–95

Declaration of Independence, 7

De Forrest, John William: and environment, 176–77; and slavery, 182; and southern poverty, 175

Discourses of Difference (Mills), 12–13, 106

Discoverers, Explorers, Settlers (Franklin), 11

Domestic Manners of the American (Trollope), 105

Douglass, Frederick: "accidental" travel by, 64; appropriation of city landscape by, 73–74; and Auld, Hugh, 68, 71–72; and Auld, Sophia, 68, 71–72; and Auld, Thomas, 78; as "Bailey, Frederick," 82; and Bailey, Harriet, 82; and Canada, 78; as citizen-traveler, 80; contrasted with Northup, 67–68; and Covey, Edward, 68, 76; and Dodson, Edward,

78; escape of, 79–80; father of, 76; friendship of, with white children, 72–73; and Garrison, William Lloyd, 212–13 (n. 24); and Henry, Patrick, 81; importance of travel to, 68, 69, 74; and Jacobs, Harriet, 127, 135–36; literacy of, 73; and Lloyd, Colonel, 68, 74, 77–78; and master's sailboat, 74–75, 78; mother of, 68, 82; *My Bondage and My Freedom*, 100; optimism of, 100; relationship of, to language, 70–71; as representative American, 69, 81–82; and Sandy, 79; and slave songs, 67; soldiers compared with, 166; and subjectivity, creation of, 71; and tourism, 100; as traveler, 16, 67, 73–82; as trickster, 70; and Underground Railroad, 212 (n. 23). See also *Narrative of the Life of Frederick Douglass, an American Slave* (Douglass)

Dred Scott v. John F. A. Sandford, 63–64, 66, 102

Eakin, Sue, 84, 227 (n. 14)
Earnest, Ernest, 44
Edwards, Justin, 5, 201 (n. 17)
Egan, Ken, Jr., 104
Emerson, John, 63

Fein, Albert, 141
Fish, Cheryl J., 13
Foote, Shelby, 166, 168, 186, 227 (n. 8)
Fothergill, John, 42
Fox-Genovese, Elizabeth: on household, 104, 115, 121–22, 125, 219 (n. 35); and Northup, Solomon, 213 (n. 29); on women's relationship to master, 110
Franklin, Wayne, 11
Fryer, Judith, 126
"Fugitive slave," definition of, 65–66
Fugitive Slave Law, 66, 101–2
Fussell, Paul, 10

Gates, Henry Louis, Jr., 70, 71
Gellner, Ernest, 6
Gibson, Donald, 81, 219 (n. 42), 220 (n. 47)
Gilroy, Paul, 13–14
Goodloe, Daniel, 145
Grabo, Norman, 38,
Greenblatt, Stephen, 11

Hall, Basil, 5, 105
Hall, Catherine, 7
Hall, Lee, 155–56, 221 (n. 5)
Hayden, Dolores, 104, 125, 216–17 (n. 18)
Herbst, Josephine, 42
Higginson, Thomas Wentworth: as commander, 182, 189; and environment, 175–76, 177; and Kemble, Fanny, 227 (n. 11); and northern enterprise, 174; and travel, 227 (n. 6); on Union sympathy, 228 (n. 17); and work ethic, southern, 174
Holbo, Christine, 32, 202 (nn. 2, 3), 204 (n. 12)
Home: as alternative to men's domains, 111; as broad concept, 104; contrasted with household, 103, 104; as domain of women, 103; as haven, 104; and intranational travel, 104; and Kemble, Fanny, 125; nation as, 112–14; and plantation, 104, 121; and politics, 111–14
Homes of the New World, The (Bremer), 105
Hooper, Glenn, 193
Household. *See* Home

Imperial Eyes (Pratt), 45–46, 106, 109, 164; and "capitalist vanguard," 17; and travel writing, criticism of, 10–11; and travel writing, women's, 12
Incidents in the Life of a Slave Girl (Jacobs): and Alabama, 129; Benjamin (son) in, 137; Benjamin (uncle) in, 133;

Incidents in the Life of a Slave Girl
(Jacobs) (*continued*)
and Boston, 135, 137–38; "Brent, Linda,"
in, 128, 130, 219 (n. 38); Bruce, Mr., in,
138, 139; Bruce, Mrs. (first), in, 137;
Bruce, Mrs. (second), in, 139; and
Chesapeake Bay, 136; children of Jacobs
in, 133, 137; on "domestic institution,"
130; and domestic space, 127, 131, 133;
and economics, 136–37; Ellen
(daughter) in, 133, 137; and England,
138; escape of Jacobs in, 135–36; and
family stability, 130–31; Fanny in,
135–36; Flint, Dr., in, 130, 132, 133, 134,
135, 137; Flint, Mrs., in, 128, 131; and
Fugitive Slave Law, 138, 139; garret of
Jacobs in, 133–35, 136; grandmother of
Jacobs in, 131–33; Hobbs family in, 137;
home versus household in, 105; and
legal system, 134; and Louisiana, 129;
marriage in, 132; on Martineau,
Harriet, 129; and Middle Passage, 136;
on Murray, Amelia, 129–30; and New
York, 136, 137, 139; and North, 136, 139;
Peter in, 135; and Philadelphia, 135–36;
Psyche in, 215 (n. 9); purchase of, 139;
and reader, 128, 130–31, 138–39, 140;
reception of, 128; sexual demands on
Jacobs in, 130; and topics, forbidden,
140; and travel, freedom from, 139; and
travelers, previous, 128–29; as travel
literature, 16–17, 127–31
In the Tennessee Mountains (Murfree),
194–95

Jacobs, Harriet: audience of, 108, 110; and
"Brent, Linda," 128, 130, 219 (n. 38);
Child, Lydia Marie, as editor of work
of, 219 (n. 40); citizenship of, 127; on
home, 105, 131–33, 138, 139; and legal
discourse, 107; and "loophole of
retreat," 109, 133, 134–35; physical

danger of, 127; soldiers compared with,
166; and subjectivity, creation of, 127;
tone of, in publication, 108; and travel,
16–17, 127–40 passim; and travel,
geographical, 127; and travel,
ideological, 134; and United States, 139.
See also *Incidents in the Life of a Slave
Girl* (Jacobs)
James (narrator of *Letters from an
American Farmer*): and American
Revolution, 39; in Charles Town
(Charleston), 30–31, 35–37, 38; and
children, 23, 40; contentment of, 22; as
farmer, 20, 22–26; as farmer-traveler,
38–41; and father, 23; founding new
society, 40–41; and frontier, 39–41;
Latin used by, 36; and legal system, 34;
in Nantucket, 27–30; and Native
American culture, 25, 28, 34, 39–41; and
natural law, 35; on slavery, 30–34,
36–38, 206 (n. 19); as traveler, 20, 25,
29; wife of, 32; *See also* Crèvecoeur,
J. Hector St. John de; *Letters from an
American Farmer* (Crèvecoeur)
Jefferson, Thomas, 104, 181
Johnson, Richard, 9
*Journal of a Residence on a Georgian
Plantation in 1838–1839* (Kemble):
argument of, 125; epistolary form of,
107; establishment of national
domestic space in, 105; quotations
from slaves in, 106–7, as representative
text, 115; as travel literature, 16
Journey in the Back Country, A (F. L.
Olmsted), 142, 145
Journey in the Seaboard Slave States, A
(F. L. Olmsted), 142, 145
Journey through Texas (F. L. Olmsted),
142, 145

Kemble, Fanny: as actress, 114, 119, 216
(n. 13), 218 (n. 28); audience of, 108;

and Butler, Pierce, 114, 118, 121, 124; and Butler Island, 116, 118, 124; and domestic ideology, northern, 125–27; and domestic ideology, southern, 115; and "domestic institution," 123; and domestic ritual, 123; and economics, 140; and Elizabeth, 120, 121; as Englishwoman, 121; and home, ideal, 105, 115, 121, 125; house of, 117; as intercessor, 122; and Jack, 119, 124; and labor, 119–21; as Lady Macbeth, 219 (n. 36); and legal discourse, 107; as mistress, 109, 131; narrative identity of, 114; and Ned, 120; as outsider, 119; on paths, 124; and philanthropy, 110; prejudice of, 110, 215 (n. 7); and privacy, lack of, 117; self-fashioning of, 109–10; and Shaw, Robert, 174; as slave, 126; on slave marriage, 218 (n. 29); and slave quarters, 118, 122–23; and slavery, opposition to, 114; and slave songs, 67; and southern climate, 121; on southern houses, 115; and St. Leger, Harriet, 115; and St. Simon's Island, 115, 118; and sympathy for slaves, 106; and travel, 16, 114–27 passim. See also *Journal of a Residence on a Georgian Plantation* (Kemble)

Key to Uncle Tom's Cabin, The (Stowe), 84

Kingsbury, Frederick, 142

Kolodny, Annette, 31, 205 (n. 18)

Lawrence, D. H., 19, 33

Lawson-Peebles, Robert, 7

Lee, Robert E., 180, 187

Letters from an American Farmer (Crèvecoeur): and American as traveler, 21; as American national epic, 19; and American Revolution, 39; Andrew, the Hebridean, in, 26–27; and Bartram, John, 41–42; bees and kingbird in, 33–35; critical reception of, 19, 25; dedication of, to Abbé Raynal, 31–32; and European immigrants, 24; and farming ideal, 15; and F. B., Mr., 22, 24, 32–33; letters 1–3, 25; letter 2, 32; letter 3, 26; letter 4, 27; letter 7, 28; letter 9, 25, 30–31, 35–38; letter 11, 41; letter 12, 25, 39–41; and Nantucket, 27–30; Native Americans in, 25, 28, 34; and nature, 23, 35–38; and "New Garden," 30; role of, in construction of American identity, 19; and slavery, 25, 30–32, 36–38; and the South, 35–38; as travel literature, 26. *See also* James (narrator of *Letters from an American Farmer*)

Lewis, Robert, 159

Lincoln, Abraham, 191–92

Linnaeus, 41–42; classification system of, 45, 52–53, 55

Lippincott's, 194

Literacy, as focus of Douglass criticism, 65, 67, 69

Logsdon, Joseph, 84, 227 (n. 14)

Looby, Christopher, 35, 55

MacCannell, Dean, 192, 201 (n. 16)

Martineau, Harriet, 105, 106, 129

Marvelous Possessions (Greenblatt), 11

Mason, George, 180, 181

Mason-Dixon Line, 104

Masters of Small Worlds (McCurry), 144

Masur, Louis P., 176, 182, 228 (nn. 18, 20)

McCurry, Stephanie, 144, 156–57

Medeiros, Patricia, 6, 8

Melville, Herman, 142, 196, 222 (n. 13)

Mills, Sara, 12–13, 106, 110–11, 215 (n. 8)

Missouri Compromise, 64

Mitchell, Broadus, 146, 147

Morgan, Winifred, 131

Mudimbe, V. Y., 8

Muir, John, 196

Murfree, Mary Noailles, 194–96

Murray, Amelia, 129–30
Murray, Charles Augustus, 5, 105
My Bondage and My Freedom (Douglass),
    100

*Narrative of the Life of Frederick Douglass,
    an American Slave* (Douglass): and
    abolitionists, 80, 87; and Baltimore, 69,
    74, 78; boats in, 74–75; Bondly, Beal, in,
    78; and Chesapeake Bay, 67, 75; Coffin,
    William C., in, 80; critical preference
    for, 83, 213 (n. 27); criticism of, 69–71;
    Demby in, 78; and Franklin, Benjamin,
    71; Gore, Mr., in, 78; literacy in, 73; and
    Maryland, 68; and New Bedford, 80;
    and New York, 68; and Philadelphia,
    78; prefaces to, 75; roads in, 72–73,
    77–78; speaking engagements in, 80–81;
    themes of, 67; travel in, importance of,
    16, 68
Nationalism: role of newspapers in, 6–7;
    theories of, 6
Northup, Solomon: as abolitionist, 84;
    and American Dream, 87; and
    American Revolution, 87; and
    American society, 87; and Baird, Mr.,
    87; and Brown, Lewis, 87; as citizen, 67,
    100; as coauthor, 84; and community,
    relationship with, 85, 99–100;
    contrasted with Douglass, 67–68, 93;
    and Eddy, Timothy, 87; enslavement of,
    88–102 passim; family of, 86; as farmer,
    86–87; father of, 86; free papers of, 88;
    kidnapping of, 88–102 passim; and
    Mary, 97; and McEachron, David, 87;
    and movement, 90–93; and Northup,
    Anne (wife), 86–87, 100; and Northup,
    Henry B., 87, 99–100; as "participant
    observer," 95–96; as "Platt," 82–83,
    90–91; and Proudfit, Rev., 87; and
    recovery of identity, 83; relationship of,
    to Wilson, David, 84; as slave, 67–68;

and slave response to Union Army, 182;
    soldiers compared with, 166, 182;
    struggle of, for legal recognition, 83;
    swimming ability of, 94; and Taylor,
    Isaac, 87; and travel, 16; as traveler, 67;
    and Van Nortwich, William, 87; violin
    playing of, 86–88, 93; and women's
    travel narratives, 127, 136, 138. See also
    Twelve Years a Slave (Northup)

Olmsted, Frederick Law: and
    abolitionism, 142; and "capitalist
    vanguard," 17; as Central Park
    designer, 145, 148, 221 (n. 7), 225
    (n. 29); and China, 149; and Civil
    War, 167, 226 (n. 4); class views of,
    161–63; and Dix, Edwards, and
    Company, 142; and economy,
    southern, 17; father of, 141; and free
    labor, 162, 225 (n. 29); on German
    immigrants, 144, 149, 163–64; goals
    of, 227 (n. 8); and Goodloe, Daniel,
    145; and immigration, 152, 163; and
    literary ambitions, 142–43; and New
    England, 144, 148, 155–57; and
    newspapers, 201 (n. 20); and *New-York
    Daily Times*, 142, 150, 154, 158; and *New
    York Times*, 141; "orientalist" discourse
    of, 144; and public institutions, 150;
    Puritan heritage of, 143; and *Putnam's
    Magazine*, 142; racism of, 153, 224
    (n.20); and Raymond, Henry J., 221
    (n. 2); and reform, 143, 147–48, 162, 174,
    225 (n. 29); revisions of, 142; on roads,
    149–50, 157, 174; and service, 143; and
    slavery, 145–46, 148–64; and the South,
    travel in, 158–59; on southern cities,
    150; on southern landscape, 150–53;
    Staten Island farm of, 141, 143, 144;
    and subjectivity, creation of, 160–61;
    and travel, 15, 141–64 passim; and
    Vaux, Calvert, 221 (n. 7); on Virginia,

149, 223 (n. 15); as voice of North, 148; as "Yeoman," 147; yeoman ideal of, 17, 141, 143, 144, 155–56

Olmsted, Frederick Law, works of: *A Journey in the Back Country*, 142, 145; *A Journey in the Seaboard Slave States*, 142, 145; *Journey through Texas*, 142, 145; *Slavery and the South*, 142; *Walks and Talks of an American Farmer in England*, 141, 223 (n. 15). See also *Cotton Kingdom, The* (F. L. Olmsted)

Olmsted, John, 141, 142, 222 (n. 9)

Pepper, George, 174, 177–79, 183–84, 185

Philbrick, Thomas, 36, 202 (n. 2)

Phillips, U. B., 83

Plumstead, A. W., 25, 205 (n. 17)

Porter, Carolyn, 7, 8, 137, 147, 148, 211 (n. 11)

Powell, Lawrence N., 143, 146, 147, 156, 157, 161

Pratt, Mary Louise: on "anti-conquest," 45–46; on "capitalist vanguard," 17, 145, 164; on categories of travel narratives, 105, 106; on "contact zone," 11; on expansive capitalism, 161; on natural history, 52; on social reformism, 216 (n. 15); on women travel writers, 12, 106, 109

Pratt, Mary Louise, works of: "Scratches on the Face of the Country," 105; "Travel Narrative and Imperialist Vision," 14. See also *Imperial Eyes* (Pratt)

Quint, Alonzo, 175, 183, 185–86, 229 (n. 21)

Redding, J. Saunders, 146–47

Redesigning the American Dream (Hayden), 104, 125, 216–17 (n. 18)

Regional writing, 194–96

Reising, Russell, 78

Return Passages (Ziff), 11

Rhodes, Elisha Hunt: advancement of, through ranks, 169, 226 (n. 4); and desertion, 170; and environment, 171–72, 177; and Katie (horse), 173; and movement, 168–70; and nation, diversity of, 188–90; and Richmond, 181–82; and sites visited, 168–69; and slaves, 182, 188; on the South, 173–74; and southerners, relations with, 187; and travel, 170–73, 188–89, 190; and troops, black soldiers among, 182; and Union sentiment in South, 228 (nn. 16–17); and Washington, George, 180

Rice, Grantland, 31, 203 (n. 3)

Ripley, Edward, 178, 187, 227 (n. 8)

Roberts, Diane, 106, 115, 122, 217 (n. 22), 219 (n. 41)

Romero, Lora, 113

Romines, Ann, 103, 107, 108, 112

Root, William, 182

Roper, Laura Wood, 146, 223 (n. 15)

Rybczynski, Witold, 146, 147

Sandford, John, 102

Scheper, George, 147

Schriber, Mary Suzanne, 5, 12, 103–4, 107, 110, 201 (n. 19)

Scott, Dred, 63–64, 72, 102

Scott, Harriet, 63–64, 72, 102

"Scratches on the Face of the Country" (Pratt), 105

Sedgwick, Elizabeth Dwight, 107

Seelye, John, 19, 56, 57, 61, 203 (n. 5), 206 (nn. 24, 28)

Sensational Designs (Tompkins), 216 (n. 17)

Shaw, Robert: and appointment of officers, 226 (n. 4); as commander, 182; and Kemble, Fanny, 174; and Olmsted, Frederick Law, 226 (n. 4); and secessionists, 185; on the South, 174

Skinfill, Mauri, 131, 140

Slaughter, Thomas, 43, 44–45, 48, 54, 208 (n. 45), 209 (n. 47)

Slave narrative: and construction of narrators as travelers, 67; criticism of, 65; and literacy, 65, 67

Slavery, American: ideology of, 68; as lack of freedom of movement, 64; and travel, 65

Slavery and the South (F. L. Olmsted), 142

Smith, Valerie, 70, 130, 134–35, 136

Society in America (Martineau), 105

Soldiers, Union: and the South, 17–18, 167, 178–82; as travel writers, 17–18. *See also* Travelers, Civil War soldiers as

Stephens, George: and landscape, 176, 178; and movement, 169; relationship of, with southern soldiers, 186; and secessionists, 185; and slave as comrade, 182; and southern past, 179; and Vernon, Mount, 180–81

Stepto, Robert, 83, 84, 210 (n. 6)

Stone, Albert E., 19, 67, 202 (n. 2)

Stowe, Harriet Beecher, 111, 142; *The Key to Uncle Tom's Cabin*, 84; *Uncle Tom's Cabin*, 112, 173, 216 (n. 17)

Stowe, William W., 12

Sumner, Charles, 146

Sundquist, Eric, 71, 81

Supreme Court, 63–64

Tate, Claudia, 139

Taylor, Susie King, 182–83, 184, 186–87, 190–91

Thoreau, Henry David, 142, 196

Tompkins, Jane, 112, 216–17 (nn. 17–18)

Travel: as broadening, 20, 29; and community, 94; as constitutive of American identity, 20; as defining characteristic of America, 1, 4, 18; and democracy, 4; and determination, 79; and Douglass, Frederick, 67–82 passim;

and expansion of knowledge, 78–79; and immigration, 4; intranational versus international, 1–2; versus movement, 64, 90–94; and Northup, Solomon, 85–102 passim; as precondition of slave narrative, 65; reading as, 72; by slaves, 64–65; as teleological, 160; and tourism, 4. *See also* Travel literature

Travelers, Civil War soldiers as, 166–92 passim; and class, 187; and desertion, 170; and the enemy, 167, 185–88; and movement, of army, 166, 168–70; and movement, of individual soldiers, 168–73; and nation, diversity of, 166, 188–89; and national identity, 166, 167–68; and Quakers, 183; and regional identity, 166; and reincorporation of the South, 167; slaves compared with, 170, 226 (n. 5); and southern distinctiveness, 173, 174; and tourism, 171, 178; and Union sentiment in the South, 182–88

Travelers and Travel Liars, 1660–1800 (P. Adams), 10

Travelers in the Confederate States (Clark), 171

Travel literature: and "contact zones," 14; as critical term, 193–94, 196–97; criticism of, 1, 9–15, 193; definition of, 1, 13–14, 193; discourses of, 14, 107; fluidity of, 196; and imperialism, 11; "informational," 105; and international travel, 1; and intranational travel, 1–2; and postcolonialism, 13; "sentimental," 105; study of, 193; and veracity, 14; women's, study of, 12–13

Travel Literature and the Evolution of the Novel (P. Adams), 10

"Travel Narrative and Imperialist Vision" (Pratt), 14

Travels (W. Bartram): and Alachua

Savanna, 48–52; and Altamaha River, 49–52; and Charleston, 52; as combining Enlightenment and proto-Romantic perspectives, 43, 49; drawings in, 48–52; Ephouskyca bird (*Tantalus pictus*) in, 53; and fountain on Saint Johns River, 60; narrator in, 45; politics of, 55; and report to Fothergill, 41–43, 45, 48–52; revisions of, 44, 209 (n. 49); rhetorical shifts in, 52, 53; role of, in production of American identity, 15–16, 19–20; and the South, 61–62

Travels in Pensilvania and Canada (J. Bartram), 42

Travel writing, women's: contrasted with men's, 105–6, 111; criticism of, 111; dialogism in, 106–7; and domesticity, 103; form of, 106–10; heteroglossia in, 107; novelistic practices in, 106; reception of, 110–11; "sentimental," 105; and sentimental novel, 111, 216 (n. 17); social concerns of, 110; and social context, 107; and subjectivity, creation of, 109; subject matter of, 105

Travers, Len, 7

Trollope, Frances, 105

Twelve Years a Slave (Northup): American society, critique of, in, 85; Bass, Samuel, in, 83, 99; boat trip in, 90; Brown, Merrill, in, 88; Burch, James H., in, 90; and Canada, 83; and the Capitol, 89; and Champlain Canal, 86; Chapin, Mr., in, 91; complexity of, 85; contrasted with Douglass's *Narrative*, 68, 85–86, 94–95, 97; critical reception of, 83; environment, role of, in, 98–99; Epps, Master, in, 92–93, 95, 98, 99–100; and escape within slavery, 94; and ethnography, 96; Ford, William, in, 91, 96, 98; Freeman, Theophilus, in, 90;

and Grand Coteau, 96; Hamilton, Abram, in, 88; and Louisiana, 95, 99; and New Orleans, 90, 97; and New York, 86, 88, 89, 97, 100; and New York Act, 101–2; plot of, as unrepresentative, 84; and Red River, 95; and risk of travel, 89; sales of, 83; and Saratoga Springs, 86–87; southerners, description of, in, 96–97; Tanner, Peter, in, 94; themes of, 67; Tibeats, Mr., in, 91–92, 93–94; and travel, 16, 68, 85–102 passim; as travel narrative, 85; and Union Army, 182; and Washington, D.C., 82, 87, 89, 97; and Wilson, David, 84; as worldly, 98

Uncle Tom's Cabin (Stowe), 112, 173, 216 (n. 17)

United States: "Age of Nationalism," 2; American Revolution, 1, 2, 6, 7, 9; Civil War, 2, 15, 165–92 passim; exploration of, 6–7; and international travel, 5; and intranational travel, 5–6; national identity, 1; and regions, 6–7; relationship of North and South in, 1–18 passim; role of struggle in, 1; role of travel in, 1; the South as problem in, 8–9

Vernon, Mount, 180–81

Walks and Talks of an American Farmer in England (F. L. Olmsted), 141, 223 (n. 15)

Washington, George, 180

Washington, Martha Custis, 180

Welter, Barbara, 112–13

Wesley, Marilyn, 135

White, Dana, 146, 148

Whitman, George, 171; and Confederate wealth, 186; and movement, 169; and the South, 175

Whitman, Walt, 171

Wilson, David, 84, 210 (n. 5). See also *Twelve Years a Slave* (Northup)

Wilson, Edmund, 146

Worley, Sam, 87, 89, 98, 211 (n. 9)

Writing Home (Schriber), 12, 103

Yellin, Jean Fagan, 132, 139

Youngs, Tim, 193

Zafar, Rafia, 70

Ziff, Larzer, 11, 20